UNITING in WORSHIP

Leader's Book

Uniting Church Press
Melbourne

Published by
The Joint Board of Christian Education
Second Floor, 10 Queen Street, Melbourne 3000, Australia

Prepared by the Assembly Commission on Liturgy
and approved by the Assembly Standing Committee for use
in the Uniting Church in Australia.

First printed 1988

Edited by Hugh McGinlay
Designed by Jennifer Richardson
Typeset by National Graphics
Printed by Singapore National Printers Ltd.

ISBN 0 85819 710 3

JB88/1318

Contents

Preface

The Uniting Church in Australia was inaugurated on 22 June 1977. It was formed by the union of the Congregational, Methodist and Presbyterian Churches. At the inaugural Assembly, a Commission on Liturgy was appointed, with the responsibility of preparing orders of worship and other resources. The first Assembly also endorsed the continuing use of orders of service and worship books that were being used by the three denominations which came into union.

However, the new church was soon looking for worship resources that would reflect its new-found unity. *The Australian Hymn Book*, prepared by an ecumenical committee over a period of nine years, was published a few months after the Inauguration of the Uniting Church. Within a year or two of its publication, most Uniting congregations had purchased the new hymn book, and it became a sign of a new phase in christian worship and witness, as well as the expression of a desire to proclaim the christian faith in the Australian cultural context.

But a new church was also requiring new orders of service, so the initial work of the Commission on Liturgy was to prepare some basic orders – Baptism, Holy Communion, Ordination and Induction. These first services were published in a simple format, and congregations and presbyteries were given permission to reproduce them for their own needs.

Then, beginning in 1980 and concluding in 1985, twenty orders of service were published in a series of eight booklets, entitled *Uniting Church Worship Services*. Over the last few years, these booklets have been purchased in large numbers and have enjoyed wide use. The preparation of these provisional services gave the Commission opportunity to note new liturgical directions, ecumenically and internationally, as well as to reflect more deeply on the rich legacy of worship inherited from former denominational practice. These 'booklet' services also gave ministers, leaders of worship and congregations an opportunity to react to the new orders, and to send their comments and suggestions to the Commission.

It was at the Third Assembly in 1982 that a resolution directed the Commission 'to begin work on the publication of a comprehensive collection of services and other resources for use in worship'. *Uniting in Worship* is the result. After examination of the possibility of paperback collections, loose-leaf binders and similar options, the most practical format turned out to be a hardback service book.

Uniting in Worship is published in two editions: People's Book and Leader's Book. The latter contains many services not included in the People's Book; it also has the full text of each service. There are liturgical reasons as well as economic ones for having two books. The chief liturgical reason is that an outline of a service, with congregational responses in full, as in the People's Book, better enables the congregation to participate in the service than a complete text. The economic reasons have to do with the omission from the People's Book of those resources, such as the Lectionary, which do not need to be in the hands of the whole congregation.

Ministers and leaders of worship will need a copy of each edition, as the People's Book has selections from the Psalms and other resources which will be useful both for formal services and less formal ones. Some church members may also desire to have a copy of each edition, as the Leader's Book gives access to 'Resources for the Liturgical Year' and 'Resources for Leading Worship', but the intention is that the People's Book will be the one generally used in the congregation.

Although both books are in hardback, liturgical work, including revision of services, will continue. The publication of *Uniting in Worship* is not so much a point of arrival as a station on the way. The needs of the church are always in process of change, and the pace of change has been particularly rapid in recent decades. The provision of new services, and the revision of some of those in *Uniting in Worship*, will be needed during the 1990s. The question of when a hardback successor to *Uniting in Worship* will appear is unanswerable at this stage, but other denominations in the English-speaking world are mentioning twelve or fifteen years as the expected life of their service books or prayer books.

Since 1977, the Commission on Liturgy has been based in South Australia, but has had the benefit of consultants in all Australian states. Most of these are Uniting Church people, but valuable help has been received from members of other denominations and this help is gratefully acknowledged. We have also benefited from published material and friendly advice from liturgical commissions in Canada, New Zealand, the United Kingdom and the United States.

As well as this lively correspondence, there have been drafting groups in several Australian cities, and these have lightened the load of the Commission considerably. Without their help, the publication date of 1988 would not have been possible. In the later stages of drafting, there have been two points of reference: the Assembly Commission on Doctrine (a national body); and the Assembly Standing Committee and its three working groups. These points of reference have enabled the Commission to propose confidently to the Assembly of 1988 that *Uniting in Worship* be authorised as 'official services of the Uniting Church in Australia'.

During the drafting process, many services have been field tested in congregations. The Commission is grateful for the co-operation of synods, presbyteries and parishes in the testing and evaluation of our work.

It can easily be seen that the process of producing *Uniting in Worship* has been an elaborate one. No book of services or prayers could claim to be without blemish, but the Commission is gratified by the keen participation of many individuals and groups within the Uniting Church and beyond. The Acknowledgments set out the published sources to which we are indebted but the individual ideas and suggestions used have been even greater in number.

The status and authority of published services is a matter of some debate within the Uniting Church. It is important to avoid both understatement and overstatement of the authority of *Uniting in Worship*. Its services and resources are not *required* to be used. Ministers and other worship leaders have the right to use other books, provided that these conform to the doctrine of the Uniting Church. On the other hand, *Uniting in Worship*, with the approval of the Assembly behind it, sets a standard for worship. It is normative in the sense that it is a standard against which other services may be measured.

This does not mean, of course, that the services in *Uniting in Worship* are intended to be used rigidly and without imagination. All worship should be geared to the particular situation of the congregation, be it large or small, urban or rural. All the resources in *Uniting in Worship* are therefore designed to be used in a flexible way. Indeed most of the services have many options within them, and there are frequent invitations to use free prayer. The Service of the Lord's Day, which is the centre-piece of the book, is a case in point. There is a variety of Great Prayers of Thanksgiving, and at other points in the service the entire content of a prayer must be provided by the leader and congregation. The funeral service contains the greatest number of options, as the Commission believes that many factors combine to make each funeral unique, one which requires careful choice between various possibilities.

But flexibility is more than choosing between printed options, or composing prayers of intercession, or other prayers for local use. Other factors such as the desired length of the service, the background and history of the congregation, and the people available for leadership will suggest variations from the printed text. This flexibility must be accompanied by responsibility, so that the congregation may be protected from worship which is idiosyncratic or insensitive.

The way in which these general principles apply to particular services and parts of services may be gleaned from *A Leader's Guide to Uniting in Worship* compiled by the Revd Robert Gribben. This volume is an important tool for all leaders of worship.

Uniting in Worship is not itself an authoritative statement of the church's doctine in the way that Assembly doctrinal pronouncements are. However the Commission has been guided by the doctrinal standards of our denomination. First among these are the Scriptures of the Old and New Testaments. The Commission has sought to use the Scripture in a way that reflects both the deep embedding of Scripture in the prayers of christian people and the development of biblical scholarship in recent decades. Second in importance comes the *Basis of Union* of the Uniting Church. Its statements on baptism and holy communion have been particularly important. Third comes the developing ecumenical consensus concerning worship and the sacraments. The crucial text here is *Baptism, Eucharist and Ministry* (World Council of Churches, 1982).

The commitment of the Uniting Church to christian unity has also meant that translations from ecumenical sources have been treated as having a strong claim for adoption in this book. The English Language Liturgical Consultation completed its work in time for its texts to be included in *Uniting in Worship* although the book of translations and commentary called *Praying Together* will not be published for some months. This international Consultation has an Australian counterpart, the Australian Consultation on Liturgy, and the discussions of that body, conducted annually since 1976, have been of great benefit to the Uniting Church.

The Commission has borrowed not only international translations but original prayers from other English-speaking churches. Some material is original to members of the Commission and other Uniting Church contributors. The style of language we have sought to adopt is contemporary but dignified, direct without being bland, and clear without being prosaic. It is not always understood that the language of worship (that is, for general use throughout the church, as distinct from the local and extempore) is not the same as everyday or conversational English. The words and many of the phrases will be common to both, but the tone and temper will be different. This means that the manner of reading is crucial. The more familiar the texts become, the greater is the possibility of good, prayerful reading.

The Commission has used inclusive language where the references are to human beings. The Assembly of the church has itself given a lead in this direction and the Commission has been glad to follow. We have not, however, extended this to include the names of God. While some female imagery is certainly appropriate with reference to God, biblical names which are male, especially Father and Son, are not to be discarded, as they belong to the heart of Trinitarian doctrine. More discussion of the use of inclusive language will take place in the church, and the Commission wishes to be part of that discussion.

Two of the services in this book are available in separate booklets, namely Baptism and Marriage. This provision is a response to pastoral experience with the use of the booklets in the *Uniting Church Worship Services* series.

It is expected that further resources, not included in *Uniting in Worship*, will follow in due time. Among these will be resources for daily prayer and Scripture reading.

There is little provision of music in *Uniting in Worship* because two other books provide this. *The Australian Hymn Book* (1977) is used widely. The supplementary book *Sing Alleluia* (1987) includes not only a good selection of contemporary christian songs but has several communion settings. These settings are recommended to ministers, musicians and congregations as a means to congregational participation in the prayers and proclamation of the eucharist.

Music and hymns, orders of service and resources for worship have power both to shape faith and to kindle devotion. But because they are human creations and words, they have their limitations. Aids to worship are signposts for christian pilgrims, not the goal of their journey. Only the grace of Jesus Christ and the power of the Holy Spirit can bring human words and works to life, enabling us to be true worshippers who worship the Father in spirit and in truth.

In offering *Uniting in Worship* to the church in the early part of our history as a denomination within the Church catholic, the Commission on Liturgy affirms Paragraph 18 of the *Basis of Union*:

The Uniting Church affirms that she belongs to the people of God on the way to the promised end. She prays God that, through the gift of the Spirit, he will constantly correct that which is erroneous in her life, will bring her into deeper unity with other churches, and will use her worship, witness and service to his eternal glory through Jesus Christ the Lord.   Amen.

D'Arcy Wood
Chairperson
Assembly Commission on Liturgy

March, 1988

Members of the Assembly Commission on Liturgy, 1983-1988

Deaconess Pat Baker
Revd John Bentley
Revd David Brown
Ms Jessie Byrne-Hoffmann
Mr Graham Canty
Revd Grant Dunning
   Secretary
Revd Robert Gribben
Mr Trevor Kitto

Revd Norah Norris
Miss Katherine O'Neill
Revd Dr Brian Phillips
Revd Michael Sawyer
Revd Graham Vawser
Revd John Watt
Revd Rob Williams
Revd Dr D'Arcy Wood
   Chairperson

Baptism and Related Services

Baptism
and the Reaffirmation of Baptism
Called Confirmation

NOTES

i   The service of baptism and/or confirmation takes place immediately
    after the Preaching of the Word.

ii This order provides for a number of people to make their profession of
    faith in Christ, either in baptism or in confirmation. If only one
    person is to make a profession of faith, the text and rubrics will need to
    be adapted in some places.

iii 'The Uniting Church will baptise those who confess the Christian
    faith, and children who are presented for baptism and for whose
    instruction and nourishment in the faith the Church takes
    responsibility.' (*Basis of Union,* paragraph 7)

iv Baptism, except in unusual circumstances, shall be administered
    during a regular Sunday service of the congregation.

v   'Normally the sacrament of baptism shall be administered in the
    presence of the Congregation within whose life the candidates are
    currently or promise in the future to be involved.' (Regulation
    1.1.3(c))

vi The council of elders normally is required to give prior approval for
    baptism and confirmation of the candidates. (Regulation 1.1.3(a) and
    3.1.9(h))

vii The elders responsible for the candidates should share with the
    minister in preparing them for their baptism or confirmation, not
    only in the instruction of the candidates in the faith in the
    confirmation group, but also in their devotional preparation for the
    service. The rubrics in this order identify those parts where it is
    appropriate for elders to lead or share in the worship.

viii Baptism is administered by totally immersing the candidate in water or
    by pouring water on the head of the candidate. Sprinkling water on
    the head of the candidate has also been recognised and practised by the
    church through many centuries. Because sprinkling is a less adequate
    use of the sign of water, its practice in the Uniting Church is

discouraged. Sprinkling is regarded as valid baptism in the Uniting Church, but it should be noted that some other denominations no longer permit baptism to be administered by this mode.

ix The baptismal font should be visible during all services and of such size that in the sacrament of baptism a generous quantity of water may be poured into it, and the minister may scoop water from it when baptising.

x If all candidates in the group are already baptised, sections 6 and 7 in this order are omitted.

xi It is required by the Regulations of the Uniting Church that all candidates be confirmed, whether baptised earlier in the service or previously. The laying on of hands is a good apostolic practice, referred to frequently in the Acts of the Apostles. The prayer in 9, Laying On of Hands, asks that the baptised person may be *strengthened* by the Holy Spirit — which is an appropriate request for all baptised christians, at whatever stage. The words spoken during the laying on of hands are a charge to that person, a commissioning to christian discipleship.
While there are good biblical and theological reasons for affirming that baptism on profession of faith makes a person both a member of the body of Christ and a confirmed member of the church, the Constitution and Regulations of the Uniting Church, as they stand at present, require the act of confirmation for a person to be recognised as a confirmed member of the Uniting Church. (Constitution 5(b) and Regulations 1.1.8 and 1.1.9)

xii A confirmed member of another denomination transferring membership to the Uniting Church should not be reconfirmed, but welcomed according to the provisions in the order Reception of a Member by Transfer. (Constitution 5(c)) Similarly, a person transferring membership to the Uniting Church from a church which practices only baptism on profession of faith should be regarded as a confirmed member of that church and should not be required to receive confirmation in the Uniting Church.

xiii In this order of service, NNN denotes the full name of a person, NN the christian names and N the christian name by which the person is called.

xiv The Apostles' Creed is set in the form of answers to three questions. This possibly reflects the earliest use of the creed as an affirmation of faith prior to baptism. The regular form of the Apostles' Creed or any other statement of faith should therefore be omitted from the worship when this order is used.

xv It is not permissable for a person to be baptised a second time. If a person does not know whether or not he/she has been baptised, and if there is reasonable doubt after all appropriate enquiries have been made, conditional baptism is administered. The usual procedures are followed in the preparation of the candidate for baptism, and the council of elders gives prior approval for baptism. The complete order of service is followed, except that this form of words is used for the act of baptism:

'NN, if you are not already baptised,
I baptise you
in the name of the Father,
and of the Son,
and of the Holy Spirit.'

xvi If a person receives emergency baptism and recovers, the baptism shall be recognised at a public celebration of the sacrament. The baptised person shall participate in all parts of the baptismal service, except for the baptism in water itself. Such a service may be referred to as *Welcome of a Baptised Person into the Congregation*. The Reaffirmation of Baptism called Confirmation may also be appropriate.

xvii If the readings for the day in the lectionary are not being used, the following passages are appropriate:

First Reading:	Isaiah 11:1-3a	Ezekiel 36:25-28
	Jeremiah 31:31-34	Joel 2:26-29
Second Reading:	Acts 1:3-8	1 Corinthians 12:4-13
	Acts 8:14-17	Galatians 5:16-25
	Romans 5:1-5	Ephesians 4:1-6
	Romans 8:12-17	
Gospel:	Matthew 5:1-12	John 15:1-11
	Matthew 16:24-28	John 16:5-15
	John 14:15-21	

Baptism
and the Reaffirmation of Baptism
Called Confirmation

This order is used immediately after the Preaching of the Word.

1 HYMN

A hymn or song on baptism or commitment to discipleship may be sung.

2 PRESENTATION

(See People's Book, p. 15.)

The elder responsible for the care of each person brings the person forward and introduces him/her to the congregation.

At the baptism of a person who is professing his/her faith, the elder says:

NNN has come today for baptism.

At the profession of faith of one already baptised, the elder says:

**NNN has come today to affirm the faith
into which he/she was baptised.**

3 SCRIPTURE

The minister or an elder shall read one or both of the following on all occasions:

**Hear the words of the Lord Jesus Christ:
All authority in heaven and on earth
has been given to me.
Go therefore and make disciples of all nations,
baptising them in the name of the Father
and of the Son and of the Holy Spirit,
teaching them to observe all that I have commanded you;
and lo, I am with you always, to the close of the age.**

Matthew 28:18-20

The apostle Paul said:
Do you not know that all of us
who have been baptised into Christ Jesus
were baptised into his death?
We were buried therefore with him by baptism into death,
so that as Christ was raised from the dead
by the glory of the Father,
we too might walk in newness of life.

Romans 6:3-4

In addition, the minister or an elder may read one or more of the
following:

The last two passages are suitable when there are candidates for
confirmation only.

Jesus said:
Truly, truly, I say to you,
unless you are born of water and the Spirit,
you cannot enter the kingdom of God.

John 3:5

In the letter to the Galatians, we read:
For as many of you as were baptised into Christ
have put on Christ.
There is neither Jew nor Greek,
there is neither slave nor free,
there is neither male nor female,
for you are all one in Christ Jesus.

Galatians 3:27-28

In the letter to Titus, we read:
When the goodness and loving kindness
of God our Saviour appeared, he saved us,
not because of deeds done by us in righteousness,

but in virtue of his own mercy,
by the washing of regeneration and renewal
in the Holy Spirit.

Titus 3:4-5

In the first letter of Peter, we read:
For Christ died for sins once for all,
the righteous for the unrighteous,
that he might bring us to God,
being put to death in the flesh
but made alive in the spirit;
in which he went and preached to the spirits in prison,
who formerly did not obey,
when God's patience waited in the days of Noah,
during the building of the ark,
in which a few, that is, eight persons,
were saved through water.
Baptism, which corresponds to this, now saves you,
not as a removal of dirt from the body
but as an appeal to God for a clear conscience,
through the resurrection of Jesus Christ.

1 Peter 3:18-21

Jesus said:
You did not choose me,
but I chose you and appointed you
that you should go and bear fruit
and that your fruit should abide;
so that whatever you ask the Father in my name,
he may give it to you.
This I command you, to love one another.

John 15:16-17

The apostle Paul said:
I appeal to you, therefore, by the mercies of God,
to present your bodies as a living sacrifice,
holy and acceptable to God,
which is your spiritual worship.

Romans 12:1

4   THE MEANING OF BAPTISM AND CONFIRMATION

The minister says:

Obeying the word of the Lord Jesus,
and confident of his promises,
the church baptises those whom he has called.

Baptism is the sign of new life in Christ Jesus.
By water and the Holy Spirit
we are brought into union with Christ
in his death and resurrection.
In baptism we are sealed with the Holy Spirit,
made members of the body of Christ,
and called to his ministry in the world.

In confirmation we acknowledge what God is doing for us;
we renew in faith the covenant declared in our baptism;
and we are commissioned for our ministry in the world.

5   RENUNCIATION AND AFFIRMATION

The minister says to all the candidates:

Through baptism
we enter the covenant which God has established;
and in confirmation
we affirm that we belong to God's covenant people.

In the light of the gospel we proclaim,
I ask you now:

The minister addresses each candidate in turn:

N, do you repent of your sins?

I repent of my sins.

Do you turn to Jesus Christ,
who has defeated the power of sin and death
and brought us new life?

I turn to Christ.

Do you pledge yourself to God,
trusting in Jesus Christ as Saviour and Lord
and in the Holy Spirit as Counsellor and Guide?

I pledge myself to God.

The minister may touch each candidate's ears and mouth, saying:

N, may the Lord open your ears to receive his word,
and your mouth to proclaim his praise.

The minister says to the candidates and the congregation:

Let us confess the faith into which we are baptised.

The people stand.

Do you believe in God,
who made you and loves you?

**I believe in God, the Father almighty,
   creator of heaven and earth.**

Do you believe in Jesus Christ,
your Saviour and Lord?

**I believe in Jesus Christ, God's only Son, our Lord,
   who was conceived by the Holy Spirit,
   born of the Virgin Mary,
   suffered under Pontius Pilate,
   was crucified, died, and was buried;
   he descended to the dead.
   On the third day he rose again;
   he ascended into heaven,
   he is seated at the right hand of the Father,
   and he will come to judge the living and the dead.**

Do you believe in the Holy Spirit,
and the continuing work of our salvation?

**I believe in the Holy Spirit,
   the holy catholic Church,
   the communion of saints,
   the forgiveness of sins,
   the resurrection of the body,
   and the life everlasting. Amen.**

The people remain standing.

The candidates for confirmation return to their places.

6   PRAYER OF THANKSGIVING

The elder pours water into the font.
The minister says:

The Lord be with you.
And also with you.

Lift up your hearts.
We lift them to the Lord.

Let us give thanks to the Lord our God.
It is right to give our thanks and praise.

The minister offers one of the following prayers:

Eternal God,
we thank you for the gift of water:
in the beginning you moved over the waters
to bring order out of chaos;
from the great flood in the days of Noah
you saved those on the ark;
through the Red Sea you led your people to freedom
from slavery in Egypt;
across the river Jordan you led Israel
to the land you promised;
in the waters of the Jordan
our Lord was baptised by John
and anointed by the Spirit.

By the power of the Holy Spirit, bless this water
and those/this person who are/is baptised in it;
that they/he/she may be born anew
of water and the Spirit,
be raised to new life in Christ,
and continue to be his faithful disciple(s);
through Jesus Christ our Lord,
to whom with you and the Holy Spirit
be all honour and glory, now and for ever.
Amen.

or

Gracious God,
we thank you for the gift of water:
through the waters of the Red Sea
you led your people Israel out of slavery
into the freedom of the land you promised;
in the waters of the Jordan
your Son was baptised
and anointed by the Spirit.

By the power of the Holy Spirit, bless this water
and those/this person who are/is baptised in it;
that they/he/she may die to sin,
be raised to new life,
and strengthened to serve you in the world,
until that day when you make all things new.
To you, Father, Son and Holy Spirit, one God,
be all praise and glory, now and for ever.
Amen.

7   THE BAPTISM

The people remain standing for the act of baptism.

If the mode of immersion is used, the candidate is dipped in water three times, once at each name of the Trinity.

If the mode of pouring is used, the candidate bows his/her head over the font. The minister pours water visibly and generously on the candidate's head three times, once at each name of the Trinity.

In baptising, the minister shall use the following words:

**NN, I baptise you
in the name of the Father,
and of the Son,
and of the Holy Spirit.**

The people respond:

Amen.

The minister marks the sign of the cross on the forehead of the newly-baptised person, and may say:

**NN, from this day on
the sign of the cross is upon you.**

The minister presents the baptised member to the congregation, saying:

**N is now received into the holy catholic Church
according to Christ's command.**

8   HYMN

A hymn or song to the Holy Spirit, or on the theme of commitment to discipleship may be sung.

During the singing of the hymn, candidates for confirmation come forward and stand with those newly baptised.

The people sit at the conclusion of the hymn.

9   LAYING ON OF HANDS

(See People's Book, p. 18.)

The minister says to the candidates:

**Always remember you are baptised,
and be thankful.**

The candidates kneel.

Elders and other members appointed by the council of elders to lay on hands come forward and stand around the candidates.

The minister calls the people to silent prayer, after which one or more people may offer free prayer.

The minister, with both hands extended over the candidates, offers this prayer:

**By the Holy Spirit, Lord,
strengthen these your servants,
and set their hearts on fire with love for you.
Increase in them your gifts of grace:
the spirit of wisdom and understanding,
the spirit of counsel and might,
the spirit of knowledge and wonder in your presence,
the spirit of joy and delight in your service,
now and for ever.
Amen.**

Based on Isaiah 11:2

The minister, elders and any others appointed lay hands on the
head of each candidate in turn, and the minister says:

**N, by the power of the Holy Spirit,
be a faithful witness to Christ
all the days of your life.**

The candidates and the people respond each time this is said:

Amen.

When all have received the laying on of hands, the newly-
confirmed members stand.

The Aaronic Blessing may be said or sung by the people
(*Australian Hymn Book, 572*), or said by the minister.

**The Lord bless you and keep you;
the Lord make his face to shine upon you,
and be gracious unto you;
the Lord lift up his countenance upon you,
and give you peace.**

Numbers 6:24-26

10   RESPONSES

One or more of the newly-confirmed members may make a brief
statement of faith.

The newly-confirmed members standing, the minister says:

**I ask you now to pledge yourself
to christian discipleship:**

The newly-confirmed members answer together these questions:

Do you promise to follow Christ
in your daily life?

**With God's help,
I will seek to love and obey Christ,
and to grow in my relationship with God
through prayer and study of the Bible.**

Do you promise to be a faithful member
of the christian community?

**With God's help,
I will share in the worship of the church,
and support its work
with my time, talents and money.**

Do you promise to participate
in God's mission to the world?

**With God's help,
I will witness to Christ in word and deed,
and look for the coming of his kingdom.**

The minister addresses the people:

I charge you,
the people of this congregation,
to love, encourage and support
these brothers and sisters in faith,
that they may continue to grow
in the grace of the Lord Jesus Christ
and the knowledge and love of God.

**With God's help,
we will live out our baptism
as a loving community in Christ:
nurturing one another in faith,
upholding one another in prayer,
and encouraging one another in service.**

11   PRESENTATIONS

Gifts from the congregation, including the presentation of
baptism and/or confirmation certificates, may be made.

12   OFFERING

13   NOTICES AND CONCERNS OF THE CHURCH

14   PRAYERS OF THE PEOPLE

One of the following prayers may be included in the
intercessions:

God, the Father of all,
with your sons and daughters
who have been baptised and confirmed this day,
we rejoice in the gift of the Holy Spirit.
We thank you that the Spirit
awakens us to new truth,
strengthens us in our daily pilgrimage,
and inspires us to venture out into life.
We thank you for your church,
and for our fellowship with Christ
who shows us the way of discipleship.
Praise be to God,
the Father, the Son and the Holy Spirit.
Amen.

or

Loving God,
we praise you for calling us to be your servant people,
and for gathering us into the body of Christ.
We thank you for strengthening our brothers and sisters,
and commissioning them to serve you through the church.
Together may we live in the Spirit,
loving one another and all people.
May the mind of Christ our Lord be in us;
to him be honour and glory for ever.
Amen.

or

Almighty God,
we give you thanks and praise
for all that you have done for us.
We thank you for calling our brothers and sisters
into your family;
may they continue as Christ's faithful disciples.
We pray for ourselves who so easily forget your grace,
that by sharing in this mystery
we may recall our own baptism,
and continue to walk in the light of Christ
and the fellowship of the Holy Spirit.
Amen.

The Sacrament of the Lord's Supper

During the Setting of the Table, the newly-confirmed members
may present the offerings of bread and wine.

The Sending Forth of the People of God

15   HYMN

16   BAPTISMAL CANDLE

The newly-confirmed members and their elders may gather at the front of the church.

The elder of each person, both those previously baptised and those newly baptised, may take a white candle, light it from the Easter candle standing near the font and present it, saying:

**N, you belong to Christ,
the light of the world.**

When all have received a lighted candle, the minister says:

**Let your light so shine before the world
that all may see your good works
and give glory to our Father who is in heaven.**

Matthew 5:16

17   WORD OF MISSION

**Go forth into the world in peace;
be of good courage;
hold fast that which is good;
render to no one evil for evil;
strengthen the faint-hearted;
support the weak;
help the afflicted;
honour all people;
love and serve the Lord,
rejoicing in the power of the Holy Spirit.**

18 BLESSING

And the blessing of God almighty,
the Father, the Son and the Holy Spirit,
be upon you and remain with you always.
Amen.

> The new members, holding their lighted candles, may process
> out of the church together with their elders and the leaders of
> worship.

Baptism of a Child

i   Normally the sacrament of baptism follows the Preaching of the Word. However it may be placed before The Service of the Word if children and young people leave the service.

ii This order provides for one child to be baptised. If more than one child is to be baptised, the text and rubrics will need to be adapted in some places.

iii 'The Uniting Church will baptise those who profess the Christian faith, and children who are presented for baptism and for whose instruction and nourishment in the faith the Church takes responsibility.' (*Basis of Union,* paragraph 7)

iv Baptism, except in unusual circumstances, shall be administered during a regular Sunday service of the congregation.

v   'Normally the sacrament of baptism shall be administered in the presence of the Congregation within whose life the candidate or the parents of the candidate are currently or promise in the future to be involved.' (Regulation 1.1.3(c))

vi The council of elders normally is required to give prior approval for baptism of the candidate. (Regulation 1.1.3(a) and 3.1.9(h))

vii The family's elder should share with the minister both in the pre-baptismal counselling of the parents and in the preparation of the parents for their participation in the service.

viii Baptism is administered by pouring water on the head of the candidate. The other two modes used by the church are total immersion and sprinkling. In the case of a baby or young child, immersion is not recommended. Sprinkling water on the head of the candidate has been recognised and practised by the church through many centuries, but because sprinkling is a less adequate use of the sign of water than the other two modes, its practice in the Uniting Church is discouraged. Sprinkling is regarded as valid baptism in the Uniting Church, but it should be noted that some other denominations no longer permit baptism to be administered by this mode.

ix The baptismal font should be visible during all services and of such size that in the sacrament of baptism a generous quantity of water may be poured into it, and the minister may scoop water from it when baptising.

x In this order, NN denotes the christian names of the child and N the christian name by which the child is called. N and N denotes the christian names of the parents.

xi The Apostles' Creed is set in the form of answers to three questions. This possibly reflects the earliest use of the creed as an affirmation of faith prior to baptism. The regular form of the Apostles' Creed or any other statement of faith should therefore be omitted from the worship when this order is used.

xii It is appropriate but not necessary for holy communion to be celebrated following the baptism of a child.

xiii If a newly-born child receives emergency baptism and lives, or a sick child receives emergency baptism and recovers, the baptism shall be recognised at a public celebration of the sacrament. The complete order of service is used, except for the baptism in water itself. In some places, the text will need to be adapted to make it clear that baptism has already been administered; for example, the first question to the parents should be reworded to read:

'N and N,
what have you asked of God's church for N?'

Such a service may be referred to as *Welcome of a Baptised Child into the Congregation*.

Baptism of a Child

1 HYMN

A hymn or song on baptism may be sung.

2 PRESENTATION

(See People's Book, p. 23.)

The elder responsible for the care of the family brings the parent(s), the child to be baptised and any brothers and sisters forward, and introduces them to the congregation.

The elder concludes the introduction by saying:

N and N have come today
to present their son/daughter NN for baptism.

3 SCRIPTURE

The minister or elder shall read one or both of the following:

Hear the words of the Lord Jesus Christ:
All authority in heaven and on earth
has been given to me.
Go therefore and make disciples of all nations,
baptising them in the name of the Father
and of the Son and of the Holy Spirit,
teaching them to observe all that I have commanded you;
and lo, I am with you always, to the close of the age.

Matthew 28:18-20

The apostle Paul said:
Do you not know that all of us
who have been baptised into Christ Jesus
were baptised into his death?
We were buried therefore with him by baptism into death,
so that as Christ was raised from the dead
by the glory of the Father,
we too might walk in newness of life.

Romans 6:3-4

In addition, the minister or elder may read
one or more of the following:

The apostle Peter said:
Repent, and be baptised every one of you
in the name of Jesus Christ
for the forgiveness of your sins;
and you shall receive the gift of the Holy Spirit.
For the promise is to you and to your children
and to all that are far off,
every one whom the Lord our God calls to him.

Acts 2:38-39

In the letter to the Ephesians we read:
There is one body and one Spirit,
just as you were called to the one hope
that belongs to your call,
one Lord, one faith, one baptism,
one God and Father of us all,
who is above all and through all and in all.

Ephesians 4:4-6

In the letter to the Colossians we read:
In Christ also you were circumcised
with a circumcision made without hands,
by putting off the body of flesh
in the circumcision of Christ;
and you were buried with him in baptism,
in which you were also raised with him
through faith in the working of God,
who raised him from the dead.

Colossians 2:11-12

4   THE MEANING OF BAPTISM

The minister says:

Obeying the word of the Lord Jesus,
and confident of his promises,
the church baptises those whom he has called.

Baptism is the sign of new life in Christ Jesus.
By water and the Holy Spirit
we are brought into union with Christ
in his death and resurrection.
In baptism we are sealed with the Holy Spirit,
made members of the body of Christ,
and called to his ministry in the world.

5   RENUNCIATION AND AFFIRMATION

The minister says to the parent(s):

N and N
what do you ask of God's church for N?

**We ask that he/she be baptised
into the faith and family of Jesus Christ.**

In the light of the covenant promise
and of your request,
I ask you now:

Do you believe that the gospel
enables us to turn from the darkness of evil
and to walk in the light of Christ?

We do.

The minister may touch the child's ears and mouth, saying:

N, may the Lord open your ears to receive his word,
and your mouth to proclaim his praise.

The minister says to the parent(s) and the congregation:

Let us confess the faith into which we are baptised.

The people stand.

Do you believe in God,
who made you and loves you?

**I believe in God, the Father almighty,
    creator of heaven and earth.**

Do you believe in Jesus Christ,
your Saviour and Lord?

**I believe in Jesus Christ, God's only Son, our Lord,
    who was conceived by the Holy Spirit,
    born of the Virgin Mary,
    suffered under Pontius Pilate,
    was crucified, died, and was buried;
    he descended to the dead.
    On the third day he rose again;
    he ascended into heaven,
    he is seated at the right hand of the Father,
    and he will come to judge the living and the dead.**

Do you believe in the Holy Spirit,
and the continuing work of our salvation?

I believe in the Holy Spirit,
   the holy catholic Church,
   the communion of saints,
   the forgiveness of sins,
   the resurrection of the body,
   and the life everlasting. Amen.

The people remain standing.

6   PRAYER OF THANKSGIVING

The elder pours water into the font.

The minister says:

The Lord be with you.
And also with you.

Lift up your hearts.
We lift them to the Lord.

Let us give thanks to the Lord our God.
It is right to give our thanks and praise.

The minister offers one of the following prayers:

Eternal God,
we thank you for the gift of water:
in the beginning you moved over the waters
to bring order out of chaos;
from the great flood in the days of Noah
you saved those on the ark;

through the Red Sea you led your people to freedom
from slavery in Egypt;
across the river Jordan you led Israel
to the land you promised;
in the waters of the Jordan
our Lord was baptised by John
and anointed by the Spirit.

By the power of the Holy Spirit, bless this water
and this child who is baptised in it;
that he/she may be born anew
of water and the Spirit,
be raised to new life in Christ,
and continue to be his faithful disciple;
through Jesus Christ our Lord,
to whom with you and the Holy Spirit
be all honour and glory, now and for ever.
Amen.

or

Gracious God,
we thank you for the gift of water:
through the waters of the Red Sea
you led your people Israel out of slavery
into the freedom of the land you promised;
in the waters of the Jordan
your Son was baptised
and anointed by the Spirit.

By the power of the Holy Spirit, bless this water
and this child who is baptised in it;
that he/she may die to sin,
be raised to new life,
and strengthened to serve you in the world,
until that day when you make all things new.
To you, Father, Son and Holy Spirit, one God,
be all praise and glory, now and for ever.
Amen.

7 THE BAPTISM

The people remain standing for the act of baptism.

Addressing the child, the minister may say:

Little child,
for you Jesus Christ has come,
has lived, has suffered;
for you, he has endured the agony of Gethsemane
and the darkness of Calvary;
for you, he has uttered the cry, 'It is accomplished!'
For you, he has triumphed over death;
for you, he prays at God's right hand;
all for you, little child,
even though you do not know it.
In baptism,
the word of the apostle is fulfilled:
'We love, because God first loved us'.

1 John 4:19

The minister receives the child from the parents and pours water visibly and generously over the child's head three times, once at each name of the Trinity.

In baptising, the minister shall use the following words:

NN, I baptise you
in the name of the Father,
and of the Son,
and of the Holy Spirit.

Amen.

The people respond:

The minister marks the sign of the cross on the forehead of the child and may say:

NN, from this day on
the sign of the cross is upon you.

The minister presents the baptised member to the congregation, saying:

N is now received into the holy catholic Church
according to Christ's command.

The minister or elder may carry or take the child through the congregation.

When the child is returned to the place where the parents are standing, the Aaronic Blessing may be said or sung by the people (*Australian Hymn Book, 572*) or said by the minister.

The Lord bless you and keep you;
the Lord make his face to shine upon you,
and be gracious unto you;
the Lord lift up his countenance upon you,
and give you peace.

Numbers 6:24-26

The minister returns the child to the parents.

The people sit.

8   RESPONSES

The minister says to the parent(s):

N and N,
I ask you now to respond to God's graciousness to N
by making these solemn promises:

Will you provide for your child ·
a christian home of love and trust?

With God's help, we will.

Will you set before N
the example of a christian life,
and will you pray that he/she will learn the way of Christ?

With God's help, we will.

Will you encourage your child
to grow within the fellowship of the church,
so that he/she may come to faith in Christ?

With God's help, we will.

The minister addresses the people:

I charge you,
the people of this congregation,
to maintain the life of worship and service,
that this child and all the children among you
may grow in the grace of the Lord Jesus Christ
and the knowledge and love of God.

**With God's help,
we will live out our baptism
as a loving community in Christ:
nurturing one another in faith,
upholding one another in prayer,
and encouraging one another in service.**

9 POST BAPTISMAL PRAYERS

*One of the following prayers may be used, or free prayer may be
offered for the child, the parents and the congregation.*

*Alternatively, a post baptismal prayer may be included with other
intercessions in Prayers of the People.*

Almighty God,
we praise you for all that you have done for us.
We thank you for declaring your love for N today,
before he/she can understand.
As you have loved him/her from the beginning,
continue to protect and guide him/her.
May he/she become a loyal disciple of Jesus Christ.

We thank you for your goodness to N and N.
Grant your blessing upon their home,
and help them to keep the promises they have made.

We pray for ourselves who so easily forget your grace,
that by sharing in this mystery
we may recall our own baptism,
and continue to walk in the light of Christ
and the fellowship of the Holy Spirit.
Praise be to God,
the Father, the Son and the Holy Spirit.
Amen.

or

Loving Father,
you have filled the world with joy
by giving us your Son.
Bless this newly-baptised child;
may he/she never be ashamed
to confess the faith of Christ crucified.

Bless his/her parents N and N;
may they always show their gratitude
for the life you have given them
by loving and caring for N.

Bless your faithful people;
unite us in the peace of Christ
and the fellowship of the Holy Spirit.
Amen.

or

We pray for N, whom we have baptised in God's name;
that in the fullness of time
he/she may come to acknowledge Christ's lordship
over his/her life:
Lord, hear us.
Lord, hear our prayer.

We pray for God's blessing on N's family and home;
that his/her father and mother,
brother(s) and sister(s)
may continue to grow in grace
and in the love of God and of each other:
Lord, hear us.
Lord, hear our prayer.

We pray for ourselves who so easily forget God's grace;
that by sharing in this mystery
we may recall our own baptism
and continue to walk in the light of Christ
and the fellowship of the Holy Spirit:
Lord, hear us.
Lord, hear our prayer.

10 PRESENTATION

A gift from the congregation, including the presentation of the
certificate of baptism, may be made.

11 HYMN

If a baptismal hymn or song was not sung at the beginning of the
service, it may be sung here.

BAPTISMAL CANDLE

Immediately before the Word of Mission, during the singing of the final hymn of the service, the elder and the family may return to the font.

The elder may take a white candle, light it from the Easter candle standing near the font, and present it to the child, saying:

**N, you belong to Christ,
the light of the world.**

The minister says:

**N, may you always walk as a child of the light.
Let your light so shine before the world
that all may see your good works
and give glory to our Father who is in heaven.**

Matthew 5:16

BLESSING

**The blessing of God almighty,
the Father, the Son and the Holy Spirit,
be upon you and remain with you always.
Amen.**

With a parent holding the lighted candle, the family may process out of the church, together with the family's elder and the minister.

A Congregational Reaffirmation of Baptism

NOTES

i   This service is intended for occasional use by the whole congregation. The Easter Vigil, Easter Day, or any other Sunday of the Easter season, including the Day of Pentecost, is an appropriate time for the whole congregation to join in a reaffirmation of baptism.

ii The minister and council of elders should encourage the congregation to make prior spiritual preparation for this service. On the day of the service, it may be important for the minister to be sensitive to the presence of any people who have not been baptised. While some parts of the text are addressed to the baptised members, the questions asked in 2, Reaffirmation of Baptism, and to which people make a personal response are questions to which an unbaptised believer in Christ may sincerely give answer.
It may also be helpful to remind the congregation that all who are confirmed members have already made an affirmation of baptismal faith in Christ in their own confirmation.

iii This order forms part of the congregation's Sunday worship. It could appropriately be placed after the Preaching of the Word. Since the Apostles' Creed forms part of this order, a creed should not be used elsewhere in the service. It is appropriate for the order to be followed by holy communion.

A Congregational Reaffirmation of Baptism

1 INTRODUCTION

(See People's Book, p. 30.)

At Easter the minister says:

Brothers and sisters,
as we celebrate again the resurrection
of our Lord Jesus Christ,
we remember that through the mystery
of his suffering and death
we have died and been buried with him in baptism.
In our baptism
we were also raised with him to new life.
Having prepared ourselves during Lent,
we now reaffirm our baptism,
declaring our allegiance to the risen Christ
and our rejection of all that is evil.

At Pentecost the minister says:

Brothers and sisters,
as we celebrate again the festival of Pentecost,
we remember how our crucified and risen Lord
poured out his life-giving Spirit upon the waiting church.
In our baptism we were given the sign and seal
of the Holy Spirit who is with us —
to enlighten and empower us,
and to guide us in the way of Christ.
We now reaffirm our baptism,
declaring our allegiance to the risen Christ
and asking for a fresh outpouring of the Holy Spirit.

On other occasions the minister says:

Brothers and sisters,
in our baptism we died and were buried with Christ,
so that we might rise with him to new life.
We were initiated into Christ's holy church
and brought to life through water and the Spirit.
God's mighty acts of salvation for us and all people
are gracious gifts, freely given.
Today we come to reaffirm our baptism,
declaring our allegiance to the risen Christ
and seeking to be obedient to his will.

2 REAFFIRMATION OF BAPTISM

The people stand.

The minister continues:

Do you turn to Christ?

I turn to Christ.

Do you repent of your sins?

I repent of my sins.

Do you renounce evil
and the false values of this world?

I renounce them.

And now I ask you to confess the faith
into which you were baptised,
and in which you continue to live and grow:

Do you believe in God,
who made you and loves you?

**I believe in God, the Father almighty,
    creator of heaven and earth.**

Do you believe in Jesus Christ,
your Saviour and Lord?

**I believe in Jesus Christ, God's only Son, our Lord,
    who was conceived by the Holy Spirit,
    born of the Virgin Mary,
    suffered under Pontius Pilate,
    was crucified, died, and was buried;
    he descended to the dead.
    On the third day he rose again;
    he ascended into heaven,
    he is seated at the right hand of the Father,
    and he will come to judge the living and the dead.**

Do you believe in the Holy Spirit,
and the continuing work of our salvation?

**I believe in the Holy Spirit,
    the holy catholic Church,
    the communion of saints,
    the forgiveness of sins,
    the resurrection of the body,
    and the life everlasting. Amen.**

This is the faith of God's baptised people.

**We are not ashamed to confess it
in Christ our Lord.**

I ask you now to pledge yourselves
to Christ's ministry in the world:

Will you continue in the community of faith,
the apostles' teaching,
the breaking of bread and the prayers?

With God's help, we will.

Will you proclaim by word and example
the good news of God in Christ?

With God's help, we will.

Will you seek Christ in all people,
and love your neighbour as yourself?

With God's help, we will.

Will you strive for justice and peace,
and respect the dignity of every human being?

With God's help, we will.

May almighty God,
who has given us new birth by water and the Holy Spirit,
keep us steadfast in the faith,
and bring us to eternal life;
through Jesus Christ our Lord.
Amen.

3   RECOLLECTION OF BAPTISM

The people remain standing.

An elder pours water into the font.

The elder then says:

Come, Lord Jesus,
refresh the lives of all your faithful people.

*The minister says one or more of the following; and may sprinkle
water from the font by hand three times towards the people:*

Always remember you are baptised,
and be thankful.

and/or

Always remember you are baptised,
and give thanks to the risen Lord.

and/or

Always remember you are baptised,
and praise the Holy Spirit.

The minister may then say:

Today we remember that, from the time of our baptism,
the sign of the cross has been upon us.
I invite you now to join me
in tracing the sign of the cross upon your forehead,
saying — I belong to Christ. Amen.

*The minister and people may mark themselves with the sign,
saying:*

I belong to Christ. Amen.

The minister may also add:

You may trace the sign of the cross
on those around you,
saying: You belong to Christ. Amen.

The people may mark others with the sign, saying:

You belong to Christ. Amen.

4 HYMN

A seasonal hymn, a hymn in praise of the risen Lord or the Holy
Spirit, or other appropriate hymn may be sung.

At the conclusion of the hymn, the people sit.

5 OFFERING

6 NOTICES AND CONCERNS OF THE CHURCH

7 PRAYERS OF THE PEOPLE

(See People's Book, p. 34.)

Let us pray for all the baptised everywhere
and for ourselves in this congregation of God's people:

That our redemption from evil
and our rescue from the way of sin and death
may be evident in our daily living:
Lord, in your mercy,
hear our prayer.

That the Holy Spirit may continue
to open our hearts and lives
to the grace and truth we find in Jesus our Lord:
Lord, in your mercy,
hear our prayer.

That we may be kept in the faith and communion
of the holy, catholic and apostolic Church:
Lord, in your mercy,
hear our prayer.

That we may be sent into the world
to witness to the love of Christ:
Lord, in your mercy,
hear our prayer.

That we may be brought to the fullness
of God's peace and glory:
Lord, in your mercy,
hear our prayer.

Other prayers are offered for the peoples of the world,
for the nation and the community,
and for situations of need.

To conclude the prayers, the following prayer of commitment may
be said by all the people:

**Praise be to you, my Lord Jesus Christ,
for all the benefits
you have won for me,
for all the pains and insults
you have borne for me.**

**O most merciful Redeemer,
friend and brother,
may I know you more clearly,
love you more dearly,
and follow you more nearly,
day by day. Amen.**

Attributed to St Richard of Chichester

8   THE PEACE

The people stand for the greeting of peace.

The minister says:

We are the body of Christ.
In the one Spirit we were all baptised into one body.
Let us then pursue all that makes for peace
and builds up our common life.

The peace of the Lord be always with you.
And also with you.

The people may exchange a sign of peace.

The Sacrament of the Lord's Supper

The service continues from page 90 at 17 HYMN in The Service of the Lord's Day.

NOTES

i This service witnesses to the fact that the Holy Spirit given in baptism has awakened a response of faith in a person's life. It may be used to meet particular situations such as the following:

 * When a baptised and confirmed member of a congregation has come into a renewing and transforming experience of the love of Christ, and desires to witness to this experience before his/her congregation.

 * When a baptised and confirmed member has lapsed from faith and active involvement in the life of a congregation of the Uniting Church or other denomination of the church, and now desires to reaffirm allegiance to Christ.

ii This order forms part of the congregation's Sunday worship. It could appropriately be placed after the Preaching of the Word. Since the Apostles' Creed forms part of this order, a creed should not be used elsewhere in the service. It is appropriate for the order to be followed by holy communion.

iii The service provides for one person to reaffirm his/her baptism. If a small group of people wishes to make a personal reaffirmation together, the text and rubrics will need to be adapted in some places.

A Personal Reaffirmation of Baptism

1   INTRODUCTION AND WELCOME

(See People's Book, p. 38.)

The minister and an elder or another appropriate person stand with the person at the front of the church.

The elder addresses the person:

N, why have you come here today?

**I have come to reaffirm my baptism,
and to ask the congregation to pray for me.**

The minister welcomes the person, and says:

We rejoice that today N has come
to give witness to the gracious gift of God in salvation,
and with renewed faith to commit his/her life
to the service of the Lord and the work of the church.

In our baptism we die and are raised to life
through the death and resurrection of Christ.
We are made members of the family of God
and live under the lordship of Christ.

Despite our unfaithfulness,
God is always faithful,
and through the Holy Spirit reawakens faith,
leading us into new awareness
of the salvation offered in Christ.

2 WITNESS

The baptised person may give a brief testimony to his/her awakened faith.

If the person is unwilling or unable to do this, the minister, elder or other appropriate person may outline briefly the experiences which have brought the person to make a reaffirmation of baptism.

3 CONGREGATIONAL RESPONSE

The elder may make a brief response to the witness, concluding with:

**N, we rejoice in your acknowledgment
of the work of Christ in your life.
He has opened your ears to receive God's word
and your mouth to proclaim his praise.**

The people say:

**In the love of Christ we encourage you,
and pray that he will continue to bless you.
To his name be glory and praise.
Hallelujah!**

The elder may initiate applause.

4 HYMN

A hymn or song which is significant to the person may be sung.

At the conclusion of the hymn or song, all remain standing.

5   BAPTISMAL CANDLE

(See People's Book, p. 39.)

The person lights a candle from the Easter candle.

Facing the congregation, the person says:

**Since my baptism, I have belonged to Christ,
the light of the world.**

The elder says:

Let your light so shine before the world
that all may see your good works
and give glory to our Father who is in heaven.

Matthew 5:6

6   REAFFIRMATION OF BAPTISM

The minister says:

N, through your baptism you entered the covenant
which God has established with his people.

I invite you now to reaffirm your baptism
by giving answer to these questions:

Do you turn again to Christ?

I turn to Christ.

Do you repent of your sins?

I repent of my sins.

Do you renounce evil
and the false values of this world?

I renounce them.

The minister addresses the congregation:

Let us all confess the faith
into which we were baptised,
and in which we continue to live and grow:

**I believe in God, the Father almighty,
    creator of heaven and earth.**

**I believe in Jesus Christ, God's only Son, our Lord,
    who was conceived by the Holy Spirit,
    born of the Virgin Mary,
    suffered under Pontius Pilate,
    was crucified, died, and was buried;
    he descended to the dead.
    On the third day he rose again;
    he ascended into heaven,
    he is seated at the right hand of the Father,
    and he will come to judge the living and the dead.**

**I believe in the Holy Spirit,
    the holy catholic Church,
    the communion of saints,
    the forgiveness of sins,
    the resurrection of the body,
    and the life everlasting. Amen.**

The person places the lighted baptismal candle in an empty candle
holder on the communion table.

The people sit.

7 PRAYER WITH THE LAYING ON OF HANDS

Some of the congregation, family and friends may be invited to
come forward and gather around the person.

The person kneels.

*The minister invites the elder and those who have come forward
to lay hands on the person's head.*

The minister then says to the congregation:

Let us pray for N in silence.

*After a time, the minister and/or elder and/or other persons lead in
free prayer.*

The minister says one of the following:

Strengthen, Lord, your servant N
with your heavenly grace,
that he/she may continue yours for ever,
and daily increase in the Holy Spirit,
until he/she comes to your everlasting kingdom.
Amen.

or

N, you are a child of God,
a servant of Christ,
and a temple of the Holy Spirit.
May almighty God bless you
and keep you in eternal life.
Amen.

or

N, may the Father of our Lord Jesus Christ
strengthen you through the Spirit in your inner being;
that Christ may dwell in your heart through faith,
and that you may be filled with all the fullness of God.
Amen.

Based on Ephesians 3:14-19

The people may say or sing the Aaronic Blessing,
(*Australian Hymn Book, 572*).

The Lord bless you and keep you;
the Lord make his face to shine upon you,
and be gracious unto you;
the Lord lift up his countenance upon you,
and give you peace.

Numbers 6:24-26

The person stands and all return to their seats.

8   INVITATION TO DISCIPLESHIP

The minister may invite others to make a first commitment of
their life to Christ or a reaffirmation of their faith in him.

They may come forward during the singing that follows.

If people respond to the invitation, brief free prayer is offered.

9   HYMN

An appropriate hymn or song may be sung.

10   OFFERING

11   NOTICES AND CONCERNS OF THE CHURCH

12   PRAYERS OF THE PEOPLE

Prayers of intercession are offered
for the church,
for the peoples of the world,
for the nation and the community,
and for situations of need.

13 THE PEACE

The people stand for the greeting of peace.

The minister says:

We are the body of Christ.
In the one Spirit we were all baptised into one body.
Let us then pursue all that makes for peace
and builds up our common life.

The peace of the Lord be always with you.
And also with you.

The people may exchange a sign of peace.

The Sacrament of the Lord's Supper

The service continues from page 90 at 17 HYMN in The Service of the Lord's Day.

NOTES

i   This service is intended for occasional use by the whole congregation.
The first Sunday of the New Year, the Sunday on which church activities
recommence after the summer holidays, the church anniversary or any
other significant occasion in the life of the congregation is an
appropriate time for renewing the covenant with God.

ii   The minister and council of elders should encourage the congregation
to make prior spiritual preparation for the service. The covenant prayer
is nothing less than an act of complete self-abandonment to the will of
God and should not be entered upon lightly.

iii   This order, followed by holy communion, is a complete act of worship
for a Sunday service.

The Covenant Service

The Gathering of the People of God

1   CALL TO WORSHIP

(See People's Book, p. 44.)

Come, let us worship God,
who has called us to be a holy people,
and has established an everlasting covenant
through Jesus Christ our Lord.

We come in spirit and in truth.

2   ADORATION

A hymn of adoration (*e.g. Australian Hymn Book 1, 86 or 113*) is
sung and/or the following prayer, based on 'We praise you, O
God' (*Te Deum Laudamus*), is used:

(See People's Book, p. 44.)

Let us pray:

Let us adore the God of love:
who created us;
who continually preserves and sustains us;
who has loved us with an everlasting love,
and given us the light of the knowledge of his glory
in the face of Jesus Christ.

We praise you, O God,
we acclaim you as Lord.

Let us glory in the grace of our Lord Jesus Christ:
though he was rich, yet for our sakes he became poor;
he was tempted in all points as we are, yet without sin;
he went about doing good
and preaching the gospel of the kingdom;

he became obedient to death, death on the cross;
he was dead and is alive for evermore;
he has opened the kingdom of heaven to all believers;
he is seated at God's right hand in glory;
he will come again to be our judge.

You are the king of glory, O Christ.

Let us rejoice in the fellowship of the Holy Spirit,
the Lord, the giver of life:
whose witness confirms us;
whose wisdom teaches us;
whose power enables us.
By the Spirit we are born into the family of God,
and made members of Christ's body.

All praise to you, O Holy Spirit.

3 CONFESSION

Let us humbly confess our sins to God:

Merciful God,
you have set forth the way of life for us
in your beloved Son.
We confess with shame our slowness to learn of him,
our failure to follow him,
our reluctance to bear the cross.

Have mercy on us, Lord, and forgive us.

or

Lord, have mercy. *(sung)*

We confess the poverty of our worship,
our neglect of the christian community
and of the means of grace,
our hesitating witness for Christ,
our evasion of responsibilities in your service,
our imperfect stewardship of your gifts.

Have mercy on us, Lord, and forgive us.

or

Christ, have mercy. *(sung)*

We confess that so little of your love
has reached others through us;
that we have cherished things
which divide us from others;
that we have made it hard for others to live with us;
that we have been thoughtless in our judgments,
hasty in condemnation,
and grudging in forgiveness.

Have mercy on us, Lord, and forgive us.

or

Lord, have mercy. *(sung)*

Let each of us in silence make confession to God.

After a time the minister says:

This is the message we have heard from Christ
and proclaim to you,
that God is light and in him is no darkness at all.
If we walk in the light, as God is in the light,
we have fellowship with one another,
and the blood of Jesus his Son cleanses us from all sin.

If we say we have no sin,
we deceive ourselves, and the truth is not in us.
If we confess our sins,
God is faithful and just, and will forgive our sins
and cleanse us from all unrighteousness.

1 John 1:5, 7-9

Hear then Christ's word of grace to us:
Your sins are forgiven.
Thanks be to God.

4   COLLECT

Almighty God,
you have appointed our Lord Jesus Christ
as mediator of a New Covenant.
Give us grace to draw near with full assurance of faith,
and rejoice in our continuing covenant with you;
through Christ your Son.
Amen.

5   HYMN

A hymn or anthem may be sung.

The Service of the Word

6   FIRST READING

Jeremiah 31:31-34, or the lectionary reading for the day, or other
appropriate reading.

7 PSALM

8 SECOND READING

Hebrews 12:22-24, or the lectionary reading for the day, or other appropriate reading.

9 GOSPEL

John 15:1-11, or the lectionary reading for the day, or other appropriate reading.

The following may be used after this final reading:

This is the word of the Lord.
Thanks be to God.

10 HYMN

11 PREACHING OF THE WORD

After the preaching, silence may be kept for meditation.

12 OFFERING

The gifts of money are presented and a prayer offered.

13 NOTICES AND CONCERNS OF THE CHURCH

14 PRAYERS OF THE PEOPLE

Prayers of intercession are offered
   for the church,
   for the peoples of the world,
   for the nation and the community,
   and for situations of need.

15 HYMN

The Covenant

16 INTRODUCTION

(See People's Book, p. 48.)

The minister says:

In the Old Covenant,
God chose Israel as his people
and gave them the gift of the Law.
In the New Covenant,
he made the gift of his Son Jesus Christ,
who fulfils the Law for us.
We stand within the New Covenant
and we bear the name of Christ.

God promises us new life in him.
We receive this promise
and pledge to live not for ourselves but for God.
This covenant is renewed each time we meet
at the table of the Lord.

Today we meet, as generations before us have met,
to renew that which bound them and now binds us to God.

The people stand.

The minister continues:

Beloved in Christ,
let us again claim this covenant for ourselves,
and take the yoke of Christ upon us.

To take this yoke upon us means that we are content
that he appoint us our place and work,
and that he himself be our reward.

Christ has many services to be done:
some are easy, others are difficult;
some bring honour, others bring reproach;
some are suitable to our natural inclinations
and material interests,
others are contrary to both.
In some we may please Christ and please ourselves;
in others we cannot please Christ
except by denying ourselves.
Yet the power to do all these things
is given us in Christ, who strengthens us.

Therefore let us make this covenant with God our own,
trusting in the eternal promises
and relying on divine grace.

17 THE COVENANT PRAYER

Let us pray:

Lord God,
in baptism you brought us into union with Christ
who fulfils your gracious covenant;
and in bread and wine
we receive the fruit of his obedience.
So with joy
we take upon ourselves the yoke of obedience,
and commit ourselves to seek and do your perfect will.

Silence is kept for a time.

The minister says:

I am no longer my own, but yours.

The minister and people say together:

**I am no longer my own, but yours.
Put me to what you will,
rank me with whom you will;
put me to doing, put me to suffering;
let me be employed for you or laid aside for you;
exalted for you or brought low for you;
let me be full, let me be empty;
let me have all things, let me have nothing;
I freely and wholeheartedly yield all things
to your pleasure and disposal.**

**And now, glorious and blessed God,
Father, Son and Holy Spirit,
you are mine and I am yours,
to the glory and praise of your name. Amen.**

18 THE PEACE

The minister says:

We are the body of Christ.
The Spirit is with us.

The peace of the Lord be always with you.
And also with you.

The people may exchange a sign of peace.

The Sacrament of The Lord's Supper

The service continues from page 90 at 17 HYMN in The Service
of the Lord's Day.

The Service of the Lord's Day

The Service of the Lord's Day

NOTES

i   Christian worship is God's gift whereby we participate through the Spirit in the Son's communion with the Father. Thus we are called as the people of God with the gifts the Spirit has distributed among us, to take part in what Christ, our one Mediator and High Priest, has done and continues to do for us. So the bread which we break is a participation in the body of Christ and the cup we take is a participation in the blood of Christ.

ii   Since New Testament times, the Lord's people have gathered at the Lord's table on the Lord's day. This is to remember Christ's death and resurrection and to celebrate the sacraments as signs of the last day, the day of consummation. Through the ages the basic structure of christian worship has remained the same. In Reformed practice, despite variations for historical reasons, this pattern has been maintained.

iii   The following order of service reflects this basic structure and may be used whether or not the eucharist is celebrated. When the section entitled 'The Sacrament of the Lord's Supper' is omitted, other acts of thanksgiving and dedication such as those in Resources for Leading Worship are used.

iv   This service has four parts:

The Gathering of the People of God
Summoned by God's good news, we come together to offer our praise to God, to confess the grace of our Lord Jesus Christ in the forgiveness of sin, and to hear God's word.

The Service of the Word
The Scriptures of the Old and New Testaments are read and proclaimed; and in grateful response we make an offering of faith in a creed, an offering of our concern for others in prayers of intercession, and an offering of money as our participation in the mission of Christ in the whole world.

The Sacrament of the Lord's Supper
God feeds his baptised people in the Spirit with the body and blood of Christ. In the breaking of the bread, the church acknowledges the presence of Christ, who re-presents himself to his disciples as the risen crucified One. In communion with Christ, we make our sacrifice of praise and thanksgiving and proclaim the Lord's death until he comes.

The Sending Forth of the People of God

Having been nourished, we are drawn into Christ's mission in the world, and God sends us forth in the power of the Spirit to love and serve all people.

v   It is the particular privilege and responsibility of a minister of the Word to preside at the Lord's table. This includes the offering of the Great Prayer of Thanksgiving and The Breaking of the Bread. Ministers and other leaders should discern the gifts of the people and encourage their participation in such ministries as welcoming the people, offering prayer, reading the Scriptures, making music, giving notices, taking up the offering, preparing the Lord's table and assisting the minister with the distribution of holy communion.

vi In every service of the Lord's supper, bread and wine shall be set apart with the use of Christ's words of institution as found in the gospels or epistle, and the manual acts there commanded: the breaking of the bread, the taking of the cup, and participation in both kinds by minister and people. (Appendix I to the *Basis of Union*, 2. (ii))

vii Music is an important part of the service. It can deepen our prayer and enhance our praise. Leaders and musicians should choose hymns with care as to their place in the service, their relation to the readings, and the theme of the day or season. As well as hymns, much of the service can be sung: 'Lord, have mercy', 'Glory to God in the highest' or other doxologies, the responses before and after the readings, the psalm, a creed, and the responses after prayers; and in The Sacrament of the Lord's Supper, 'Holy, holy, holy Lord' and 'Lamb of God'. Anthems and instrumental items may also be added at other points in the service where they are appropriate.

viii Silence is an important part of worship. Some appropriate places are indicated by rubrics, but a period of silence is often helpful before or after any prayer or reading or the sermon. Because some congregations are unfamiliar with the practice of silence, leaders may need to direct how the silence should be used.

ix When the Lord's supper is celebrated, the Nicene Creed, by tradition, is used. When baptism is celebrated, the Apostles' Creed is included in the order for baptism. No other creed or statement of faith is needed at any other place in these services. These creeds are authoritative statements of faith and have a special place in worship. *(Basis of Union, para. 9)* At other services, congregations may use other statements of faith.

x By using the lectionary for The Service of the Word, leaders of worship can ensure that the people regularly hear the testimony of the whole of Scripture. The Revised Standard Version is recommended. The lectionary assists the observance of the Liturgical Year, through which the church recalls the story of God's saving work. Readings are provided for Sundays and other principal days, and also for other occasions in the congregation.

xi Where liturgical colours are used for the minister's stoles, book marks, lectern and/or pulpit falls, table frontals and banners, the sequence of colours set out in The Calendar and Lectionary of the Uniting Church should be followed.

xii After the greetng of The Peace, the people may exchange a sign of peace by a handclasp or according to other local custom.

xiii The Fourth Assembly of the Uniting Church (1985) encouraged all congregations to arrange their furnishings in such a way that the communion table is free-standing, accessible on all sides, conspicuous and of adequate size to accommodate all the elements of bread and wine required for the distribution of holy communion to all present, together with the offering of the people.

xiv The minister should stand behind the table, facing the people. The table furnishings should be placed in such a way that the people have an uninterrupted view of the liturgical action.

xv The table should be laid with a clean white cloth. The bread and wine may be brought to the table by members of the congregation at The Setting of the Table, or they may be placed on the table before the service and covered with a white cloth which is removed at The Setting of the Table.

xvi It is the responsibility of the minister with the council of elders to determine whether the bread used is leavened or unleavened, pre-cut or an unbroken loaf; and whether the wine used is fermented or unfermented, offered in individual cups or in a common cup. They also decide how the elements are to be distributed during the service, and how the elements remaining after the service are to be disposed of, whether by eating and drinking or some other reverent means.

xvii If pre-cut bread is used, a slice or loaf of bread should be provided for The Breaking of the Bread. The pre-cut pieces of bread should be of generous size. Those responsible for preparing the bread and wine should ensure that adequate provisions are made, while avoiding over-supply. A chalice containing wine for lifting up and drinking should be placed centrally on the table.

Prayers Before the Service

A

Lord Jesus Christ,
by your Holy Spirit,
be present with us now. Amen.

B   This prayer may be used at 1.

(See People's Book, p. 58.)

Almighty God,
to whom all hearts are open,
all desires known,
and from whom no secrets are hidden:
cleanse the thoughts of our hearts
by the inspiration of your Holy Spirit,
that we may perfectly love you,
and worthily magnify your holy name;
through Christ our Lord. Amen.

C   This prayer may be used before 6, or before or after 11.

(See People's Book, pp. 61-2.)

O Lord our God,
you have given your word
to be a lamp to our feet and a light to our path.
Grant us grace to receive your truth in faith and love,
that we may be obedient to your will
and live always for your glory;
through Jesus Christ our Lord. Amen.

D   This may be used as a prayer of approach at 18 in The Sacrament of
the Lord's Supper.

(See People's Book, p. 65.)

Be present, risen Lord Jesus,
as you were with your disciples,
and make yourself known to us
in the breaking of the bread;
for you live and reign with the Father and the Holy Spirit,
one God, for ever and ever. Amen.

E   This may be used as a prayer of approach at 18 in The Sacrament of
the Lord's Supper.

(See People's Book, p. 65.)

We do not presume
to come to your table, merciful Lord,
trusting in our own righteousness,
but in your manifold and great mercies.
We are not worthy
so much as to gather up the crumbs under your table.
But you are the same Lord
whose nature is always to have mercy.
Grant us, therefore, gracious Lord,
so to eat the flesh of your dear Son Jesus Christ,
and to drink his blood,
that we may evermore dwell in him,
and he in us. Amen.

A Service of Word and Sacrament

The Gathering of the People of God

The people may stand as the open Bible is carried in and placed on the lectern or pulpit.

1   CALL TO WORSHIP

Let us worship God.

One or more Scripture sentences may be said.

2   HYMN

After the hymn, the people remain standing.

(See People's Book, p. 58.)

3   GREETING

The grace of the Lord Jesus Christ
and the love of God
and the fellowship of the Holy Spirit
be with you all.
And also with you.

2 Corinthians 13:14

The people sit.

A brief introduction to the theme of the service may be given.

4 PRAYERS OF ADORATION AND CONFESSION

Silence may be kept after an invitation to prayer.

A prayer of adoration such as the following is offered:

Eternal God, Lord of heaven and earth,
we praise you for your greatness.
Your wisdom is seen in all your works.
Your grace and truth are revealed
in Jesus Christ your Son.
Your presence and power are given to us
through the Holy Spirit.
Therefore, O blessed Trinity,
we worship and adore you for ever and ever.
Amen.

A prayer of confession is offered, the leader first saying words such as:

In penitence and faith,
let us confess our sins to almighty God.

After a time of silence, one of the following forms may be used, or free prayer offered.

(See People's Book, p. 58.)

Let us pray:

Merciful God,
our maker and our judge,
we have sinned against you in thought, word, and deed:
we have not loved you with our whole heart,
we have not loved our neighbours as ourselves;
we repent, and are sorry for all our sins.
Father, forgive us.
Strengthen us to love and obey you in newness of life;
through Jesus Christ our Lord. Amen.

or

The following responses may be said or sung:

(See People's Book, p. 59.)

Let us pray:

The first petition is offered.

Lord, have mercy.
Lord, have mercy.

A second petition is offered.

Christ, have mercy.
Christ, have mercy.

A third petition is offered.

Lord, have mercy.
Lord, have mercy.

DECLARATION OF FORGIVENESS

Before the declaration of forgiveness, the leader says a Scripture sentence such as:

The saying is sure and worthy of full acceptance,
that Christ Jesus came into the world to save sinners.

1 Timothy 1:15

or

If we confess our sins,
God is faithful and just, and will forgive our sins
and cleanse us from all unrighteousness.

1 John 1:9

The leader says:

Hear then Christ's word of grace to us:
Your sins are forgiven.
Thanks be to God.

5 DOXOLOGY

One of these doxologies may be said or sung, the people standing:

(See People's Book, p. 60.)

**Glory to God in the highest,
and peace to God's people on earth.**

**Lord God, heavenly King,
almighty God and Father,
  we worship you, we give you thanks,
  we praise you for your glory.**

**Lord Jesus Christ, only Son of the Father,
Lord God, Lamb of God,
you take away the sin of the world:
  have mercy on us;
you are seated at the right hand of the Father:
  receive our prayer.**

**For you alone are the Holy One,
you alone are the Lord,
you alone are the Most High,
  Jesus Christ,
  with the Holy Spirit,
  in the glory of God the Father. Amen.**

or

**Now to him who loved us, gave us
every pledge that love could give,
freely shed his blood to save us,
gave his life that we might live,
be the kingdom
and dominion
and the glory evermore.**

A.H.B., 576

The Service of the Word

If a brief address is to be given to young people, it is appropriate at this point or after a Scripture reading.

The address may be followed by a hymn or song.

A brief introduction may be given to the readings of the day.

Before the readings, a prayer for illumination or the collect of the day may be offered, or the following may be said or sung:

Your word, O Lord, is a lamp to our feet:
a light to our path.

6   FIRST READING

7   PSALM

8   SECOND READING

9   GOSPEL

After the final reading, one of the following may be said or sung:

This is the word of the Lord.
Thanks be to God.

or

Lord, may your word live in us:
and bear much fruit to your glory.

10 HYMN

11 PREACHING OF THE WORD

After the preaching, an Ascription of Glory may be said.

Silence may be kept for meditation.

> *If there is no celebration of The Sacrament of the Lord's Supper, the Service of the Lord's Day continues on page 131. (People's Book, page 69.)*

12 AFFIRMATION OF FAITH

(See People's Book, pp. 62-3.)

A creed of the church may be said or sung

The people stand.

We believe in one God,
the Father, the Almighty,
maker of heaven and earth,
of all that is, seen and unseen.

We believe in one Lord, Jesus Christ,
the only Son of God,
eternally begotten of the Father,
God from God, Light from Light,
true God from true God,
begotten, not made,
of one Being with the Father;
through him all things were made.
For us and for our salvation
he came down from heaven,
was incarnate by the Holy Spirit of the Virgin Mary
and became truly human.
For our sake he was crucified under Pontius Pilate;
he suffered death and was buried.
On the third day he rose again
in accordance with the Scriptures;
he ascended into heaven
and is seated at the right hand of the Father.
He will come again in glory
to judge the living and the dead,
and his kingdom will have no end.

We believe in the Holy Spirit, the Lord, the giver of life,
who proceeds from the Father,
who with the Father and the Son
is worshipped and glorified,
who has spoken through the prophets.
We believe in one holy catholic and apostolic Church.
We acknowledge one baptism for the forgiveness of sins.
We look for the resurrection of the dead,
and the life of the world to come. Amen.

Nicene Creed

The people sit.

13 OFFERING

A Scripture sentence may be used before the gifts of money are collected.

The gifts are presented and a prayer is offered.

14 NOTICES AND CONCERNS OF THE CHURCH

15 PRAYERS OF THE PEOPLE

Prayers are offered for the church,
for the peoples of the world,
for the nation and the community,
and for situations of need.

After each prayer the people may say or sing: **Amen.**

A response may be said or sung such as:

Lord, in your mercy,
hear our prayer.
or
Lord, hear us.
Lord, hear our prayer.

The prayers may conclude with
a commemoration of the faithful departed,
the collect of the day,
or some other appropriate collect.

The Sacrament of the Lord's Supper

16 THE PEACE

The people stand for the greeting of peace.

**The peace of the Lord be always with you.
And also with you.**

The people may exchange a sign of peace.

17 HYMN

18 SETTING OF THE TABLE

During the hymn, the gifts of bread and wine are brought to the table; or, being already in place, are uncovered and made ready for use.

An invitation to the Lord's table may be given.

A prayer of approach may be offered.

19 GREAT PRAYER OF THANKSGIVING

(See People's Book, p. 65.)

A Great Prayer of Thanksgiving shall be offered.

The structure of the first Great Prayer of Thanksgiving provides for the Narrative of the Institution of the Lord's Supper either to be read first, or else to form part of the prayer itself.

If Alternative Prayer A, D, E, F, or H is used, the Narrative of the Institution is not read at this point.

If Alternative Prayer B, C, or G is used, the Narrative of the Institution as follows shall be read first.

NARRATIVE OF THE INSTITUTION OF THE LORD'S SUPPER

Hear the words of institution of this sacrament
as recorded by the apostle Paul:

For I received from the Lord
what I also delivered to you,
that the Lord Jesus,
on the night when he was betrayed,
took bread,
and when he had given thanks,
he broke it and said:
This is my body which is for you.
Do this for the remembrance of me.

In the same way also the cup,
after supper, saying:
This cup is the new covenant in my blood.
Do this, as often as you drink it,
for the remembrance of me.

For as often as you eat this bread
and drink the cup,
you proclaim the Lord's death until he comes.

1 Corinthians 11:23-26

The minister may say:

With this bread and this cup
we do as our Saviour commands:
we set them apart for the holy supper
to which he calls us,
and we come to God with our prayers of thanksgiving.

THE GREAT PRAYER OF THANKSGIVING

The people stand.

The minister says:

The Lord be with you.
And also with you.

Lift up your hearts.
We lift them to the Lord.

Let us give thanks to the Lord our God.
It is right to give our thanks and praise.

Thanks and praise, glory and honour are rightly yours,
our Lord and God,
for you alone are worthy.

In time beyond our dreaming
you brought forth light out of darkness,
and in the love of Christ your Son
you set man and woman at the heart of your creation.

A seasonal or other special thanksgiving may be offered.

If there is no seasonal thanksgiving, the minister continues:

And so we praise you
with the faithful of every time and place,
joining with choirs of angels and the whole creation
in the eternal hymn:

Holy, holy, holy Lord . . .

The Great Prayer of Thanksgiving continues on page 102.

Advent

We thank you for the true light
that enlightens the whole world.
    In the preaching of John the Baptist
or, In the annunciation to Mary
you prepared the way of the Lord Jesus Christ.

And so we praise you
with the faithful of every time and place,
joining with choirs of angels and the whole creation
in the eternal hymn:

Holy, holy, holy Lord . . .

The Great Prayer of Thanksgiving continues on page 102.

Christmas

When the right time had come
you sent your Son Jesus.
By the power of the Holy Spirit
he was incarnate of the Virgin Mary,
and became truly human.

And so we praise you
with the faithful of every time and place,
joining with choirs of angels and the whole creation
in the eternal hymn:

Holy, holy, holy Lord . . .

The Great Prayer of Thanksgiving continues on page 102.

Epiphany

We give you thanks through your beloved child Jesus,
whom you revealed to the whole world
as Saviour and Redeemer,
the light of all the nations.

And so we praise you
with the faithful of every time and place,
joining with choirs of angels and the whole creation
in the eternal hymn:

Holy, holy, holy Lord . . .

The Great Prayer of Thanksgiving continues on page 102.

Baptism of Jesus

The Spirit moved over the water in the beginning.
Through the Sea you led the children of Israel
to freedom and the Promised Land.
When Jesus was baptised in Jordan
the Spirit came upon your Beloved,
in whom you were well pleased.

And so we praise you
with the faithful of every time and place,
joining with choirs of angels and the whole creation
in the eternal hymn:

Holy, holy, holy Lord . . .

The Great Prayer of Thanksgiving continues on page 102.

Lent

You make us your disciples
and call us to deny ourselves,
to take up our cross and follow Jesus.

And so we praise you
with the faithful of every time and place,
joining with choirs of angels and the whole creation
in the eternal hymn:

Holy, holy, holy Lord . . .

The Great Prayer of Thanksgiving continues on page 102.

Holy Week

In humility your Servant entered Jerusalem
to cries of Hosanna!
When the cries turned to Crucify!
he was taken outside the city
and lifted up as King of glory.

And so we praise you
with the faithful of every time and place,
joining with choirs of angels and the whole creation
in the eternal hymn:

Holy, holy, holy Lord . . .

The Great Prayer of Thanksgiving continues on page 102.

Holy Thursday

In Egypt your people ate the bitter bread of slavery.
In the desert you gave them fresh water
and manna for their daily bread.
You led them to a land of milk and honey.

And so we praise you
with the faithful of every time and place,
joining with choirs of angels and the whole creation
in the eternal hymn:

Holy, holy, holy Lord . . .

The Great Prayer of Thanksgiving continues on page 102.

Good Friday: Easter Day

The tree of life in the midst of the garden
was the tree of our defeat.
Christ was lifted up on the tree of victory;
and where life was lost,
there life has been restored.

And so we praise you
with the faithful of every time and place,
joining with choirs of angels and the whole creation
in the eternal hymn:

Holy, holy, holy Lord . . .

The Great Prayer of Thanksgiving continues on page 102.

Easter Day: Easter Season

You loved the world so much
that you sent your only Son
to bring us life eternal.
Dying he destroyed our death, alleluia.
Rising he restored our life, alleluia.

And so we praise you
with the faithful of every time and place,
joining with choirs of angels and the whole creation
in the eternal hymn:

Holy, holy, holy Lord . . .

The Great Prayer of Thanksgiving continues on page 102.

Ascension

You have revealed your glory
in the One who humbled himself.
You have exalted him to your right hand
where he lives for ever to pray for us.

And so we praise you
with the faithful of every time and place,
joining with choirs of angels and the whole creation
in the eternal hymn:

Holy, holy, holy Lord . . .

The Great Prayer of Thanksgiving continues on page 102.

Pentecost

By the gift of the Spirit
you bring to completion the work of your Son.
You lead us into all truth
and give us power to proclaim the gospel
to the whole world.

And so we praise you
with the faithful of every time and place,
joining with choirs of angels and the whole creation
in the eternal hymn:

Holy, holy, holy Lord . . .

The Great Prayer of Thanksgiving continues on page 102.

Trinity Sunday

You call us to proclaim the mystery of our faith:
the Lord our God, the Lord is One,
Father, Son and Holy Spirit,
Trinity of love,
equal in majesty,
undivided in splendour,
worshipped and adored for ever.

And so we praise you
with the faithful of every time and place,
joining with choirs of angels and the whole creation
in the eternal hymn:

Holy, holy, holy Lord . . .

The Great Prayer of Thanksgiving continues on page 102.

Confirmation

You make covenant with us in Christ
and incorporate us into his body by baptism.
By the Spirit we are enabled
to live no longer for ourselves
but for him who died and rose again,
and we are commissioned as his servants in the world.

And so we praise you
with the faithful of every time and place,
joining with choirs of angels and the whole creation
in the eternal hymn:

Holy, holy, holy Lord . . .

The Great Prayer of Thanksgiving continues on page 102.

Marriage

You formed us in your image,
and gave the covenant of marriage,
that in the union of husband and wife
we might share in the self-giving love
of Christ for the church.

And so we praise you
with the faithful of every time and place,
joining with choirs of angels and the whole creation
in the eternal hymn:

Holy, holy, holy Lord . . .

The Great Prayer of Thanksgiving continues on page 102.

Funeral

In death we return to the dust from which we were made,
trusting in your promise:
nothing can separate us from your love in Christ Jesus,
neither death nor life,
nor things present, nor things to come.

And so we praise you
with the faithful of every time and place,
joining with choirs of angels and the whole creation
in the eternal hymn:

Holy, holy, holy Lord . . .

The Great Prayer of Thanksgiving continues on page 102.

Ordination

In every age Christ the Good Shepherd
calls his faithful servants to preach the gospel,
celebrate the sacraments of the new covenant
and build up his people in faith and love.
For he came not to be served, but to serve,
and to give his life a ransom for many.

And so we praise you
with the faithful of every time and place,
joining with choirs of angels and the whole creation
in the eternal hymn:

Holy, holy, holy Lord . . .

The Great Prayer of Thanksgiving continues on page 102.

The Great Prayer of Thanksgiving continues, all singing or saying:

Holy, holy, holy Lord, God of power and might,
heaven and earth are full of your glory.
   Hosanna in the highest.

Blessed is he who comes in the name of the Lord.
   Hosanna in the highest.

We thank you that you called a covenant people
to be a light to the nations.
Through Moses you taught us to love your law,
and in the prophets you cried out for justice.

In the fullness of your mercy
you became one with us in Jesus Christ,
who gave himself up for us on the cross.
You make us alive together with him,
that we may rejoice in his presence
and share his peace.

By water and the Spirit
you open the kingdom to all who believe,
and welcome us to your table:
for by grace we are saved, through faith.

The following Narrative of the Institution of the Lord's Supper shall be read here if it has not been read before The Great Prayer of Thanksgiving.

We bless you, Lord God, king of the universe,
through our Lord Jesus Christ,
who on the night of his betrayal
took bread,
gave you thanks,
broke it,
and gave it to his disciples, saying:

Take this and eat it.
This is my body given for you.
Do this for the remembrance of me.

In the same way, after supper,
he took the cup,
gave thanks,
and gave it to them, saying:
Drink from this, all of you.
This is my blood of the new covenant
poured out for you and for everyone
for the forgiveness of sins.
Do this, whenever you drink it,
for the remembrance of me.

With this bread and this cup
we do as our Saviour commands:
we celebrate the redemption he has won for us.

Pour out the Holy Spirit on us
and on these gifts of bread and wine,
that they may be for us the body and blood of Christ.

Make us one with him,
one with each other,
and one in ministry in the world,
until at last we feast with him in the kingdom.

Through your Son, Jesus Christ,
in your holy church,
all honour and glory is yours, Father almighty,
now and for ever.
Amen.

The service continues with The Lord's Prayer on page 126.

ALTERNATIVE GREAT PRAYER OF THANKSGIVING   A

The Narrative of the Institution is included in this prayer.

The people stand.

The minister says:

The Lord be with you.
And also with you.

Lift up your hearts.
We lift them to the Lord.

Let us give thanks to the Lord our God.
It is right to give our thanks and praise.

All thanks and praise, glory and honour,
be yours at all times, and in every place,
creator Lord, holy Father, true and living God.

We praise you that through your eternal Word
you brought the universe into being
and made us in your own image.
You have given us this earth to care for and delight in,
and with its bounty you preserve our life.

We thank you that you bound yourself to all people
with the promises of a gracious covenant,
and called us to serve you in love and peace.

Above all, we give you thanks for your Son,
our Saviour Jesus Christ;
by the power of the Holy Spirit
he was born a man and lived our common life;
to you he offered his life in perfect obedience and trust;
he has delivered us from our sins, brought us new life,
and reconciled us to you, Father, and to one another.

And so we praise you
with the faithful of every time and place,
joining with choirs of angels and the whole creation
in the eternal hymn:

**Holy, holy, holy Lord, God of power and might,
heaven and earth are full of your glory.
Hosanna in the highest.**

**Blessed is he who comes in the name of the Lord.
Hosanna in the highest.**

And now, Father, we thank you
for these gifts of your creation, this bread and this wine,
and we pray that we who eat and drink them
in the fellowship of the Holy Spirit
in obedience to our Saviour Christ
may be partakers of his body and blood,
and be made one with him and with each other
in peace and love.

For on the night he was betrayed he took bread;
and when he had given you thanks
he broke it, and gave it to his disciples, saying:
Take, eat. This is my body which is given for you.
Do this in remembrance of me.

After supper, he took the cup;
and again giving you thanks
he gave it to his disciples, saying:
Drink from this, all of you.
This is my blood of the new covenant
which is shed for you and for all people
for the remission of sins.
Do this, as often as you drink it, in remembrance of me.

With this bread and this cup
we show forth Christ's death
until he comes in glory.

With thanksgiving, Father, for the gift of your Son,
we proclaim his passion and death,
his resurrection and ascension,
the outpouring of his Spirit,
and his presence with his people.

Renew us by your Holy Spirit
that we may be united in the body of your Son
and serve you as a royal priesthood
in the joy of your eternal kingdom.

Receive our praises, Father almighty,
through Jesus Christ our Lord,
with whom and in whom,
by the power of the Holy Spirit,
we worship you in songs of never-ending praise:

Blessing and honour and glory and power
are yours for ever and ever.
Amen.

The service continues with The Lord's Prayer on page 126.

ALTERNATIVE GREAT PRAYER OF
THANKSGIVING **B**

The Narrative of the Institution shall be read before this prayer.

The people stand.

The minister says:

The Lord be with you.
And also with you.

Lift up your hearts.
We lift them to the Lord.

Let us give thanks to the Lord our God.
It is right to give our thanks and praise.

It is right that we should always offer thanks, O God,
because you have created and sustained us
and all things.

And so we praise you
with the faithful of every time and place,
joining with choirs of angels and the whole creation
in the eternal hymn:

Holy, holy, holy Lord, God of power and might,
heaven and earth are full of your glory.
　　Hosanna in the highest.

Blessed is he who comes in the name of the Lord.
　　Hosanna in the highest.

We praise you, O God,
that in your mercy you gave your only Son, Jesus Christ,
that whoever believes in him
should not perish but have eternal life.

We give thanks for his humble birth,
for his life and ministry of love,
for his sufferings and death on the cross,
for his glorious resurrection and ascension,
and for the promise that he will come again.

O God, by your word and Spirit
bless and sanctify this bread and this wine,
that they may be for us
the communion of the body and blood of Christ,
and that he may ever live in us
and we in him.

Father, accept us,
as we offer and present ourselves, our souls and bodies,
to be a holy and living sacrifice;
through Jesus Christ our Lord,
to whom with you and the Holy Spirit
be all honour and glory, now and for ever.
Amen.

The service continues with The Lord's Prayer on page 126.

ALTERNATIVE GREAT PRAYER OF THANKSGIVING   C

The Narrative of the Institution shall be read before this prayer.

This short prayer is especially suitable for use with the sick, in which case the responses may be omitted.

The people stand.

The minister says:

The Lord be with you.
And also with you.

Lift up your hearts.
We lift them to the Lord.

Let us give thanks to the Lord our God.
It is right to give our thanks and praise.

Holy God, we praise you.
Let the heavens be joyful,
and the earth be glad.

We bless you for creating the whole world,
for your promises to your people Israel,
and for the life we know in Jesus Christ your Son.

Born of Mary, he shares our life.
Eating with sinners, he welcomes us.
Leading his followers, he guides us.
Dying on the cross, he rescues us.
Risen from the dead, he gives new life.

And so we praise you
with the faithful of every time and place,
joining with choirs of angels and the whole creation
in the eternal hymn:

**Holy, holy, holy Lord, God of power and might,
heaven and earth are full of your glory.**
   Hosanna in the highest.

Blessed is he who comes in the name of the Lord.
   Hosanna in the highest.

With thanksgiving we take this bread and this cup
and proclaim his death and resurrection.
Receive our sacrifice of praise.

Send to us the Holy Spirit,
that this meal may be holy
and your people may become one.
Unite us in faith, inspire us to love,
encourage us with hope,
that we may receive Christ
as he comes to us in this holy banquet.

We praise you, almighty Father,
through Christ your Son,
in the Holy Spirit.
Amen.

The service continues with The Lord's Prayer on page 126.

ALTERNATIVE GREAT PRAYER OF THANKSGIVING   D

The Narrative of the Institution is included in this prayer.

This prayer is especially suitable for use when children are present. The optional responses (in brackets) may be led by a choir.

The people stand.

The minister says:

The Lord be with you.
And also with you.

Lift up your hearts.
We lift them to the Lord.

Let us give thanks to the Lord our God.
It is right to give our thanks and praise.

We thank you, God,
that from the beginning
you made the world and all its creatures.
You made people to live for you and each other.
(We praise you, O God.)

You created Adam and Eve and gave them a garden;
you showed Noah a rainbow;
you gave strength to Moses to free his people
and taught Miriam to sing;
you gave courage to Esther and loyalty to Ruth;
you helped David defeat the giant
and gave him a harp to sing with.
(We praise you, O God.)

And yet even they turned away from you
and forgot about you, as we do too.
But you did not forget;
you sent your only child Jesus to the world
to show how much you love us
and to bring us back to you again.
(We praise you, O God.)

As one of us he came; at first a helpless infant,
then a child, a youth, and an adult.
He rejoiced with those who rejoiced
and wept with those who wept.
To the despairing he spoke a word of hope;
to the sick he gave healing;
to the rejected he was a friend.
And yet he was betrayed and nailed to a cross.
But he was lifted from the grave and restored to life
that he might be with us and we with him,
alive for evermore.

And so we praise you
with the faithful of every time and place,
joining with the choirs of angels and the whole creation
in the eternal hymn:

**Holy, holy, holy Lord, God of power and might,
heaven and earth are full of your glory.
   Hosanna in the highest.**

**Blessed is he who comes in the name of the Lord.
   Hosanna in the highest.**

On the night before Jesus died,
he had supper with his disciples.
He took bread,
thanked you, as we have thanked you,
broke the bread,
and gave the bread to his friends, saying:
This is my body given for you.
Each time you do this, remember me.

After supper he took the wine,
thanked you for it,
and passed a cup of wine to his friends, saying:
This cup is the new promise God has made with you
in my blood.
Each time you do this and drink from the cup,
remember me.

Remembering his death and celebrating his resurrection,
we await with hope his coming again
to bring peace and justice to the earth.
(Come, Lord Jesus.)

We pray you, God of love,
send your Holy Spirit upon us and what we do here;
that we and these signs, touched by your Spirit,
may be signs of life and love to each other
and to all the world.

Through Christ, with Christ, and in Christ,
in the unity of the Holy Spirit,
all glory is yours, God most holy,
now and for ever.
Amen.

The service continues with The Lord's Prayer on page 126.

ALTERNATIVE GREAT PRAYER OF THANKSGIVING   E

The Narrative of the Institution is included in this prayer.

This prayer is suitable for use on the occasion of a baptism and/or confirmation.

The people stand.

The minister says:

The Lord be with you.
And also with you.

Lift up your hearts.
We lift them to the Lord.

Let us give thanks to the Lord our God.
It is right to give our thanks and praise.

We give thanks to you, Lord God,
for the gift of creation and life.
You divided the light from the darkness
and the water from the dry land;
you made us in the image of yourself,
and breathed into us the breath of life.

We thank you for the gifts of mercy and new life.
Through the waters of the Red Sea
you delivered us from suffering and servitude;
at the foot of your sacred mountain
you called us to truth and holiness;
in the words of your holy prophets
you called us to justice and compassion;
through the lives of your blessed saints and martyrs
you taught us wisdom and faithfulness.

We thank you for the gift of Jesus, your only-begotten.
He is the newness of your promise to us,
the brightness of our hope in you;
for he emptied himself,
taking upon himself our bondage,
bearing our sins,
carrying the sorrows of our pilgrimage.
He was torn from the land of the living
for his witness to your holy teachings,
for fulfilment of your holy law;
and has become the first fruit of earth in your kingdom,
the One in whom your will is done.

And so we praise you
with the faithful of every time and place,
joining with choirs of angels and the whole creation
in the eternal hymn:

**Holy, holy, holy Lord, God of power and might,
heaven and earth are full of your glory.
   Hosanna in the highest.**

**Blessed is he who comes in the name of the Lord.
   Hosanna in the highest.**

On the night before he died,
Jesus and his friends gathered together in the Upper Room.
During supper he took some bread, saying:
Blessed is the Holy One of Israel,
Sovereign of all that is,
who brings forth bread from the earth.
After the blessing, he broke the bread
and gave it to the disciples, and said:
Take this and eat it; this is my body.

Then he took a cup, saying:
Blessed is the Holy One of Israel,
Sovereign of all that is,
who creates the fruit of the vine.
Having offered thanks,
he gave the cup to them, saying:
Drink from it, all of you;
this is my blood of the new covenant,
shed for all people for the forgiveness of sins.
I tell you,
never again shall I drink from the fruit of the vine
until that day when I drink it anew with you
in the kingdom of my Father.

Loving God,
we offer you this bread and this cup,
remembering his death and celebrating his resurrection.
You have made him the light of the nations
and the bearer of justice to the ends of the earth.

Send the Holy Spirit upon us and upon these gifts.
Make us one with Christ in his self-giving,
that through us he may bind up the broken hearted,
comfort the mourners, open the eyes of the blind,
and proclaim liberty to the captives;
until justice rolls down like waters,
and righteousness like an everflowing stream.
In this hope, and as your people, we praise you.

Through Christ, with Christ, and in Christ,
in the unity of the Holy Spirit,
all glory is yours, God most holy.
Amen.

The service continues with The Lord's Prayer on page 126.

ALTERNATIVE GREAT PRAYER OF THANKSGIVING   **F**

The Narrative of the Institution is included in this prayer.

The people stand.

The minister says:

The Lord be with you.
And also with you.

Lift up your hearts.
We lift them to the Lord.

Let us give thanks to the Lord our God.
It is right to give our thanks and praise.

Father, all-powerful and everliving God,
it is indeed right,
it is our joy and our salvation
always and everywhere to give you thanks and praise
through Jesus Christ, your Son, our Lord.
You created all things and made us in your image.
When we had fallen into sin,
you gave your only Son to be our Saviour.

He shared our human nature, and died on the cross.
You raised him from the dead,
and exalted him to your right hand in glory,
where he lives for ever to pray for us.
Through him you sent your holy and life-giving Spirit
and made us your people, a royal priesthood,
to stand before you to proclaim your glory
and to celebrate your mighty acts.

And so we praise you
with the faithful of every time and place,
joining with choirs of angels and the whole creation
in the eternal hymn:

**Holy, holy, holy Lord, God of power and might,
heaven and earth are full of your glory.
Hosanna in the highest.**

**Blessed is he who comes in the name of the Lord.
Hosanna in the highest.**

We praise you, Lord God, King of the universe,
through our Lord Jesus Christ,
who, on the night in which he was betrayed,
took bread,
gave thanks,
broke it and gave it to his disciples, saying:
Take this and eat it.
This is my body given for you.
Do this in remembrance of me.

In the same way, after supper,
he took the cup,
gave thanks,
and gave it to them, saying:
Drink from it, all of you.
This is my blood of the new covenant
poured out for you and for all people
for the forgiveness of your sins.
Do this, whenever you drink it,
in remembrance of me.

Therefore, Father, as he has commanded us,
we do this in remembrance of him;
and we ask you to accept our sacrifice of praise
and thanksgiving.

Send upon us the Holy Spirit,
that we who receive your gifts
may share in the body and blood of Christ.
Make us one body with him.

Accept us as we offer ourselves to be a living sacrifice,
and bring us with the whole creation
to your heavenly kingdom.

We ask this through your Son, Jesus Christ our Lord.
Through him, with him, in him,
in the unity of the Holy Spirit,
all honour and glory be given to you, almighty Father,
from all who dwell in earth and in heaven
throughout all ages.
Amen.

The service continues with The Lord's Prayer on page 126.

ALTERNATIVE GREAT PRAYER OF THANKSGIVING   G

The Narrative of the Institution shall be read before this prayer.

The people stand.

The minister says:

The Lord be with you.
And also with you.

Lift up your hearts.
We lift them to the Lord.

Let us give thanks to the Lord our God.
It is right to give our thanks and praise.

Almighty Father, creator and sustainer of life,
your majesty and power, your continued blessings
and your great goodness fill us with wonder.
We are unworthy of the pardon you have in mercy given.
We can bring only our thanks,
putting our trust in your Son, who alone saves us from evil.

And so we praise you
with the faithful of every time and place,
joining with choirs of angels and the whole creation
in the eternal hymn:

**Holy, holy, holy Lord, God of power and might,
heaven and earth are full of your glory.
    Hosanna in the highest.**

**Blessed is he who comes in the name of the Lord.
    Hosanna in the highest.**

God of glory,
in thanks we remember how Jesus broke bread and gave the cup
to make us partakers of his body and blood,
so that he might live in us and we in him.

God of mercy,
in thanks we remember how Jesus invites us to his table,
imprinting on our hearts his sacrifice on the cross.
In gratitude we bow before the Righteous One,
declaring his resurrection and glory,
and knowing that his prayers alone
make us worthy to partake of his spiritual meal.

Almighty God,
pour out the Holy Spirit upon us,
that, as we receive bread and wine,
we may be assured
that Christ's promise in these signs will be fulfilled.

Eternal Father,
lift our hearts and minds on high
where, with Christ your only Son,
and with the Holy Spirit,
all glory is yours, now and for evermore.
Amen.

The service continues with The Lord's Prayer on page 126.

ALTERNATIVE GREAT PRAYER OF THANKSGIVING   H

The Narrative of the Institution is included in this prayer.

The people stand.

The minister says:

The Lord be with you.
And also with you.

Lift up your hearts.
We lift them to the Lord.

Let us give thanks to the Lord our God.
It is right to give our thanks and praise.

It is right to glorify you, Father,
and to give you thanks;
for you alone are God, living and true,
dwelling in light inaccessible
from before time and for ever.
Fountain of life and source of all goodness,
you made all things
and fill them with your blessing;
you created them to rejoice
in the splendour of your radiance.

And so we praise you
with the faithful of every time and place,
joining with choirs of angels and the whole creation
in the eternal hymn:

**Holy, holy, holy Lord, God of power and might,
heaven and earth are full of your glory.**
Hosanna in the highest.

Blessed is he who comes in the name of the Lord.
Hosanna in the highest.

We acclaim you, holy Lord, glorious in power;
your mighty works reveal your wisdom and love.
You formed us in your own image,
giving the whole world into our care,
so that, in obedience to you, our Creator,
we might rule and serve all your creatures.
When our disobedience took us far from you,
you did not abandon us to the power of death.
In your mercy you came to our help,
so that in seeking you we might find you.
Again and again
you called us into covenant with you,
and through the prophets
you taught us to hope for salvation.

Father, you loved the world so much
that in the fullness of time
you sent your only Son to be our Saviour.
Incarnate by the Holy Spirit,
born of the Virgin Mary,
he lived as one of us, yet without sin.
To the poor he proclaimed the good news of salvation;
to prisoners, freedom;
to the sorrowful, joy.
To fulfil your purpose
he gave himself up to death
and, rising from the grave, destroyed death
and made the whole creation new.

And that we might live no longer for ourselves,
but for him who died and rose for us,
he sent the Holy Spirit,
his own first gift for those who believe,
to complete his work in the world,
and to bring to fulfilment the sanctification of all.

We bless you, Lord God, king of the universe,
through our Lord Jesus Christ,
who on the night of his betrayal
took bread,
gave you thanks,
broke it,
and gave it to his disciples, saying:
Take this and eat it.
This is my body given for you.
Do this for the remembrance of me.

In the same way, after supper,
he took the cup,
gave thanks,
and gave it to them, saying:
Drink from this, all of you.
This is my blood of the new covenant
poured out for you and for all people
for the forgiveness of sins.
Do this, whenever you drink it,
for the remembrance of me.

Father,
we now celebrate the memorial of our redemption.
Recalling Christ's death
and descent among the dead,
proclaiming his resurrection
and ascension to your right hand,
awaiting his coming in glory;
and offering to you,
from the gifts you have given us,
this bread and this cup,
we praise you and we bless you.

Lord,
we pray that in your goodness and mercy
your Holy Spirit may descend upon us,
and upon these gifts,
sanctifying them and showing them
to be holy gifts for your holy people,
the bread of life and the cup of salvation,
the body and blood of your Son Jesus Christ.

Grant that all who share this bread and this cup
may become one body and one spirit,
a living sacrifice in Christ
to the praise of your name.

Through Christ, and with Christ, and in Christ,
all honour and glory are yours,
almighty God and Father,
in the unity of the Holy Spirit,
for ever and ever.
Amen.

The service continues with The Lord's Prayer on page 126.

THE LORD'S PRAYER

(See People's Book, p. 66.)

Our Father in heaven,
  hallowed be your name,
  your kingdom come,
  your will be done,
    on earth as in heaven.
Give us today our daily bread.
Forgive us our sins
  as we forgive those who sin against us.
Save us from the time of trial
  and deliver us from evil.

For the kingdom, the power, and the glory are yours
  now and for ever. Amen.

The people sit.

20 THE BREAKING OF THE BREAD

The minister takes the bread and breaks it in full view of the people, in silence or saying:

The bread we break
is a sharing in the body of Christ.

The minister lifts the cup in full view of the people, in silence or saying:

The cup we take
is a sharing in the blood of Christ.

The minister holds out the bread and the cup to the people and says:

The gifts of God for the people of God.

21 LAMB OF GOD

This litany may be said or sung here, or sung during the distribution of holy communion.

(See People's Book, p. 66.)

Jesus, Lamb of God,
have mercy on us.

Jesus, bearer of our sins,
have mercy on us.

Jesus, redeemer of the world,
grant us peace.

or

Lamb of God, you take away the sin of the world,
have mercy on us.

Lamb of God, you take away the sin of the world,
have mercy on us.

Lamb of God, you take away the sin of the world,
grant us peace.

22 THE COMMUNION

The minister receives, then those assisting with the distribution, then the people according to local custom.

If the people are to serve one another, receiving in silence, the minister may first say to all:

**Receive this holy sacrament
of the body and blood of Christ,
and feed on him in your hearts
by faith with thanksgiving.**

Words such as the following are said before or during the distribution:

**The body of Christ, given for you.
Amen.**

and

**The blood of Christ, given for you.
Amen.**

or

**The body of Christ keep you in eternal life.
Amen**

and

**The blood of Christ keep you in eternal life.
Amen.**

After all have received, a time of silence may be kept.

23 PRAYER AFTER COMMUNION

The minister may offer a prayer such as one of the following, or the service continues from The Sending Forth of the People of God, page 130.

Let us pray:

We thank you, God our Father,
that through word and sacrament
you have given us your Son
who is the true bread of heaven
and food of eternal life.

So strengthen us in your service
that our daily living may show our thanks;
through Jesus Christ our Lord.
Amen.

or

Let us pray:

Father of all,
we give you thanks and praise
that when we were still far off
you met us in your Son and brought us home.
Dying and living, he declared your love,
gave us grace, and opened the gate of glory.
May we who share Christ's body live his risen life;
we who drink his cup bring life to others;
we whom the Spirit lights give light to the world.
Anchor us in this hope that we have grasped;
so we and all your children shall be free,
and the whole earth live to praise your name;
through Jesus Christ our Lord.
Amen.

The Sending Forth of the People of God

24 HYMN

25 WORD OF MISSION

A verse of Scripture, e.g. the sentence of the day or a verse from the readings of the day, or a brief charge to the people may be given.

26 BLESSING

May almighty God bless you,
the Father, the Son and the Holy Spirit.
Amen.

or

The blessing of God almighty,
the Father, the Son and the Holy Spirit,
be upon you and remain with you always.
Amen

27 DISMISSAL

If there has been no Word of Mission at 25, the following dismissal may be given:

Go in peace to love and serve the Lord:
In the name of Christ. Amen.

> *If there is no celebration of The Sacrament of the Lord's Supper, the Service of the Lord's Day continues from here.*

12 AFFIRMATION OF FAITH

A creed of the church or one of the statements of faith (*People's Book, pp. 122-134*) may be used.

The people stand.

13 HYMN

14 OFFERING

A Scripture sentence may be used before the gifts of money are collected.

The gifts are presented and a prayer is offered.

15 NOTICES AND CONCERNS OF THE CHURCH

16 PRAYERS OF THE PEOPLE

(See People's Book, p. 69.)

Prayers of thanksgiving and intercession are offered.

The intercessions may include prayers
> for the church,
> for the peoples of the world,
> for the nation and the community,
> and for situations of need.

After each prayer, the people may say or sing: **Amen.**

A response may be said or sung such as:

Lord, in your mercy,
hear our prayer.

or

Lord, hear us.
Lord, hear our prayer.

The prayers may conclude with
a commemoration of the faithful departed,
the collect of the day,
or some other appropriate collect.

THE LORD'S PRAYER

**Our Father in heaven,
hallowed be your name,
your kingdom come,
your will be done,
on earth as in heaven.
Give us today our daily bread.
Forgive us our sins
as we forgive those who sin against us.
Save us from the time of trial
and deliver us from evil.**

**For the kingdom, the power, and the glory are yours
now and for ever. Amen.**

The Sending Forth of the People of God

17 HYMN

18 WORD OF MISSION

A verse of Scripture, e.g. the sentence of the day or a verse from the readings of the day, or a brief charge to the people may be given.

19 BLESSING

May almighty God bless you,
the Father, the Son and the Holy Spirit.
Amen.

or

The blessing of God almighty,
the Father, the Son and the Holy Spirit,
be upon you and remain with you always.
Amen.

20 DISMISSAL

If there has been no word of mission at 18, the following dismissal may be given:

Go in peace to love and serve the Lord:
In the name of Christ. Amen.

NOTES

i   It is important that church members should not be deprived of hearing the Word and receiving holy communion because sickness or some other reason prevents them from joining in Sunday worship with the congregation.

ii   Normally, during a pastoral visit to such people, the minister will give communion, using a brief but complete order of service. However, in some parishes the minister and elders may decide to allow elders or other lay people appointed by the council of elders to take some of the bread and wine from the communion in the church to people at home or in hospital after the service. This order of service is designed for such use.

iii   Wherever possible, this ministry should take place on the Sunday and is to be regarded as part of the worship of the whole congregation. It would be appropriate to read one of the Bible readings used in the congregation (or at least some of the verses from that reading) and for the visitor to share some points from the sermon.

iv   The length of the service and what is to be included will depend on the situation of the person(s) visited. In some cases of sickness brevity is essential. For some housebound people their sense of isolation is eased by sharing in a longer service.

v   Prior arrangements should be made for each visit. Before the first such visit to any person(s), the purpose of the service and the procedure to be followed should be explained and the person(s) given the opportunity to accept or reject this form of ministry.

vi   The minister should prepare the visitors for this ministry. Spiritual preparation for conducting the service and general advice about visiting can be offered. The minister may also want to suggest the Bible reading to be used and points to be included in the Reflection and Prayers.

vii   Care should be taken that the bread and wine are taken in adequate containers and can be served in an appropriate manner. Following the visit, or the last visit if a series of calls is made on the day, any remaining bread or wine should be consumed or otherwise disposed of in a reverent manner.

viii   It would be appropriate for the congregation to know who are to be visited with the communion and who are to make the visits. All these can be remembered in the prayers of the congregation.

Communion Beyond the Gathered Congregation

GREETING

(See People's Book, p. 74.)

The grace of the Lord Jesus Christ
and the love of God
and the fellowship of the Holy Spirit
be with you.
And also with you.   *2 Corinthians 13:14*

PRAYER

The elder or other lay person may offer free prayer.

The theme of the prayer(s) may include the invocation and adoration of God and the confession of sin.

BIBLE READING

The theme of the day may be introduced and/or one of the readings of the day may be used.

REFLECTION

A brief reflection on the reading or a brief summary of the preaching in the congregation may be given.

PRAYERS OF THE PEOPLE

Greetings from the congregation and news of the congregation may be given.

Prayers of intercession may be offered here or during the Prayer after Communion.

The prayers may include intercessions for the church and the world, for the home or hospital and the person(s) being visited, and for the congregation.

The collect of the day and/or the Lord's Prayer may conclude Prayers of the People.

Our Father in heaven,
   hallowed be your name,
   your kingdom come,
   your will be done,
      on earth as in heaven.
Give us today our daily bread.
Forgive us our sins
   as we forgive those who sin against us.
Save us from the time of trial
   and deliver us from evil.

For the kingdom, the power, and the glory are yours
   now and for ever. Amen.

or

Our Father, who art in heaven,
   hallowed be thy name,
   thy kingdom come,
   thy will be done
      on earth as it is in heaven.
Give us this day our daily bread.
And forgive us our trespasses,
   as we forgive those who trespass against us.
And lead us not into temptation,
   but deliver us from evil.

For thine is the kingdom, the power and the glory,
   for ever and ever. Amen.

RECEPTION OF COMMUNION

The elder or other lay person says:

In obedience to the Lord Jesus,
our congregation has shared today in holy communion,
as christians have done through the ages.

This bread and this wine
have been brought from the communion table
so that you also may receive Christ's body and blood,
and be nourished for eternal life.

So let us lift our hearts to the Lord,
and receive this sacrament with thanksgiving.

The following prayer may be said together, or by the leader only.

Let us pray:

**Father, we thank you
that you feed us in these holy mysteries
with the spiritual food
of the body and blood of our Saviour, Jesus Christ.
We thank you for this assurance
of your goodness and love,
and that we are living members of his body
and heirs of his eternal kingdom.
May the Holy Spirit be upon us now,
that as we receive this bread and wine
we may know the presence and power
of Christ our Lord. Amen.**

The following is said with the giving of the bread:

The body of Christ, given for you.
Amen.

or

The body of Christ keep you in eternal life.
Amen.

The following is said with the giving of the cup:

The blood of Christ, given for you.
Amen.

or

The blood of Christ keep you in eternal life.
Amen.

PRAYER AFTER COMMUNION

After a time of silence, a prayer of thanksgiving and commitment may be offered.

THE PEACE

The peace of the Lord be always with you.
And also with you.

A sign of peace may be exchanged.

BLESSING

The blessing of God almighty,
the Father, the Son and the Holy Spirit,
be upon us and remain with us always.
Amen.

Resources for
the Liturgical Year

The Calendar and Lectionary of the Uniting Church

THE CALENDAR

The worship of the church celebrates the central mystery of our faith: the life, death and resurrection of the Lord Jesus Christ.

The foundation of the calendar is what the New Testament calls the Lord's Day (Revelation 1:10), the first day of each week. On the first day of creation God separated light from darkness. (Genesis 1:3-5) All four gospels state that it was in the morning of the first day of the week that the empty tomb of Jesus was discovered. (Matthew 28:1, Mark 16:2, Luke 24:1, John 20:1) The gospels go on to affirm that the risen Christ appeared to the disciples on that first day of the week and also on the eighth day — that is, the next Sunday. (John 20:26) Acts 2 states that on the Day of Pentecost (the fiftieth day), the Sunday seven weeks after Christ's resurrection, the disciples were filled with the Holy Spirit and the church was empowered to proclaim the gospel. The early christians also saw the Lord's Day as the eighth day of creation when God, after having rested on the seventh day, began to create anew. Anyone who is in Christ is 'a new creation'. (2 Corinthians 5:17) On this day they celebrated the whole saving work of Christ, including passion and death as well as resurrection; and they claimed the promise that the risen Christ would be in their midst. (Matthew 18:20, 28:20).

Each Sunday is therefore the weekly commemoration of that mystery of Christ. Christians gather each Lord's Day to celebrate, in word and sacrament, their participation in Christ. This is central to our understanding of the Liturgical Year (also known as the Christian Year and the Church Year), because it means that whenever we gather for worship on Sunday the most important thing to remember is not what season or day it is in the Liturgical Year but the fact that it is the Lord's Day. Every Sunday we celebrate the whole gospel, the whole good news of salvation, whatever may be the particular emphasis of that day or season.

Each year the weekly commemoration of the Lord's Day is celebrated with particular joy when the church keeps Easter. The Easter observance includes forty days of preparation in Lent and fifty days of celebration in the Easter season. Easter is the central festival of the Liturgical Year.

The commemoration of the birth of Jesus at Christmas provides the focus for the other seasons of the Liturgical Year. This festival, much later in origin than Easter, is preceded by a period of four weeks of preparation called Advent.

Sundays which are not immediately related to Christmas or Easter are known as Sundays after Epiphany and Sundays after Pentecost.

LITURGICAL COLOURS

There is a basic common pattern in the use of liturgical colours in the various denominations, although a number of small variations exist. For ministers of the Word who wear liturgical stoles and for congregations which have book marks, pulpit falls, communion table hangings and banners in liturgical colours, the following guidelines are suggested:

Violet or Purple:

These are the colours symbolising repentance and sorrow. They are used in the penitential seasons of Advent and Lent.

White or Gold:

These are the colours which symbolise rejoicing and celebration. They are used in the joyful seasons of Christmas and Easter.

Green:

This is the colour of growth. It is used in the seasons after The Epiphany and after The Day of Pentecost when the significance of Christ's incarnation and resurrection is applied to our christian life and witness.

Violet, white and green are the three principal liturgical colours. In both the Christmas Cycle (from the First Sunday in Advent through to the Last Sunday after Epiphany) and the Easter Cycle (from Ash Wednesday through to The Festival of Christ the King), the colours violet, white and green are used in that order. A time of preparation (violet) leads us into a season of celebration (white) which challenges us to a time of recommitment and growth in Christ (green).

Red:

This is the colour of fire, symbolising the presence and power of the Holy Spirit. It is used on The Day of Pentecost and other specific days in the life and witness of the church and of the congregation. Such days may include Synod Sunday, Mission Sunday, Church Anniversary etc.

Particular Services

There is much more variation among the denominations regarding the use of liturgical colours for particular services. Without wishing to limit local initiative and creativity, the following guidelines may promote uniformity of practice in our denomination:

Baptism:	White, or the seasonal colour of the day
Confirmation:	Red, or the seasonal colour of the day
Marriage:	White, or the seasonal colour of the day
Funeral:	Violet, or the seasonal colour of the day (Some use white, symbolising witness to Christ's resurrection, others use green, symbolising continuing growth in Christ)
Ordination:	Red
Induction:	Red

Installation of a Moderator of Synod
or Chairperson of Presbytery: Red
Commissioning of a Lay Preacher: Red
Commissioning of Elders: Red, or the seasonal colour of the day

TITLES OF THE SEASONS, SUNDAYS AND OTHER PRINCIPAL DAYS

Advent Season　　　　　　*Colour: Violet*
First Sunday in Advent
Second Sunday in Advent
Third Sunday in Advent
Fourth Sunday in Advent

Christmas Season　　　*Colour: White*
Christmas Eve　　　　　　　　　　*24 December*
Christmas Day: The Day of Christ's Birth　*25 December*
First Sunday of Christmas
The Naming of Jesus　　　　　　　*1 January*
Second Sunday of Christmas
The Epiphany of the Lord　　　　　*6 January*

Season after Epiphany　　*Colour: Green,*
　　　　　　　　　　　　　unless otherwise indicated

First Sunday after Epiphany: The Baptism of Jesus　*White*
Second Sunday through to a possible Eighth Sunday after
Epiphany
Last Sunday after Epiphany: The Transfiguration of Jesus　*White*

Lenten Season　　　　　*Colour: Violet*

Ash Wednesday: The First Day in Lent
First Sunday in Lent
Second Sunday in Lent
Third Sunday in Lent
Fourth Sunday in Lent
Fifth Sunday in Lent

Holy Week

Sixth Sunday in Lent: The Sunday of the Passion: Passion Sunday:
(also known as Palm Sunday)
Monday in Holy Week
Tuesday in Holy Week
Wednesday in Holy Week
Holy Thursday
Good Friday: The Day of Christ's Death   *No Colour*
Holy Saturday   *No colour*

Easter Season   *Colour: White,*
                                       unless otherwise indicated

Easter Eve
Easter Day: The Day of Christ's Resurrection
Second Sunday of Easter
Third Sunday of Easter
Fourth Sunday of Easter
Fifth Sunday of Easter
Sixth Sunday of Easter
Ascension Day: The Ascension of the Lord
Seventh Sunday of Easter
The Day of Pentecost   *Red*

Season after Pentecost   *Colour: Green,*
                                     unless otherwise indicated

First Sunday after Pentecost: Trinity Sunday   *White*
Second Sunday through to a possible Twenty Seventh Sunday
after Pentecost
Last Sunday after Pentecost: The Festival of Christ the
King   *White*

Other Principal Days

The Annunciation of Jesus to Mary   *25 March*   *White*
All Saints' Day   *1 November*   *White*

THE LECTIONARY

The lectionary contains the Scripture readings and a sentence and collect for every Sunday in a three-year cycle. The lections are taken from *Common Lectionary,* prepared by an ecumenical body, the Consultation on Common Texts. The Consultation based its work on the *Roman Lectionary* of 1969, which must be accounted as one of the foremost gifts of the Second Vatican Council to the Church catholic. The readings from *Common Lectionary* are set out under Year A, Year B, and Year C.

The lectionary also provides readings, a sentence and collect for other days which celebrate the mystery of Christ. Those days are: Christmas Day, *25 December;* The Naming of Jesus, *1 January;* The Epiphany of the Lord, *6 January;* Ash Wednesday; The Annunciation of Jesus to Mary, *25 March;* the Week Days of Holy Week; Ascension Day; and All Saints' Day.

Sundays and Other Principal Days

First Sunday in Advent — Year A

Sentence

O house of Jacob, come,
let us walk in the light of the Lord.   *Isaiah 2:5*

Collect

Almighty God,
give us grace that we may cast away the works of darkness
and put on the armour of light
now in the time of this mortal life
in which your Son Jesus Christ came among us
in great humility;
that on the last day,
when he comes again in his glorious majesty
to judge the living and the dead,
we may rise to the life immortal;
through him who lives and reigns with you and the Holy Spirit,
now and for ever.

Readings

Isaiah 2:1-5   Psalm 122

Romans 13:11-14   Matthew 24:36-44

Second Sunday in Advent — Year A

Sentence

The voice of one crying in the wilderness:
Prepare the way of the Lord,
make his ways straight.   *Matthew 3:3*

Collect

Gracious Father,
by whose tender compassion
the light of Christ has dawned upon us:
open our hearts,
so that, joyfully receiving Christ,
we may declare his glory to the ends of the earth.
He lives and reigns with you and the Holy Spirit,
one God, for ever and ever.

Readings

Isaiah 11:1-10   Psalm 72:1-8

Romans 15:4-13   Matthew 3:1-12

Third Sunday in Advent — Year A

Sentence

Strengthen the weak hands,
and make firm the feeble knees.
Say to those who are of feeble heart:
Be strong, fear not.   *Isaiah 35:3, 4*

Collect

Sustain us, Father, with the power of your love
on our journey to meet the One who is coming;
strengthen our weak hands,
make firm our feeble knees,
and open blind eyes to the dawning of your kingdom;
that our hearts may rejoice with joy and singing
as we behold the majesty of our God.
We ask this through your Son, our Lord Jesus Christ,
who lives and reigns with you and the Holy Spirit,
one God, for ever and ever.

Readings

Isaiah 35:1-10

Psalm 146:5-10

James 5:7-10

Matthew 11:2-11

Fourth Sunday in Advent — Year A

Sentence

Behold, a young woman shall conceive and bear a son,
and shall call his name: Immanuel.

Isaiah 7:14

Collect

Let us pray (for grace to accept God's will for us):

Heavenly Father,
who chose the Virgin Mary, full of grace,
to be the mother of our Lord and Saviour:
fill us with your grace,
that in all things we may accept your holy will
and with her rejoice in your salvation;
through Jesus Christ our Lord.

Readings

Isaiah 7:10-16	Psalm 24
Romans 1:1-7	Matthew 1:18-25

Christmas — Years A, B, C   *24, 25 December*

Sentence

In the early evening of Christmas Eve

The people who walked in darkness have seen a great light;
those who dwelt in a land of deep darkness,
on them has light shined.   *Isaiah 9:2*

Christmas Eve at midnight and on Christmas Day

Behold, I bring you news of a great joy
which will come to all the people;
for to you is born this day in the city of David
a Saviour, who is Christ the Lord.   *Luke 2:10-11*

Collect

For Christmas Eve

Father,
you make this holy night radiant
with the splendour of Jesus Christ our light.
We welcome him as Lord, the true light of the world.
Bring us to eternal joy in the kingdom of heaven,
where he lives and reigns with you and the Holy Spirit,
one God, for ever and ever.

or

Father,
we rejoice this night
in the birth of our Saviour,
through whom you have rescued us
from the dominion of darkness
and brought us into the kingdom of light.
Let the grace and truth of Christ so fill our hearts
that we may gladly proclaim the gospel of peace,
and, with the choirs of angels,
give glory to you in highest heaven;
where with the Son and the Holy Spirit
you live and reign,
one God, for ever and ever.

or

Eternal God,
who made this most holy night
to shine with the brightness of your one true light:
bring us, who have known the revelation
of that light on earth,
to see the radiance of your heavenly glory;
through Jesus Christ our Lord.

Let us pray (for the peace that comes
from the Prince of Peace):

Almighty God and Father of light,
a Child is born for us and a Son is given to us.
Your eternal Word leaped down from heaven
in the silent watches of the night,
and now your church is filled with wonder
at the nearness of her God.
Open our hearts to receive his life
and increase our vision with the rising of dawn,
that our lives may be filled with his glory and his peace,
who lives and reigns for ever and ever.

or

O God our Father,
whose Word has come among us
in the Holy Child of Bethlehem:
may the light of faith illumine our hearts
and shine in our words and deeds;
through him who is Christ our Lord,
who lives and reigns with you and the Holy Spirit,
one God, now and for ever.

or

Gracious Father,
your love for us shines forth in Christ,
the Word made flesh.
Grant us his humble spirit,
that, by recognising your presence
in those whose lives we touch,
we may honour you by serving them;
through Jesus Christ our Lord,
who lives and reigns with you and the Holy Spirit,
one God, for ever and ever.

Readings for Christmas Eve and Christmas Day

Isaiah 9:2-7	Psalm 96
Titus 2:11-14	Luke 2:1-20

Optional readings

Isaiah 62: 6, 7, 10-12	Psalm 97
Titus 3:4-7	Luke 2:8-20

or

Isaiah 52:7-10	Psalm 98
Hebrews 1:1-12	John 1:1-14

First Sunday of Christmas — Year A

Sentence

I will recount the steadfast love of the Lord,
the praises of the Lord,
according to all the Lord has granted us.   *Isaiah 63:7*

Collect

Let us pray (for peace in our families):

Father,
help us to live as the holy family,
united in respect and love.
Bring us to the joy and peace of your eternal home.
Grant this through our Lord Jesus Christ, your Son,
who lives and reigns with you and the Holy Spirit,
one God, for ever and ever.

or

O God,
who wonderfully created, and yet more wonderfully restored,
the dignity of human nature:
grant that we may share the divine life
of him who humbled himself to share our humanity,
your Son Jesus Christ;
who lives and reigns with you
in the unity of the Holy Spirit,
one God, for ever and ever.

Readings

Isaiah 63:7-9	Psalm 111
Hebrews 2:10-18	Matthew 2:13-15, 19-23

The Naming of Jesus
Years A, B, C

Sentence

You shall call his name Jesus,
for he will save his people from their sins. *Matthew 1:21*

Collect

Eternal Father,
you gave to your incarnate Son
the holy name of Jesus
to be a sign of our salvation.
Plant in every heart, we pray,
the love of him who is the Saviour of the world,
our Lord Jesus Christ;
who lives and reigns with you and the Holy Spirit,
one God, in glory everlasting.

Readings

Numbers 6:22-27   Psalm 67

Galatians 4:4-7 *or*   Luke 2:15-21
Philippians 2:9-13

154   UNITING IN WORSHIP

Second Sunday of Christmas — Years A, B, C

Sentence

To all who received him, who believed in his name,
Christ gave power to become children of God.   *John 1:12*

Collect

Almighty God,
you have filled us with the new light of the Word
who became flesh and lived among us.
Let the light of faith
shine in all that we do;
through your Son, Jesus Christ our Lord,
who lives and reigns with you and the Holy Spirit,
one God, now and for ever.

Readings

Jeremiah 31:7-14   Psalm 147:12-20

Ephesians 1:3-6, 15-18   John 1:1-18

The Epiphany of the Lord
Years A, B, C

Sentence

When Jesus was born in Bethlehem,
wise men came from the East, saying:
Where is he who is born king of the Jews?
For we have seen his star in the East,
and have come to worship him.

Matthew 2:1, 2

Collect

Father,
you revealed your Son to the nations
by the guidance of a star.
Lead us to your glory in heaven
by the light of faith.
We ask this through our Lord Jesus Christ, your Son,
who lives and reigns with you and the Holy Spirit,
one God, for ever and ever.

or

Almighty God,
your Son our Saviour Jesus Christ
is the light of the world.
May your people,
illumined by your word and sacraments,
shine with the radiance of his glory,
that he may be known, worshipped, and obeyed
to the ends of the earth;
who lives and reigns with you and the Holy Spirit,
one God, now and for ever.

or

Lord God,
on this day you revealed your Son to the nations
by the leading of a star.
Lead us now by faith
to know your presence in our lives,
and bring us at last to the full vision of your glory;
through your Son, Jesus Christ our Lord,
who lives and reigns with you and the Holy Spirit,
one God, now and for ever.

Readings

Isaiah 60:1-6   Psalm 72:1-14

Ephesians 3:1-12   Matthew 2:1-12

First Sunday after Epiphany – Sunday 1 Year A

(The Baptism of Jesus)

Sentence

When Jesus was baptised, the heavens were opened
and he saw the Spirit of God descending like a dove;
and there was a voice from heaven, saying:
This is my beloved Son.   *Matthew 3:16, 17*

Collect

Almighty, eternal God,
when the Spirit descended upon Jesus
at his baptism in the Jordan,
you revealed him as your own beloved Son.
Keep us, your children born of water and the Spirit,
faithful to our calling.
We ask this through our Lord Jesus Christ, your Son,
who lives and reigns with you and the Holy Spirit,
one God for ever and ever.

Readings

Isaiah 42:1-9   Psalm 29

Acts 10:34-43   Matthew 3:13-17

Second Sunday after Epiphany – Sunday 2
Year A

Sentence

Behold, the Lamb of God,
who takes away the sin of the world. *John 1:29*

Collect

Heavenly Father,
you have called us to serve you in the world.
Bend our hearts to your will,
that we may gladly follow Christ,
and strive ceaselessly for your kingdom
of righteousness and peace;
through Jesus Christ our Lord,
who lives and reigns with you and the Holy Spirit,
one God, for ever and ever.

Readings

Isaiah 49:1-7   Psalm 40:1-11

1 Corinthians 1:1-9   John 1:29-34

Third Sunday after Epiphany – Sunday 3 Year A

Sentence

The people who sat in darkness have seen a great light,
and for those who sat in the region and shadow of death,
light has dawned. *Matthew 4:16*

Collect

O loving God,
you are the light of the minds that know you,
the life of the souls that love you,
and the strength of the hearts that serve you.
Help us so to know you
that we may truly love you;
and so to love you
that we may faithfully serve you,
whom to serve is perfect freedom;
through Jesus Christ our Lord.

Readings

Isaiah 9:1-4

Psalm 27:1-6

1 Corinthians 1:10-17

Matthew 4:12-23

Fourth Sunday after Epiphany – Sunday 4
Year A

Sentence

Commit your way to the Lord and put your trust in him,
and he will bring it to pass.
Be still before the Lord, and wait patiently for him.

Psalm 37:5,7

Collect

Father in heaven,
from the days of Abraham and Moses
until this gathering of your church in prayer,
you have formed a people in the image of your Son.
Bless this people with the gift of your kingdom.
May we serve you with our every desire
and show love for one another,
even as you have loved us;
through Jesus Christ our Lord.

Readings

Micah 6:1-8   Psalm 37:1-11

1 Corinthians 1:18-31   Matthew 5:1-12

Fifth Sunday after Epiphany – Sunday 5 Year A

Sentence

Jesus said:
You are the light of the world.
Let your light so shine before the world
that all may see your good works
and give glory to your Father who is in heaven.

Matthew 5:14, 16

Collect

O God,
who in the folly of the cross
reveals how great is the distance
between your wisdom and human understanding:
open our minds to the simplicity of Christ's gospel,
so that, fervent in faith and tireless in love,
we may become light and salt for the world.
We ask this through our Lord Jesus Christ, your Son,
who lives and reigns with you
in the unity of the Holy Spirit,
one God, for ever and ever.

Readings

Isaiah 58:3-9a   Psalm 112:4-9

1 Corinthians 2:1-11   Matthew 5:13-16

Sixth Sunday after Epiphany – Sunday 6
Year A

Sentence

Happy are they whose way is blameless,
who walk in the law of the Lord!
Happy are they who observe his decrees,
and seek him with all their hearts! *Psalm 119:1, 2*

Collect

Let us pray (that everything we do
will be guided by God's law of love):

God our Father,
you have promised to remain for ever
with those who do what is just and right.
Help us to live in your presence.
We ask this through our Lord Jesus Christ, your Son,
who lives and reigns with you and the Holy Spirit,
one God, for ever and ever.

Readings

Deuteronomy 30:15-20	Psalm 119:1-8
1 Corinthians 3:1-9	Matthew 5:17-26

Seventh Sunday after Epiphany – Sunday 7
Year A

Sentence

For God alone my soul in silence waits;
from him comes my salvation.
He alone is my rock and my salvation.   *Psalm 62:1, 2*

Collect

Let us pray (to have life more abundantly):

Set us free, O God,
from the bondage of our sins,
and give us, we pray, the liberty of that abundant life
which you have made known to us in your Son,
our Saviour Jesus Christ;
who lives and reigns with you
in the unity of the Holy Spirit,
one God, now and for ever.

Readings

Isaiah 49:8-13   Psalm 62:5-12

1 Corinthians 3:10, 11, 16-23   Matthew 5:27-37

Eighth Sunday after Epiphany – Sunday 8
Year A

Sentence

Jesus said:
Love your enemies
and pray for those who persecute you,
so that you may be children of your Father
who is in heaven   *Matthew 5:44, 45*

Collect

O God,
in the passion and death of your dear Son
you have revealed to the world your limitless love.
Renew us by the power of Christ's cross
and break the chains of hatred and violence,
so that, in the victory of good over evil,
we may bear witness to your gospel of reconciliation.
We ask this through our Lord Jesus Christ,
who lives and reigns with you and the Holy Spirit,
one God, for ever and ever.

Readings

Leviticus 19: 1, 2, 9-18   Psalm 119:33-40

1 Corinthians 4:1-5   Matthew 5:38-48

Last Sunday after Epiphany
Sunday before Ash Wednesday – Year A

(The Transfiguration of Jesus)

Sentence

Jesus was transfigured before them,
and a voice from the cloud said:
This is my beloved Son, with whom I am well pleased;
listen to him.   *Matthew 17:2, 5*

Collect

O God,
who before the passion of your only-begotten Son
revealed his glory upon the holy mountain:
Grant to us that we,
beholding by faith the light of his countenance,
may be strengthened to bear our cross,
and be changed into his likeness from glory to glory;
through Jesus Christ our Lord,
who lives and reigns with you and the Holy Spirit,
one God, for ever and ever.

Readings

Exodus 24:12-18	Psalm 2:6-11
2 Peter 1:16-21	Matthew 17:1-9

Ash Wednesday – Years A, B, C

Sentence

Have mercy on me, O God, according to your loving-kindness;
in your great compassion blot out my offences.
Create in me a clean heart, O God,
and renew a right spirit within me.   *Psalm 51:1, 10*

Collect

Father,
by obedience, even to the point of death,
your Son, our Saviour, has overcome the world.
Grant us his grace,
that we may not yield to evil,
but remain steadfast in doing your good and perfect will;
through Jesus Christ our Lord,
who lives and reigns with you and the Holy Spirit,
one God, for ever and ever.

or

Almighty and everlasting God,
you despise nothing that you have made
and forgive the sins of all who are penitent.
Create and make in us new and contrite hearts,
that we, worthily lamenting our sins
and acknowledging our brokenness,
may obtain of you, the God of all mercy,
perfect remission and forgiveness;
through Jesus Christ our Lord,
who lives and reigns with you and the Holy Spirit,
one God, for ever and ever.

or

Let us pray (that God will make us worthy to serve him):

Remember, O Lord, what you have wrought in us,
and not what we deserve;
and as you have called us to your service,
make us worthy of our calling;
through Jesus Christ our Lord.

Readings

Joel 2:1, 2, 12-17a

2 Corinthians 5:20b to 6:2 (3-10)

Psalm 51:1-12

Matthew 6:1-6, 16-21

First Sunday in Lent – Year A

Sentence

If because of one man's trespass,
death reigned through that one man Adam,
much more will those who receive the abundance of grace
and the free gift of righteousness
reign in life through the one man, Jesus Christ.   *Romans 5:17*

Collect

Almighty God,
whose blessed Son was led by the Spirit
to be tempted by Satan:
come quickly to help us who are assaulted by many temptations;
and, as you know the weaknesses of each of us,
let each one find you mighty to save;
through Jesus Christ your Son, our Lord,
who lives and reigns with you and the Holy Spirit,
one God, now and for ever.

Readings

Genesis 2:4b-9, 15-17, 25 to 3:7   Psalm 130

Romans 5:12-19   Matthew 4:1-11

Second Sunday in Lent — Year A

Sentence

Our soul waits for the Lord;
he is our help and our shield.
Indeed, our heart rejoices in him,
for in his holy name we put our trust.   *Psalm 33:20, 21*

Collect

O God of Abraham, Isaac and Jacob,
you called our ancestors to a journey of faith;
and in your Son, lifted up on the cross,
you opened for us the path to eternal life.
Grant that, being born again of water and the Spirit,
we may joyfully serve you in newness of life
and faithfully walk in your holy ways;
through Jesus Christ our Lord.

Readings

Genesis 12:1-8	Psalm 33:12-22
Romans 4:1-5 (6-12) 13-17	John 3:1-17

Third Sunday in Lent – Year A

Sentence

God shows his love for us in that,
while we were yet sinners, Christ died for us.   *Romans 5:8*

Collect

O God, the fountain of life,
to a humanity parched with thirst
you offer the living water of grace
which springs up from the rock, our Saviour Christ.
Grant your people the gift of the Spirit,
that we may profess our faith with courage
and announce with joy the wonders of your love.
We ask this through our Lord Jesus Christ, your Son,
who lives and reigns with you
in the unity of the Holy Spirit,
one God, for ever and ever.

Readings

Exodus 17:3-7   Psalm 95

Romans 5:1-11   John 4:5-26 (27-42)

Fourth Sunday in Lent – Year A

Sentence

Jesus said:
As long as I am in the world,
I am the light of the world.

John 9:5

Collect

Let us pray (that our human weakness
may be transformed into God's strength):

Almighty God,
in Christ you make all things new:
transform the poverty of our nature
by the riches of your grace,
and in the renewal of our lives
make known your heavenly glory;
through Jesus Christ our Lord.

Readings

1 Samuel 16:1-13	Psalm 23
Ephesians 5:8-14	John 9:1-41 *or*
	9:1, 6-9, 13-17, 34-38

Fifth Sunday in Lent – Year A

Sentence

I love the Lord,
because he has heard the voice of my supplication,
because he has inclined his ear to me
whenever I called upon him.   *Psalm 116:1*

Collect

Loving God our Father,
we see your compassion revealed
in the tears of Jesus for Lazarus his friend.
Look today upon the distress of your church,
mourning and praying for your children dead in their sins.
By the power of your Spirit call them back to life.
We ask this through our Lord Jesus Christ, your Son,
who lives and reigns with you
in the unity of the Holy Spirit,
one God, for ever and ever.

Readings

Ezekiel 37:1-14   Psalm 116:1-9

Romans 8:6-11   John 11:(1-16) 17-45 *or*
                                 11:3-7, 17, 20-27, 33b-45

Sixth Sunday in Lent – Year A

Sentence

(when observed as The Sunday of the Passion: Passion Sunday)

Have mercy on me, O Lord, for I am in trouble.
But I have trusted in you, O Lord.
I have said: You are my God. *Psalm 31:9, 14*

(when observed as Palm Sunday)

Tell the daughter of Zion:
Behold, your king is coming to you,
humble and mounted on an ass,
and on a colt, the foal of an ass. *Matthew 21:5*

Collect

(when observed as The Sunday of the Passion: Passion Sunday)

Almighty and everlasting God,
in your tender love for the human race
you sent your Son our Saviour Jesus Christ
to take upon him our nature,
and to suffer death upon the cross,
giving us the example of his great humility.
Mercifully grant that we may walk in the way of his suffering,
and also share in his resurrection;
through Jesus Christ our Lord,
who lives and reigns with you and the Holy Spirit,
one God, for ever and ever.

O Lord Jesus Christ,
who as on this day entered the rebellious city
where you were to die,
enter into our hearts and subdue them wholly to yourself.
And, as your faithful disciples blessed your coming,
and spread their garments in the way,
covering it with palm branches,
make us ready to lay at your feet
all that we have and are,
and to bless you, the One who comes in the name of the Lord.

Readings

(when observed as The Sunday of the Passion: Passion Sunday)

Isaiah 50:4-9a	Psalm 31:9-16
Philippians 2:5-11	Matthew 26:14 to 27:66 *or* 27:11-54

(when observed as Palm Sunday)

Isaiah 50:4-9a	Psalm 118:19-29
Philippians 2:5-11	Matthew 21:1-11

Monday in Holy Week – Years A, B, C

Sentence

The Son of man must be lifted up,
that whoever believes in him may have eternal life. *John 3:14, 15*

Collect

Almighty God,
whose Son was crucified yet entered into glory:
may we, walking in the way of the cross,
find it to be the way of life;
through Jesus Christ our Lord,
who is alive and reigns with you and the Holy Spirit,
one God, now and for ever.

or

Almighty and eternal God,
who in your tender love for the world
sent your Son, our Saviour Jesus Christ,
to take our flesh upon himself
and to suffer death on the cross:
grant that we may follow the example
of his patience and humility,
and also be made partakers of his resurrection;
through Jesus Christ our Lord.

Readings

Isaiah 42:1-9	Psalm 36:5-10
Hebrews 9:11-15	John 12:1-11

Tuesday in Holy Week – Years A, B, C

Sentence

The word of the cross is folly to those who are perishing,
but to us who are being saved it is the power of God.

1 Corinthians 1:18

Collect

O God,
by the passion of your blessed Son
you made an instrument of shameful death
to be for us the means of life.
Grant us so to glory in the cross of Christ,
that we may gladly suffer shame and loss
for the sake of your Son our Saviour Jesus Christ,
who lives and reigns with you and the Holy Spirit,
one God, for ever and ever.

or

Lord Jesus,
you have called us to follow you.
Grant that our love may not grow cold
in your service,
and that we may not fail or deny you
in the hour of trial.

Readings

Isaiah 49:1-7   Psalm 71:1-12

1 Corinthians 1:18-31   John 12:20-36

Wednesday in Holy Week — Years A, B, C

Sentence

Let all who seek you rejoice and be glad in you;
let those who love your salvation say for ever:
Great is the Lord!

Psalm 70:4

Collect

Lord God,
your Son our Saviour gave his body to be whipped
and turned his face for men to spit upon.
Give your servants grace to accept suffering for his sake,
confident of the glory that will be revealed,
through Jesus Christ our Lord,
who is alive and reigns with you and the Holy Spirit,
one God, now and for ever.

or

Father,
in your plan of salvation
your Son Jesus Christ accepted the cross
and freed us from the power of the enemy.
May we come to share the glory of his resurrection,
for he lives and reigns with you and the Holy Spirit,
one God, for ever and ever.

Readings

Isaiah 50:4-9a

Psalm 70

Hebrews 12:1-3

John 13:21-30

Holy Thursday — Year A

Sentence

Jesus said:
If I, your Lord and Teacher, have washed your feet,
you also ought to wash one another's feet.
For I have given you an example,
that you also should do as I have done to you. *John 13:14, 15*

Collect

Let us pray (that we may be Christ's agents in the world):

Grant, Lord, that we who receive
the body and blood of our Lord Jesus Christ
may be the means by which the work of his salvation
shall go forward;
take, consecrate, break and distribute us,
to be for all people a means of your grace,
and vehicles of your eternal love;
through Jesus Christ our Lord.

Readings

Exodus 12:1-14   Psalm 116:12-19

1 Corinthians 11:23-26   John 13:1-15

Good Friday — Years A, B, C

Sentence

All we like sheep have gone astray;
we have turned every one to his own way;
and the Lord has laid on him
the iniquity of us all.

Isaiah 53:6

or

God so loved the world that he gave his only Son,
that whoever believes in him should not perish
but have eternal life.

John 3:16

or

They took Jesus, and he went out, bearing his own cross,
to the place called the place of a skull,
which is called in Hebrew, Golgotha.
There they crucified him:

John 19:17, 18

Collect

Lord,
by shedding his blood for us,
your Son, Jesus Christ, saved us from eternal death.
In your compassion send us your grace,
and in your mercy watch over us always;
through Jesus Christ our Lord,
who lives and reigns with you and the Holy Spirit,
one God, for ever and ever.

or

Almighty God,
look graciously, we pray, on this your family,
for whom our Lord Jesus Christ was willing to be betrayed
and given into the hands of sinners.
Grant that, through faith in him
who suffered death on the cross for our salvation,
we may know the power of his resurrection;
who now lives and reigns with you and the Holy Spirit,
one God, for ever and ever.

or

Lord Jesus,
you carried our sins in your own body on the tree
so that we might have life.
May we and all who remember this day
find new life in you, now and in the world to come,
where you live and reign with the Father and the Holy Spirit,
one God, for ever and ever.

Readings

Isaiah 52:13 to 53:12   Psalm 22:1-18

Hebrews 4:14-16; 5:7-9   John 18:1 to 19:42 *or*
                                            19:17-30

Holy Saturday — Years A, B, C

Sentence

Christ became obedient unto death, even death on a cross.
Therefore God has highly exalted him
and bestowed on him the name which is above every name.

Philippians 2:8, 9

Collect

O God, creator of heaven and earth,
as the crucified body of your dear Son
was laid in the tomb and rested on this holy sabbath,
so may we await with him the coming of the third day,
and rise with him to newness of life;
who now lives and reigns with you and the Holy Spirit,
one God, for ever and ever.

Readings

Job 14:1-14   Psalm 31:1-4, 15-16

1 Peter 4:1-8   Matthew 27:57-66 *or*
                               John 19:38-42

Easter Vigil — Years A, B, C

Sentence

God is our refuge and strength,
a very present help in trouble.
Therefore we will not fear, though the earth be moved,
and though the mountains be toppled
into the depths of the sea.   *Psalm 46:1, 2*

Collect

Eternal Giver of life and light,
this holy night shines with the radiance of Jesus Christ.
Renew your church with the Spirit given to us in baptism,
that we may worship you in sincerity and truth,
and shine as lights in the world;
through Jesus Christ our Lord,
who is alive and reigns with you and the Holy Spirit,
one God, now and for ever.

Readings

*Old Testament Readings
and Psalms (A, B, C)*

Genesis 1:1, 26-31a
  Psalm 33:1-11

Genesis 22:1, 2, 9-18   *Second Reading (A, B, C)*
  Psalm 33:12-22   Romans 6:3-11
                              Psalm 114
Exodus 14:15 to 15:1
  Exodus 15:2-6, 17-18

Isaiah 54:5-14
   Psalm 30:4-12

Isaiah 55:1-11
   Isaiah 12:2-6

Zephaniah 3:14-20
   Psalm 98

Gospel
Matthew 28:1-10 (Year A)
Mark 16:1-8 (Year B)
Luke 23:55 to 24:9 (Year C)

Easter Day — Year A

Sentence

If you have been raised with Christ,
seek the things that are above, where Christ is,
seated at the right hand of God.   *Colossians 3:1*

Collect

O God,
you gave your only Son
to suffer death on the cross for our redemption,
and by his glorious resurrection
you delivered us from the power of death.
May we die every day to sin,
so that we may live with him for ever
in the joy of the resurrection;
through Jesus Christ our Lord,
who lives and reigns with you and the Holy Spirit,
one God, now and for ever.

Readings

Acts 10:34-43 *or*
Jeremiah 31:1-6

Psalm 118:14-24

Colossians 3:1-4 *or*
Acts 10:34-43

John 20:1-18 *or*
Matthew 28:1-10

If the Old Testament passage is chosen for the first reading, the
Acts passage is used as the second reading in order to initiate the
sequential reading of Acts during the fifty days of Easter.

Evening of Easter Day — Years A, B, C

Sentence

Jesus said:
It is written, that the Christ should suffer
and on the third day rise from the dead,
and that repentance and forgiveness of sins
should be preached in his name to all nations.   *Luke 24:46*

Collect

God our Father,
by raising Christ your Son
you conquered the power of death
and opened for us the way to eternal life.
Let our celebration today renew our lives
by the Holy Spirit who is given to us.
Grant this through our Lord Jesus Christ, your Son,
who lives and reigns with you and the Holy Spirit,
one God, for ever and ever.

or

Lord God almighty,
the radiance of your glory lights up our hearts.
Enable us truly to understand
the waters in which we were cleansed,
the Spirit by which we were reborn,
and the blood by which we were redeemed;
that in our earthly pilgrimage
we may walk more closely with our risen Saviour and Lord;
who lives and reigns with you and the Holy Spirit,
one God, for ever and ever.

Readings

Acts 5:29-32 *or*   Psalm 150
Daniel 12:1-3

1 Corinthians 5:6-8 *or*   Luke 24:13-49
Acts 5:29-32

If the first reading is from the Old Testament, the reading from Acts
should be second.

Second Sunday of Easter — Year A

Sentence

Blessed be the God and Father of our Lord Jesus Christ!
By his great mercy
we have been born anew to a living hope
through the resurrection of Jesus Christ from the dead.

1 Peter 1:3

Collect

Let us pray (that Christ will give us
a share in his glory):

God our Father,
may we look forward with hope to our resurrection,
for you have made us your sons and daughters,
and restored the joy of our youth.
We ask this through our Lord Jesus Christ, your Son,
who lives and reigns with you and the Holy Spirit,
one God, for ever and ever.

Readings

Acts 2:14a, 22-32	Psalm 16:5-11
1 Peter 1:3-9	John 20:19-31

Third Sunday of Easter — Year A

Sentence

I will offer you the sacrifice of thanksgiving
and call upon the name of the Lord.
I will fulfil my vows to the Lord
in the presence of all his people.

Psalm 116:17, 18

or

Lord Jesus, open to us the Scriptures;
make our hearts burn within us while you speak.

Based on Luke 24:32

O God,
on this day you gather together
your pilgrim church throughout the world
to keep the memory of the Lord's resurrection.
Pour out the Holy Spirit on us now,
that in the celebration of the eucharist
we may recognise the crucified and risen Christ,
who opens our hearts to understand the Scriptures
and who reveals himself in the breaking of the bread:
for he lives and reigns with you and the Holy Spirit,
one God, for ever and ever.

Readings

Acts 2:14a, 36-41	Psalm 116:12-19
1 Peter 1:17-23	Luke 24:13-35

Fourth Sunday of Easter — Year A

Sentence

I am the good shepherd, says the Lord:
I know my own and my own know me.   *John 10:14*

or

Christ himself bore our sins in his body on the tree,
that we might die to sin and live to righteousness.
By his wounds you have been healed.   *1 Peter 2:24*

Collect

O God,
whose Son Jesus is the good shepherd of your people:
Grant that when we hear his voice
we may know him who calls us each by name,
and follow where he leads;
who, with you and the Holy Spirit, lives and reigns,
one God, for ever and ever.

Readings

Acts 2:42-47   Psalm 23

1 Peter 2:19-25   John 10:1-10

Fifth Sunday of Easter — Year A

Sentence

I am the way, the truth, and the life, says the Lord;
no one comes to the Father, but by me.   *John 14:6*

Collect

O God,
form the minds of your faithful people
into a single will.
Make us love what you command and desire what you promise,
that, amid all the changes of this world,
our hearts may be fixed where true joys are found;
through your Son, Jesus Christ our Lord,
who lives and reigns with you and the Holy Spirit,
one God, now and for ever.

Readings

Acts 7:55-60   Psalm 31:1-8

1 Peter 2:2-10   John 14:1-14

Sixth Sunday of Easter — Year A

Sentence

In your hearts reverence Christ as Lord.
Always be prepared to make a defence to anyone
who calls you to account for the hope that is in you.

1 Peter 3:15

Collect

God our Father,
you have redeemed us in Jesus your Son,
and given to your church the Holy Spirit, the Counsellor,
to dwell with us for ever.
Strengthen us by your Spirit of truth,
that we may show our love for Christ
by keeping his commandments,
and by always being ready to give an account
of the hope that is in us.
We ask this through Jesus Christ our Lord.

Readings

Acts 17:22-31   Psalm 66:8-20

1 Peter 3:13-22   John 14:15-21

Ascension Day — Years A, B, C

Sentence

Go and make disciples of all nations, says the Lord;
I am with you always, to the close of the age. *Matthew 28:19, 20*

or

Since we have a great high priest
who has passed through the heavens, Jesus, the Son of God,
let us with confidence draw near to the throne of grace,
that we may receive mercy
and find grace to help in time of need.

Hebrews 4:14, 16

Collect

Almighty and everlasting Father,
you raised our Lord Jesus Christ
to your right hand on high.
As we rejoice in his exaltation,
fill us with his Spirit,
that we may go out into all the world
and faithfully proclaim his gospel.
He lives and reigns with you and the Holy Spirit,
one God, for ever and ever.

or

Let us pray (to our Father
who has raised us to new life in Christ):

Eternal Father,
reaching from end to end of the universe
and ordering all things with your mighty arm:
for you, time is the unfolding of truth
that already is,
the enveiling of beauty that is yet to be.
Your Son has saved us in history
by rising from the dead,
so that, transcending time,
he might free us from death.
May his presence among us
lead to the vision of unlimited truth
and unfold the beauty of your love

or

Let us pray (for the subjection of all things
to Christ our King):

Eternal Father,
whose Son Jesus Christ ascended to the throne of heaven
that he might rule over all things as Lord:
keep the church in the unity of the Spirit
and in the bond of his peace,
and bring the whole created order to worship at his feet;
who lives and reigns with you and the Holy Spirit,
one God, now and for ever.

Readings

Acts 1:1-11	Psalm 47
Ephesians 1:15-23	Luke 24:46-53 *or* Mark 16:9-16, 19, 20

Some or all of these readings may be used on the Seventh Sunday of Easter.

Seventh Sunday of Easter — Year A

Sentence

I will not leave you desolate, says the Lord;
I will come to you.   *John 14:18*

or

Humble yourselves under the mighty hand of God,
that in due time he may exalt you.
Cast all your anxieties on him,
for he cares about you.   *1 Peter 5:6, 7*

Collect

Almighty and eternal God,
your Son our Saviour is with you in eternal glory.
Give us faith to see that, true to his promise,
he is among us still,
and will be with us to the end of time;
who lives and reigns with you and the Holy Spirit,
one God, now and for ever.

Readings

Acts 1:6-14   Psalm 68:1-10

1 Peter 4:12-14; 5:6-11   John 17:1-11

The Day of Pentecost — Year A

Sentence

When the day of Pentecost had come,
they were all together in one place.
And they were all filled with the Holy Spirit
and began to speak in other tongues,
as the Spirit gave them utterance.   *Acts 2:1, 4*

or

Come, Holy Spirit, fill the hearts of your faithful people;
and kindle in us the fire of your love.

Collect

Let us pray (for the power of the Holy Spirit):

Almighty God,
who on the day of Pentecost
sent your Holy Spirit to the disciples
with the wind from heaven and with tongues of flame,
filling them with joy and boldness to preach the gospel:
send us out in the power of the same Spirit
to witness to your truth
and to draw everyone to the fire of your love;
through Jesus Christ our Lord.

Readings

Acts 2:1-21 *or*   Psalm 104:24-34
Isaiah 44:1-8

1 Corinthians 12:3b-13 *or*   John 20:19-23 *or* 7:37-39
Acts 2:1-21

If the Old Testament passage is chosen for the first reading, the Acts passage is used as the second reading.

Trinity Sunday — Year A

Sentence

Holy, holy, holy is the Lord of hosts;
the whole earth is full of his glory. *Isaiah 6:3*

or

The grace of the Lord Jesus Christ
and the love of God
and the fellowship of the Holy Spirit
be with you all. *2 Corinthians 13:14*

Collect

Almighty and eternal God,
you have revealed yourself as Father, Son and Holy Spirit.
Enable us to live by the Spirit,
that, walking with Christ and rejoicing in your fatherly love,
we may become partakers of the mystery of your divine being;
through Jesus Christ our Lord,
who lives and reigns with the Father
in the unity of the Holy Spirit,
three persons in one indivisible God, for ever and ever.

Readings

Deuteronomy 4:32-40   Psalm 33:1-11

2 Corinthians 13:5-14   Matthew 28:16-20

Sunday 9 — Year A

(Sunday between 29 May and 4 June inclusive, if after Trinity Sunday)

* If there is a very early Easter and a Sunday between 24 and 28 May inclusive follows Trinity Sunday, use the resources for Sunday 8.

Sentence

Happy is the nation whose God is the Lord!
Happy the people he has chosen to be his own!
Let your loving-kindness, O Lord, be upon us,
as we have put our trust in you.   *Psalm 33:12, 22*

Collect

Lord God of the nations,
you have revealed your will to all people
and promised us your saving help.
May we hear and do what you command,
that the darkness may be overcome
by the power of your light;
through your Son, Jesus Christ our Lord,
who lives and reigns with you and the Holy Spirit,
now and for ever.

Readings

Genesis 12:1-9   Psalm 33:12-22

Romans 3:21-28   Matthew 7:21-29

Sunday 10 — Year A

(Sunday between 5 and 11 June inclusive, if after Trinity Sunday)

Sentence

The Lord has anointed me
to preach good news to the poor
and release to the captives.   *Luke 4:18*

Collect

O God,
the strength of those who hope in you:
be present and hear our prayers;
and because of the weakness of our mortal nature
we can do nothing good without you,
give us the help of your grace,
so that, in keeping your commandments,
we may please you in will and deed;
through your Son, Jesus Christ our Lord.

Readings

Genesis 22:1-18   Psalm 13

Romans 4:13-18ˊ   Matthew 9:9-13

Sunday 11 — Year A

(Sunday between 12 and 18 June inclusive, if after Trinity Sunday)

Sentence

Jesus said:

The harvest is plentiful, but the labourers are few;
pray therefore the Lord of the harvest
to send out labourers into the harvest.   *Luke 9:37, 38*

Collect

God of all creation,
you reach out to call people of all nations
to your kingdom.
As you gather disciples from near and far,
count us also among those who boldly confess
your Son, Jesus Christ, as Lord.

Readings

Genesis 25:19-34   Psalm 46

Romans 5:6-11   Matthew 9:35 to 10:8

Sunday 12 — Year A

(Sunday between 19 and 25 June inclusive, if after Trinity Sunday)

Sentence

Those who dwell in the shelter of the Most High,
abide under the shadow of the Almighty.
They shall say to the Lord:
You are my refuge and my stronghold,
my God in whom I put my trust.   *Psalm 91:1, 2*

Collect

Let us pray (for release from anxiety):

Grant us, Lord,
not be anxious about earthly things,
but to love things heavenly;
and even now,
while we are placed among things that are passing away,
to hold fast to those things that shall abide;
through Jesus Christ our Lord.

Readings

Genesis 28:10-17	Psalm 91:1-10
Romans 5:12-19	Matthew 10:24-33

Sunday 13 — Year A

(Sunday between 26 June and 2 July inclusive)

Sentence

Do you not know that all of us who have been baptised
into Christ Jesus were baptised into his death?
We were buried therefore with him by baptism into death,
so that, as Christ was raised from the dead
by the glory of the Father,
we too might walk in newness of life.   *Romans 6:3, 4*

Collect

Pour forth upon us, Father,
the power and wisdom of your Spirit,
that we may walk with Christ the way of the cross,
ready to offer even the gift of our lives
to show forth to the world our hope in your kingdom.
We ask this through our Lord Jesus Christ, your Son,
who lives and reigns with you
in the unity of the Holy Spirit,
one God, for ever and ever.

Readings

Genesis 32:22-32   Psalm 17:1-7

Romans 6:3-11   Matthew 10:34-42

Sunday 14 — Year A

(Sunday between 3 and 9 July inclusive)

Sentence

Our help is in the name of the Lord,
the maker of heaven and earth.   *Psalm 124:8*

Collect

Almighty God,
your Son Jesus Christ has taught us
that what we do for the least of your children
we do also for him.
Give us the will to serve others
as he was the servant of all,
who gave up his life and died for us,
but lives and reigns with you and the Holy Spirit,
one God, now and for ever.

Readings

Exodus 1: 6-14, 22 to 2:10	Psalm 124
Romans 7:14-25a	Matthew 11:25-30

Sunday 15 — Year A

(Sunday between 10 and 16 July inclusive)

Sentence

If the Spirit of him who raised Jesus from the dead
dwells in you, he who raised Christ Jesus from the dead
will give life to your mortal bodies also
through his Spirit who dwells in you.   *Romans 8:11*

Collect

Let us pray (to be faithful to the light we have received,
and to the name we bear):

Father,
let the light of your truth
guide us to your kingdom
through a world filled with lights contrary to your own.
Christian is the name and the gospel we glory in.
May your love make us what you have called us to be;
through Jesus Christ our Lord.

Readings

Exodus 2:11-22	Psalm 69:6-15
Romans 8:9-17	Matthew 13:1-9, 18-23

Sunday 16 — Year A

(Sunday between 17 and 23 July inclusive)

Sentence

Bless the Lord, O my soul,
and all that is within me, bless his holy name.
Bless the Lord, O my soul,
and forget not all his benefits.   *Psalm 103:1, 2*

Collect

O God,
you have prepared for those who love you
joys beyond understanding.
Pour into our hearts such love for you
that, loving you above all things,
we may obtain your promises,
which exceed all that we can desire;
through your Son, Jesus Christ our Lord.

Readings

Exodus 3:1-12   Psalm 103:1-13

Romans 8:18-25   Matthew 13:24-30, 36-43

Sunday 17 — Year A

(Sunday between 24 and 30 July inclusive)

Sentence

We know that in everything
God works for good with those who love him,
who are called according to his purpose.   *Romans 8:28*

Collect

O Father, fount of wisdom,
you have revealed to us in Christ
the hidden treasure and the pearl of great price.
Grant us the Spirit's gift of discernment,
that, in the midst of the things of this world,
we may learn to appreciate the priceless value of the kingdom,
and be willing to renounce everything joyfully
for the sake of gaining the gift you offer.
We ask this through our Lord Jesus Christ, your Son,
who lives and reigns with you
in the unity of the Holy Spirit,
one God, for ever and ever.

Readings

Exodus 3:13-20   Psalm 105:1-11
Romans 8:26-30   Matthew 13:44-52

Sunday 18 — Year A

(Sunday between 31 July and 6 August inclusive)

Sentence

Lord, hear my prayer,
and in your faithfulness heed my supplications;
answer me in your righteousness.   *Psalm 143:1*

Collect

Let us pray (to find our fulfilment in God):

Grant, Lord,
that we may see in you
the fulfilment of our need;
and may turn from all false satisfactions
to feed on that true and living bread
which you have given us in your Son Jesus Christ;
who lives and reigns with you and the Holy Spirit,
one God, now and for ever.

Readings

Exodus 12:1-14   Psalm 143:1-10

Romans 8:31-39   Matthew 14:13-21

Sunday 19 — Year A

(Sunday between 7 and 13 August inclusive)

Sentence

Hallelujah!
Give thanks to the Lord, for he is good,
for his mercy endures for ever.   *Psalm 106:1*

Collect

Mighty God and ruler of all creation,
give new strength to our faith
and grant that we may recognise your presence
in all of life and of history,
so that we may face all trials with serenity
and walk with Christ toward your peace.
We ask this through our Lord Jesus Christ, your Son,
who lives and reigns with you
in the unity of the Holy Spirit,
one God, for ever and ever.

Readings

Exodus 14:19-31   Psalm 106:4-12

Romans 9:1-5   Matthew 14:22-33

Sunday 20 — Year A

(Sunday between 14 and 20 August inclusive)

Sentence

Come now, let us reason together, says the Lord:
though your sins are like scarlet,
they shall be as white as snow;
though they are red like crimson,
they shall become like wool.

Isaiah 1:18

Collect

Let us pray (that all races and creeds may find in Christ
the fulfilment of their longings):

Almighty God,
who in the incarnation of your eternal Word
revealed the source and perfection of all true religion:
grant us so fully to manifest Christ in our lives
that people of all races and creeds
may be drawn to him who is their whole salvation,
our Saviour Jesus Christ,
who lives and reigns with you and the Holy Spirit,
one God, now and for ever.

Readings

Exodus 16:2-15	Psalm 78:1-3, 10-20
Romans 11:13-16, 29-32	Matthew 15:21-28

Sunday 21 — Year A

(Sunday between 21 and 27 August inclusive)

Sentence

Come, let us bow down, and bend the knee,
and kneel before the Lord our Maker.
For he is our God,
and we are the people of his pasture
and the sheep of his hand.

Psalm 95:6, 7

Collect

O Father, fount of all wisdom,
in the humble witness of the apostle Peter
you have shown the foundation of our faith.
Give to all the light of your Spirit,
that, recognising in Jesus of Nazareth
the Son of the living God,
they may become living stones
for the building up of your holy church.
We ask this through our Lord Jesus Christ, your Son,
who lives and reigns with you
in the unity of the Holy Spirit,
one God, for ever and ever.

Readings

Exodus 17:1-7

Psalm 95

Romans 11:33-36

Matthew 16:13-20

Sunday 22 — Year A

(Sunday between 28 August and 3 September inclusive)

Sentence

Jesus said:
If people would come after me,
let them deny themselves, and take up their cross,
and follow me.

Matthew 16:24

Collect

Almighty and everlasting God,
you are always more ready to hear than we to pray,
and to give more than we either desire or deserve.
Pour upon us the abundance of your mercy,
forgiving us those things
of which our conscience is afraid,
and giving us those good things
for which we are not worthy to ask,
except through the merits of your Son,
Jesus Christ our Lord.

Readings

Exodus 19:1-9	Psalm 114
Romans 12:1-13	Matthew 16:21-28

Sunday 23 — Year A

(Sunday between 4 and 10 September inclusive)

Sentence

This is the day which the Lord has made;
we will rejoice and be glad in it. *Psalm 118:24*

Collect

Let us pray (that we may realise the freedom
God has given us in making us sons and daughters):

God our Father,
you redeem us
and make us your children in Christ.
Look on us,
give us true freedom,
and bring us to the inheritance you promised.
Grant this through our Lord Jesus Christ, your Son,
who lives and reigns with you and the Holy Spirit,
one God, for ever and ever.

Readings

Exodus 19:16-24

Psalm 115:1-11

Romans 13:1-10

Matthew 18:15-20

Sunday 24 — Year A

(Sunday between 11 and 17 September inclusive)

Sentence

A new commandment I give to you,
that you love one another as I have loved you.   *John 13:34*

Collect

O God of justice and love,
you pardon us if we pardon our brothers and sisters:
Create in us a new heart
in the image of your Son,
a heart ever greater than any offence it suffers,
that the world may remember how much you love us.
We ask this through our Lord Jesus Christ, your Son,
who lives and reigns with you
in the unity of the Holy Spirit,
one God, for ever and ever.

Readings

Exodus 20:1-20	Psalm 19:7-14
Romans 14:5-12	Matthew 18:21-35

Sunday 25 — Year A

(Sunday between 18 and 24 September inclusive)

Sentence

Jesus said:
Come to me all who labour and are heavy laden,
and I will give you rest.
Take my yoke upon you, and learn of me;
for I am gentle and lowly in heart,
and you will find rest for your souls.   *Matthew 11:28, 29*

Collect

Loving and righteous God,
the greatness of your generosity
is beyond words to describe;
you give equally to the last worker as to the first.
By the gift of your Spirit
liberate us from all selfishness and greed;
that we may be free to love and serve others,
and in that self-giving to find our reward;
through Jesus Christ our Lord.

Readings

Exodus 32:1-4   Psalm 106:7, 8, 19-23

Philippians 1:21-27   Matthew 20:1-16

Sunday 26 — Year A

(Sunday between 25 September and 1 October inclusive)

Sentence

God is light, and in him is no darkness at all.
If we walk in the light, as God is in the light,
we have fellowship with one another,
and the blood of Jesus his Son cleanses us from all sin.

1 John 1:5, 7

Collect

O God,
you declare your almighty power
chiefly in showing mercy and pity:
Grant us the fullness of your grace,
that we, running to obtain your promises,
may become partakers of your heavenly treasure;
through Jesus Christ our Lord,
who lives and reigns with you and the Holy Spirit,
one God, for ever and ever.

Readings

Exodus 33:12-23	Psalm 99
Philippians 2:1-13	Matthew 21:28-32

Sunday 27 — Year A

(Sunday between 2 and 8 October inclusive)

Sentence

They who wait for the Lord shall renew their strength,
they shall mount up with wings like eagles,
they shall run and not be weary,
they shall walk and not faint.   *Isaiah 40:31*

Collect

Almighty God,
you have built your church
on the foundation of the apostles and prophets,
Jesus Christ himself being the chief cornerstone.
Join us together in unity of spirit by their teaching,
that we may become a holy temple, acceptable to you;
through Jesus Christ our Lord,
who lives and reigns with you and the Holy Spirit,
one God, for ever and ever.

Readings

Numbers 27:12-23   Psalm 81:1-10

Philippians 3:12-21   Matthew 21:33-43

Sunday 28 — Year A

(Sunday between 9 and 15 October inclusive)

Sentence

Rejoice in the Lord always.
Have no anxiety about anything,
but in everything by prayer and supplication with thanksgiving
let your requests be made known to God.   *Philippians 4:4, 6*

Collect

Let us pray (that God will help us
to love one another):

Lord,
our help and our guide,
make your love the fountain of our lives.
May our love for you express itself
in our eagerness to do good for others.
Grant this through our Lord Jesus Christ, your Son,
who lives and reigns with you and the Holy Spirit,
one God, for ever and ever.

Readings

Deuteronomy 34:1-12   Psalm 135:1-14

Philippians 4:1-9   Matthew 22:1-14

Sunday 29 — Year A

(Sunday between 16 and 22 October inclusive)

Sentence

Hallelujah!
Praise the Lord, O my soul!
Happy are they who have the God of Jacob for their help,
whose hope is in the Lord their God.   *Psalm 146:1, 5*

Collect

Let us pray (to the Lord
who bends close to hear our prayer):

Lord our God, Father of all,
you guard us under the shadow of your wings
and search into the depths of our hearts.
Remove the blindness that cannot know you
and relieve the fear that hides you from our sight;
through Jesus Christ our Lord.

Readings

Ruth 1:1-19a   Psalm 146

1 Thessalonians 1:1-10   Matthew 22:15-22

Sunday 30 — Year A

(Sunday between 23 and 29 October inclusive)

Sentence

Happy are they who fear the Lord,
and who follow in his ways!   *Psalm 128:1*

Collect

Lord,
you have taught us through your Son
that love is the fulfilling of the law.
Send your Holy Spirit upon us,
and pour into our hearts
that most excellent gift of love,
that we may love you with our whole being,
and our neighbours as ourselves;
through Jesus Christ our Lord.

Readings

    Ruth 2:1-13   Psalm 128

    1 Thessalonians 2:1-8   Matthew 22:34-46

Sunday 31 — Year A

(Sunday between 30 October and 5 November inclusive)

Sentence

You have one Father, who is in heaven.
You have one teacher, the Christ.   *Matthew 23:9, 10*

Collect

Almighty Father,
you are both just and rich in mercy.
So protect us from the distortions of pride,
that, being made aware of your loving purposes,
we may willingly give ourselves in service to all;
through Jesus Christ our Lord,
who lives and reigns with you and the Holy Spirit,
one God, for ever and ever.

Readings

Ruth 4:7-17   Psalm 127

1 Thessalonians 2:9-13, 17-20   Matthew 23:1-12

Sunday 32 — Year A

(Sunday between 6 and 12 November inclusive)

Sentence

Watch, for you do not know on what day
your Lord is coming.
Therefore you must be ready. *Matthew 24:42, 44*

Collect

O God,
whose blessed Son came into the world
that he might destroy the works of the devil
and make us children of God and heirs of eternal life:
grant that, having this hope,
we may purify ourselves as he is pure;
that, when he comes again with power and great glory,
we may be made like him
in his eternal and glorious kingdom;
where he lives and reigns with you and the Holy Spirit,
one God, for ever and ever.

Readings

Amos 5:18-24   Psalm 50:7-15

1 Thessalonians 4:13-18   Matthew 25:1-13

Sunday 33 — Year A

(Sunday between 13 and 19 November inclusive)

Sentence

Let us put on the breastplate of faith and love,
and for a helmet the hope of salvation.
For God has not destined us for wrath,
but to obtain salvation through our Lord Jesus Christ.

1 Thessalonians 5:8

Collect

Lord God,
so rule and govern our hearts and minds
by your Holy Spirit,
that, always keeping in mind the end of all things
and the day of judgment,
we may be stirred up to holiness of life here,
and may live with you for ever in the world to come;
through your Son, Jesus Christ our Lord.

Readings

Zephaniah 1:7, 12-18   Psalm 76

1 Thessalonians 5:1-11   Matthew 25:14-30

The Festival of Christ the King
The Last Sunday after Pentecost — Year A

(Sunday between 20 and 26 November inclusive)

Sentence

When the Son of man comes in his glory,
and all the angels with him,
then he will sit on his glorious throne.
And the King will say to those at his right hand:
Come, O blessed of my Father, inherit the kingdom
prepared for you from the foundation of the world.

Matthew 25:31, 34

Collect

Father,
you have established your Son
as only king and shepherd of all people,
to build from all the painful events of history
your kingdom of love.
Increase within us the certainty of faith:
so that we may look forward to that day
when, having destroyed our final enemy death,
Christ will hand over to you the work of his redemption,
that you may be all in all;
for he lives and reigns with you and the Holy Spirit,
one God, for ever and ever.

Readings

Ezekiel 34:11-16, 20-24   Psalm 23

1 Corinthians 15:20-28   Matthew 25:31-46

The Annunciation of Jesus to Mary
Years A, B, C   *25 March*

Sentence

The Word became flesh and dwelt among us,
full of grace and truth;
we have beheld his glory.   *John 1:14*

Collect

Pour your grace into our hearts, O Lord,
that we who have known the incarnation
of your Son Jesus Christ,
announced by an angel to the Virgin Mary,
may by his cross and passion
be brought to the glory of his resurrection;
who lives and reigns with you
in the unity of the Holy Spirit,
one God, now and for ever.

Readings

Isaiah 7:10-14   Psalm 45 *or* 40:6-11

Hebrews 10:4-10   Luke 1:26-38

All Saints' Day — Year A

Sentence

They are before the throne of God,
and he who sits upon the throne
will shelter them with his presence.
Revelation 7:15

Collect

Eternal Father,
from whose love neither death nor life can separate us:
grant us grace to follow Christ as true saints,
that here on earth we may serve you faithfully,
and in heaven rejoice with all your saints
who ceaselessly proclaim your majesty and glory;
through Jesus Christ our Lord,
who lives and reigns with you and the Holy Spirit,
one God, for ever and ever.

Readings

Revelation 7:9-17   Psalm 34:1-10

1 John 3:1-3   Matthew 5:1-12

First Sunday in Advent — Year B

Sentence

Hear, O Shepherd of Israel, leading Joseph like a flock;
shine forth, you that are enthroned upon the cherubim.
Restore us, O God of hosts;
show the light of your countenance, and we shall be saved.

Psalm 80:1, 3

Collect

Almighty God,
you have promised to make all things new.
Graciously enable us to prepare for the coming
of Christ your Son,
that he may find us waiting eagerly
in joyful prayer.
He lives and reigns with you and the Holy Spirit,
one God, for ever and ever.

Readings

Isaiah 63:16 to 64:8	Psalm 80:1-7
1 Corinthians 1:3-9	Mark 13:32-37

Second Sunday in Advent — Year B

Sentence

I will listen to what the Lord God is saying,
for he is speaking peace to his faithful people
and to those who turn their hearts to him.
Truly, his salvation is very near to those who fear him,
that his glory may dwell in our land.   *Psalm 85:8, 9*

Collect

Almighty God,
who sent your servant John the Baptist
to prepare your people for the Messiah:
inspire us, the ministers and stewards of your truth,
to turn our disobedient hearts to you,
that when the Christ shall come again to be our judge,
we may stand with confidence before him;
who is alive and reigns with you and the Holy Spirit,
one God, for ever and for ever.

Readings

Isaiah 40:1-11   Psalm 85:8-13

2 Peter 3:8-15a   Mark 1:1-8

Third Sunday in Advent — Year B

Sentence

My soul proclaims the greatness of the Lord,
my spirit rejoices in God my Saviour.
You, the Almighty, have done great things for me,
and holy is your name. *Luke 1:47, 49*

Collect

O God,
Father of the poor and lowly,
you have called all people
to share the peace and joy of your kingdom.
Show us your kindness
and grant us hearts pure and generous,
that we may prepare the way
for the Saviour who is coming,
your Son, our Lord Jesus Christ,
who lives and reigns with you
in the unity of the Holy Spirit,
one God, for ever and ever.

Readings

Isaiah 61:1-4, 8-11	Luke 1:46b-55
1 Thessalonians 5:16-24	John 1:6-8, 19-28

Fourth Sunday in Advent — Year B

Sentence

Your love, O Lord, for ever will I sing;
from age to age my mouth will proclaim your faithfulness.

Psalm 89:1

Collect

Let us pray (as Advent draws to a close
that Christ will truly come into our hearts):

Lord,
fill our hearts with your love,
and as you revealed to us by an angel
the coming of your Son as man,
so lead us through his suffering and death
to the glory of his resurrection;
for he lives and reigns with you and the Holy Spirit,
one God, for ever and ever.

Readings

2 Samuel 7:8-16	Psalm 89:1-4, 19-24
Romans 16:25-27	Luke 1:26-38

Christmas — Years A, B, C   *24, 25 December*

See Year A, page 149.

First Sunday of Christmas — Year B

Sentence

When the time had fully come,
God sent forth his Son,
born of woman, born under the law,
so that we might receive adoption as God's children.

Galatians 4:4, 5

Collect

Father,
from whom every family
in heaven and on earth derives its name:
enable us to live as your holy family,
united in respect and love;
and bring us to the joy and peace
of your eternal home;
where with the Son and the Holy Spirit
you live and reign,
one God, for ever and ever.

Readings

Isaiah 61:10 to 62:3   Psalm 111

Galatians 4:4-7   Luke 2:22-40

The Naming of Jesus
Years A, B, C *1 January*

See Year A, page 154.

Second Sunday of Christmas
Years A, B, C

See Year A, page 155.

The Epiphany of the Lord
Years A, B, C

See Year A, page 156.

First Sunday after Epiphany — Sunday 1
Year B

(The Baptism of Jesus)

Sentence

When Jesus came up out of the water,
immediately he saw the heavens opened
and the Spirit descending upon him like a dove;
and a voice came from heaven:
You are my beloved Son; with you I am well pleased.

Mark 1:10, 11

Collect

Almighty and eternal God,
who openly acknowledged Jesus as your own dear Son
at his baptism in the Jordan:
grant that we who have been baptised in his name
may be born again of water and the Holy Spirit,
and live always as your faithful children;
through Jesus Christ our Lord,
who lives and reigns with you and the Holy Spirit,
one God, for ever and ever.

Readings

Genesis 1:1-5

Psalm 29

Acts 19:1-7

Mark 1:4-11

Second Sunday after Epiphany — Sunday 2 Year B

Sentence

O God, your loving-kindness is better than life itself;
my lips shall give you praise.
So will I bless you as long as I live
and lift up my hands in your name.   *Psalm 63:3, 4*

Collect

Let us pray (for the gift of peace):

Almighty and ever-present Father,
your watchful care reaches from end to end
and orders all things in such power
that even the tensions and tragedies of sin
cannot frustrate your loving plans.
Help us to embrace your will,
and give us the strength to follow your call,
so that your truth may live in our hearts
and reflect peace to those who believe in your love;
through Jesus Christ our Lord.

Readings

1 Samuel 3:1-10 (11-20)	Psalm 63:1-8
1 Corinthians 6:12-20	John 1:35-42

Third Sunday after Epiphany — Sunday 3
Year B

Sentence

After John was arrested, Jesus came into Galilee,
preaching the gospel of God and saying:
The time is fulfilled, and the kingdom of God is at hand;
repent and believe in the gospel.   *Mark 1:14, 15*

Collect

Loving God,
through your Son you have called us
to repent of our sin, to believe the good news,
and to celebrate the coming of your kingdom.
Grant that we, like Christ's first apostles,
may hear his call to discipleship;
and, gladly forsaking our old ways,
may proclaim to a waiting world the gospel of new life
through our Lord and Saviour Jesus Christ.

Readings

Jonah 3:1-5, 10   Psalm 62:5-12

1 Corinthians 7:29-35   Mark 1:14-20

Fourth Sunday after Epiphany — Sunday 4 Year B

Sentence

Hallelujah!
I will give thanks to the Lord with my whole heart,
in the assembly of the upright, in the congregation.
His work is full of majesty and splendour,
and his righteousness endures for ever.   *Psalm 111:1, 3*

Collect

Father in heaven,
you have shown us in Christ
that your love for us is never-ending.
Enable us to love you with all our hearts
and to love one another as Christ loves us.
He lives and reigns with you and the Holy Spirit,
one God, for ever and ever.

Readings

Deuteronomy 18:15-20	Psalm 111
1 Corinthians 8:1-13	Mark 1:21-28

Fifth Sunday after Epiphany — Sunday 5
Year B

Sentence

Hallelujah!
How good it is to sing praises to our God!
Great is our Lord and mighty in power;
there is no limit to his wisdom.   *Psalm 147: 1, 5*

Collect

Almighty God,
you sent your only Son as the Word of life
for our eyes to see and our ears to hear.
Help us to believe with joy
what the Scriptures proclaim;
through Jesus Christ our Lord.

Readings

Job 7:1-7   Psalm 147:1-11

1 Corinthians 9:16-23   Mark 1:29-39

Sixth Sunday after Epiphany — Sunday 6
Year B

Sentence

Do you not know that in a race all the runners compete,
but only one receives the prize?
So run that you may obtain it.   *1 Corinthians 9:24*

Collect

Heal us once again, Father,
from the sin which divides us
and from the prejudice which isolates us from others.
Help us to recognise
in the face of those branded by society as lepers
the very image of Christ, blood-stained upon his cross.
May we share in his healing ministry
by proclaiming to all our brothers and sisters
the wonders of your tender mercy and steadfast love.
We ask this through your Son, our Lord Jesus Christ.

Readings

2 Kings 5:1-14	Psalm 32
1 Corinthians 9:24-27	Mark 1:40-45

Seventh Sunday after Epiphany — Sunday 7
Year B

Sentence

The Lord has anointed me to preach good news to the poor
and release to the captives. *Luke 4:18*

Collect

Teach us, good Lord,
to serve you as you deserve:
to give, and not to count the cost;
to fight, and not to heed the wounds;
to toil, and not to seek for rest;
to labour, and not to ask for any reward,
except that of knowing that we do your holy will;
through Jesus Christ our Lord.

Readings

Isaiah 43:18-25   Psalm 41

2 Corinthians 1:18-22   Mark 2:1-12

Eighth Sunday after Epiphany — Sunday 8
Year B

Sentence

Bless the Lord, O my soul,
and all that is within me, bless his holy name.
The Lord is full of compassion and mercy,
slow to anger and of great kindness.   *Psalm 103:1, 8*

Collect

Almighty God,
grant us the Spirit to think and do always
those things that are right,
that we who can do nothing good without you
may live according to your holy will;
through Jesus Christ our Lord,
who lives and reigns with you and the Holy Spirit,
one God, now and for ever.

Readings

Hosea 2:14-20   Psalm 103:1-13

2 Corinthians 3:1-6   Mark 2:18-22

Last Sunday after Epiphany
Sunday before Ash Wednesday — Year B

(The Transfiguration of Jesus)

Sentence

It is the God who said: Let light shine out of darkness,
who has shone in our hearts
to give the light of the knowledge of the glory of God
in the face of Christ. *2 Corinthians 4:6*

Collect

Lord,
you revealed the true splendour of Christ
in the glory of his transfiguration.
Enable us to listen carefully to his voice,
that we may be changed into his marvellous likeness.
He lives and reigns with you and the Holy Spirit,
one God, for ever and ever.

Readings

2 Kings 2:1-12a	Psalm 50:1-6
2 Corinthians 4:3-6	Mark 9:2-9

Ash Wednesday — Years A, B, C

See Year A, page 167.

First Sunday in Lent — Year B

Sentence

Christ died for sins once for all,
the righteous for the unrighteous,
that he might bring us to God.

1 Peter 3:18a

Collect

Almighty God,
whose Son fasted forty days in the wilderness,
and was tempted as we are but did not sin:
give us grace to discipline ourselves
in submission to your Spirit,
that as you know our weakness,
so we may know your power to save;
through Jesus Christ our Lord,
who lives and reigns with you and the Holy Spirit,
one God, now and for ever.

Readings

Genesis 9:8-17	Psalm 25:1-10
1 Peter 3:18-22	Mark 1:9-15

Second Sunday in Lent — Year B

Sentence

Jesus began to teach them
that the Son of man must suffer many things,
and be rejected by the elders and the chief priests
and the scribes, and be killed,
and after three days rise again.   *Mark 8:31*

Collect

God our Father,
you are all tenderness and compassion,
slow to anger, rich in graciousness,
and always ready to forgive.
Grant us grace to renounce all evil
and to cling to Christ,
that in every way
we may prove to be your loving sons and daughters;
through Jesus Christ our Lord,
who lives and reigns with you and the Holy Spirit,
one God, for ever and ever.

Readings

Genesis 17:1-10, 15-19	Psalm 105:1-11
Romans 4:16-25	Mark 8:31-38

Third Sunday in Lent — Year B

Sentence

The word of the cross is folly to those who are perishing,
but to us who are being saved it is the power of God.

1 Corinthians 1:18

Collect

Lord our God,
hallowed be your name.
Incline our hearts to your commandments,
and give us the wisdom of the cross;
so that, freed from sin
which imprisons us in our own self-centredness,
we may be open to the gift of your Spirit,
and become living temples of your love;
through our Lord Jesus Christ, your Son,
who lives and reigns with you and the Holy Spirit,
one God, for ever and ever.

Readings

Exodus 20:1-17	Psalm 19:7-14
1 Corinthians 1:22-25	John 2:13-22

Fourth Sunday in Lent — Year B

Sentence

By grace you have been saved through faith;.
and this is not your own doing, it is the gift of God.

Ephesians 2:18

Collect

Gracious Father,
you gave us our Lord Jesus Christ
as a model of humility:
in lowliness and obedience
he yielded up his life on the cross.
Enable us to follow his example,
that, in humility and obedience,
we may bear witness to your steadfast love
and attain the joy of the resurrection;
through Jesus Christ our Lord,
who lives and reigns with you and the Holy Spirit,
one God, for ever and ever.

Readings

2 Chronicles 36:14-23   Psalm 137:1-6

Ephesians 2:4-10   John 3:14-21

Fifth Sunday in Lent — Year B

Sentence

Anyone who serves me must follow me, says the Lord,
and where I am, there shall my servant be also.   *John 12:26*

Collect

Hear, O Father, the cry of your Son,
who, to establish the new and everlasting covenant,
became obedient to death upon the cross.
Grant that, through all the trials of this life,
we may come to share more intimately
in his redeeming passion;
and so obtain the fruitfulness of the seed
that falls to the earth and dies,
to be gathered as your harvest for the kingdom.
We ask this through your Son, our Lord Jesus Christ.

Readings

Jeremiah 31:31-34	Psalm 51:10-17
Hebrews 5:7-10	John 12:20-33

Sixth Sunday in Lent — Year B

Sentence

(when observed as The Sunday of the Passion: Passion Sunday)

I have trusted in you, O Lord.
I have said: You are my God.
My times are in your hand;
rescue me from the hand of my enemies,
and from those who persecute me.
Make your face to shine upon your servant,
and in your loving-kindness save me.   *Psalm 31:9-16*

(when observed as Palm Sunday)

Open for me the gates of righteousness;
I will enter them;
I will offer thanks to the Lord.   *Psalm 118:19*

Collect

(when observed as The Sunday of the Passion: Passion Sunday)

Let us pray (that we may share Christ's humility):

Father of all,
who gave your only-begotten Son
to take upon himself the form of a servant,
and to be obedient even to death on a cross:
give us the same mind that was in Christ Jesus,
that, sharing in his humility,
we may come to be with him in his glory;
who lives and reigns with you and the Holy Spirit,
one God, now and for ever.

(when observed as Palm Sunday)

Almighty God,
whose Son was crucified yet entered into glory:
may we, walking in the way of the cross,
find it to be the way of life;
through Jesus Christ our Lord,
who is alive and reigns with you and the Holy Spirit,
one God, now and for ever.

Readings

(when observed as The Sunday of the Passion: Passion Sunday)

Isaiah 50:4-9a

Philippians 2:5-11

Psalm 31:9-16

Mark 14:1 to 15:47 *or*
15:1-39

(when observed as Palm Sunday)

Isaiah 50:4-9a

Philippians 2:5-11

Psalm 118:19-29

Mark 11:1-11 *or*
John 12:12-16

Monday in Holy Week — Years A, B, C

See Year A, page 176.

Tuesday in Holy Week — Years A, B, C

See Year A, page 177.

Wednesday in Holy Week — Years A, B, C

See Year A, page 178.

Holy Thursday — Year B

Sentence

How shall I repay the Lord
for all the good things he has done for me?
I will lift up the cup of salvation
and call upon the name of the Lord.

Psalm 116:12, 13

Collect

Holy Father,
your Son gave us this sacrament
as a memorial of his death and resurrection.
Make us more responsive to his unseen presence,
that we may experience in even fuller measure
the fullness of love and life
he so graciously offers to all.
He lives and reigns with you and the Holy Spirit,
one God, for ever and ever.

Readings

Exodus 24:3-8   Psalm 116:12-19

1 Corinthians 10:16-17   Mark 14:12-26

Good Friday — Years A, B, C

See Year A, page 180.

Holy Saturday — Years A, B, C

See Year A, page 182.

Easter Vigil — Years A, B, C

See Year A, page 183.

Easter Day — Year B

Sentence

It will be said on that day:
Lo, this is our God; we have waited for him,
that he might save us.
This is the Lord; we have waited for him;
let us be glad and rejoice in his salvation.

Isaiah 25:9

Collect

Let us pray (that we may rejoice in the victory
that is won for us):

Lord of all life and power,
who through the mighty resurrection of your Son
overcame the old order of sin and death
to make all things new in him:
grant that we, being dead to sin
and alive to you in Jesus Christ,
may reign with him in glory;
to whom with you and the Holy Spirit
be praise, honour and thanksgiving,
now and in all eternity.

Readings

Acts 10:34-43 *or* Psalm 118:14-24
Isaiah 25:6-9

1 Corinthians 15:1-11 *or* John 20:1-18 *or*
Acts 10:34-43 Mark 16:1-18

> If the Old Testament passage is chosen for the first reading, the Acts
> passage is used as the second reading in order to initiate the sequential
> reading of Acts during the fifty days of Easter.

Evening of Easter Day — Years A, B, C

See Year A, page 185.

Second Sunday of Easter — Year B

Sentence

This is the message we have heard from him and proclaim to you,
that God is light,
and in him is no darkness at all.   *1 John 1:5*

Collect

Let us pray (as christians thirsting for the risen life):

Heavenly Father and God of mercy,
we no longer look for Jesus among the dead,
for he is alive and has become the Lord of life.
From the waters of death you raise us with him
and renew your gift of life within us.
Increase in our minds and hearts
the risen life we share with Christ,
and help us to grow as your people
towards the fullness of eternal life with you;
through Jesus Christ our Lord.

Readings

Acts 4:32-35	Psalm 133
1 John 1:1 to 2:2	John 20:19-31

Third Sunday of Easter — Year B

Sentence

See what love the Father has given us,
that we should be called children of God;
and so we are.   *1 John 3:1*

or

Lord Jesus, open to us the Scriptures;
make our hearts burn within us while you speak.
                                    Based on Luke 24:32

Collect

O God,
whose blessed Son made himself known to his disciples
in the breaking of the bread:
open the eyes of our faith
that we may behold him in all his redeeming work;
who lives and reigns with you,
in the unity of the Holy Spirit,
one God, now and for ever.

Readings

Acts 3:12-19	Psalm 4
1 John 3:1-7	Luke 24:35-48

Fourth Sunday of Easter — Year B

Sentence

I am the good shepherd, says the Lord:
I know my own and my own know me.   *John 10:14*

or

This is his commandment,
that we should believe in the name
of his Son Jesus Christ and love one another,
just as he has commanded us.
All who keep his commandments abide in him,
and he in them.   *1 John 3:23, 24*

Collect

O God, Creator and Father,
you show the risen Lord resplendent in glory
whenever healing is bestowed in his name
upon the infirmity of our human condition.
Gather your scattered children
into the unity of one family,
so that, following closely after Christ our good shepherd,
we may taste the joy of being your children.
We ask this through your Son, our Lord Jesus Christ.

Readings

Acts 4:8-12	Psalm 23
1 John 3:18-24	John 10:11-18

Fifth Sunday of Easter — Year B

Sentence

If you abide in me, and my words abide in you,
ask whatever you will,
and it shall be done for you.   *John 15:7*

Collect

Almighty God,
whom to know is everlasting life:
grant us so perfectly to know your Son Jesus Christ
to be the way, the truth and the life,
that we may steadfastly follow his steps
in the way that leads to eternal life;
through Jesus Christ your Son our Lord,
who lives and reigns with you,
in the unity of the Holy Spirit,
one God, for ever and ever.

Readings

Acts 8:26-40	Psalm 22:25-31
1 John 4:7-12	John 15:1-8

Sixth Sunday of Easter — Year B

Sentence

You did not choose me,
but I chose you and appointed you
that you should go and bear fruit,
and that your fruit should abide.

John 15:16

Collect

Merciful God,
you have prepared for those who love you
riches beyond imagination.
Pour into our hearts such love toward you,
that we, loving you above all things,
may obtain your promises,
which exceed all that we can desire;
through Jesus Christ our Lord,
who is alive and reigns with you and the Holy Spirit,
one God, now and for ever.

Readings

Acts 10:44-48	Psalm 98
1 John 5:1-6	John 15:9-17

Ascension Day — Years A, B, C

See Year A, page 191.

Seventh Sunday of Easter — Year B

Sentence

I will not leave you desolate, says the Lord;
I will come to you.   *John 14:18*

or

God gave us eternal life,
and this life is in his Son.   *1 John 5:11*

Collect

O God, the inexhaustible fount of life,
you accepted the offering of your Son,
sacrificed for the salvation of the world.
Consecrate us in that unity which is your Spirit's gift,
that we may abide always in your love
and become witnesses of the resurrection.
We ask this through our Lord Jesus Christ, your Son,
who lives and reigns with you
in the unity of the Holy Spirit,
one God, for ever and ever.

Readings

Acts 1:15-17, 21-26	Psalm 1
1 John 5:9-13	John 17:11b-19

The Day of Pentecost — Year B

Sentence

When the Spirit of truth comes,
he will guide you into all the truth;
for he will not speak on his own authority,
but whatever he hears he will speak,
and he will declare to you the things that are to come.

John 16:13

or

Come, Holy Spirit, fill the hearts of your faithful people;
and kindle in us the fire of your love.

Collect

Father of all light,
you are the giver of every good and perfect gift.
Let your Spirit come upon us in power,
that, afire with your love,
we may in all things proclaim the lordship of Christ,
to the honour and praise of your great and glorious name;
through Jesus Christ our Lord,
who lives and reigns with you and the Holy Spirit,
one God, for ever and ever.

Readings

Acts 2:1-21 *or*
Ezekiel 37:1-14

Psalm 104:24-34

Romans 8:22-27 *or*
Acts 2:1-21

John 15:26, 27; 16:4b-15

If the Old Testament passage is chosen for the first reading, the Acts passage is used as the second reading.

Trinity Sunday — Year B

Sentence

Holy, holy, holy is the Lord of hosts;
the whole earth is full of his glory. *Isaiah 6:3*

or

God so loved the world that he gave his only Son,
that whoever believes in him should not perish
but have eternal life.
For God sent the Son into the world,
not to condemn the world,
but that the world might be saved through him. *John 3:16, 17*

Collect

Father, we praise you:
through your Word and Holy Spirit you created all things.
You reveal your salvation in all the world
by sending to us Jesus Christ, the Word made flesh.
Through your Holy Spirit
you give us a share in your life and love.
Fill us with the vision of your glory,
that we may always serve and praise you,
Father, Son and Holy Spirit,
one God, for ever and ever.

Readings

Isaiah 6:1-8

Psalm 29

Romans 8:12-17

John 3:1-17

Sunday 9 — Year B

(Sunday between 29 May and 4 June inclusive, if after Trinity Sunday)

* If there is a very early Easter and a Sunday between 24 and 28 May
  inclusive follows Trinity Sunday, use the resources for Sunday 8.

Sentence

It is the God who said: Let light shine out of darkness,
who has shone in our hearts
to give the light of the knowledge of the glory of God
in the face of Christ.   *2 Corinthians 4:6*

Collect

Let us pray (that we may commit ourselves in faith
to God's purposes for us):

Almighty and everliving God,
increase in us your gift of faith:
that, forsaking what lies behind
and reaching out to that which is before us,
we may run the way of your commandments
and win the crown of everlasting joy;
through Jesus Christ our Lord.

Readings

    1 Samuel 16:1-13   Psalm 20

    2 Corinthians 4:5-12   Mark 2:23 to 3:6

Sunday 10 — Year B

(Sunday between 5 and 11 June inclusive, if after Trinity Sunday)

Sentence

Be merciful to me, O God, be merciful,
for I have taken refuge in you;
in the shadow of your wings will I take refuge
until this time of trouble has gone by.

Psalm 57:1

Collect

O God,
from whom all good proceeds:
grant that by your inspiration
we may think those things that are right,
and by your merciful guiding may do them;
through Jesus Christ our Lord,
who lives and reigns with you and the Holy Spirit,
one God, for ever and ever.

Readings

1 Samuel 16:14-23	Psalm 57
2 Corinthians 4:13 to 5:1	Mark 3:20-35

Sunday 11 — Year B

(Sunday between 12 and 18 June inclusive, if after Trinity Sunday)

Sentence

God is our refuge and strength,
a very present help in trouble.
The Lord of hosts is with us;
the God of Jacob is our stronghold.

Psalm 46:1, 7

Collect

Father,
with a generous hand you have sown in our hearts
the seed of truth and grace.
May we welcome it with humble confidence
and cultivate it with gospel patience,
knowing well that justice and peace
will increase in the world
as your word bears fruit in our lives.
We ask this through our Lord Jesus Christ, your Son,
who lives and reigns with you
in the unity of the Holy Spirit,
one God, for ever and ever.

Readings

2 Samuel 1:1, 17-27   Psalm 46

2 Corinthians 5:6-10, 14-17   Mark 4:26-34

Sunday 12 — Year B

(Sunday between 19 and 25 June inclusive, if after Trinity Sunday)

Sentence

God was in Christ reconciling the world to himself,
not counting our trespasses against us,
and entrusting to us the message of reconciliation.

2 Corinthians 5:19

Collect

O God our defender,
storms rage about us and cause us to be afraid.
Rescue your people from despair,
deliver your sons and daughters from fear,
and preserve us all from unbelief;
through your Son, Jesus Christ our Lord,
who lives and reigns with you and the Holy Spirit,
one God, now and ever.

Readings

2 Samuel 5:1-12	Psalm 48
2 Corinthians 5:18 to 6:2	Mark 4:35-41

Sunday 13 — Year B

(Sunday between 26 June and 2 July inclusive)

Sentence

You know the grace of our Lord Jesus Christ,
that though he was rich, yet for our sake he became poor,
so that by his poverty we might become rich.   *2 Corinthians 8:9*

Collect

Almighty God,
in whom are hidden all the treasures
of wisdom and knowledge:
open our eyes to your presence,
and make us more responsive to your call,
that we may grow in the wisdom and grace you offer us
in Christ Jesus our Lord,
who lives and reigns with you and the Holy Spirit,
one God, for ever and ever.

Readings

2 Samuel 6:1-15	Psalm 24
2 Corinthians 8:7-15	Mark 5:21-43

Sunday 14 — Year B

(Sunday between 3 and 9 July inclusive)

Sentence

Jesus said: The Spirit of the Lord is upon me,
because he has anointed me to preach good news to the poor.
He has sent me to proclaim release to the captives,
and recovering of sight to the blind,
to set at liberty those who are oppressed,
to proclaim the acceptable year of the Lord.   *Luke 4:18, 19*

Collect

Remove, O Father, the veil from our eyes,
and grant us the light of the Spirit;
that we may learn to recognise your glory
in the humiliation of your Son,
and experience in the weakness of our own human nature
the surpassing power of his resurrection.
We ask this through our Lord Jesus Christ, your Son,
who lives and reigns with you
in the unity of the Holy Spirit,
one God, for ever and ever.

Readings

2 Samuel 7:1-17   Psalm 89:20-37

2 Corinthians 12:1-10   Mark 6:1-6

Sunday 15 — Year B

(Sunday between 10 and 16 July inclusive)

Sentence

Blessed be the God and Father of our Lord Jesus Christ,
who has blessed us in Christ
with every spiritual blessing in the heavenly places,
even as he chose us in him
before the foundation of the world.   *Ephesians 1:3, 4a*

Collect

Almighty God,
you have made us for yourself,
and our hearts are restless
until they find their rest in you.
May we find peace in your service now,
and in the world to come, see you face to face;
through Jesus Christ our Lord,
who lives and reigns with you and the Holy Spirit,
one God, now and for ever.

Readings

2 Samuel 7:18-29   Psalm 132:11-18

Ephesians 1:1-10   Mark 6:7-13

Sunday 16 — Year B

(Sunday between 17 and 23 July inclusive)

Sentence

Jesus said: My sheep hear my voice,
and I know them, and they follow me;
and I give them eternal life.   *John 10:27, 28a*

Collect

Lord God most high,
you have come in Christ to redeem your people.
Graciously visit us now,
that the radiance of your glory may light up our minds,
and fill our hearts with joy and peace;
through Jesus Christ our Lord,
who lives and reigns with you and the Holy Spirit,
one God, for ever and ever.

Readings

2 Samuel 11:1-15	Psalm 53
Ephesians 2:11-22	Mark 6:30-34

Sunday 17 — Year B

(Sunday between 24 and 30 July inclusive)

Sentence

Be glad, you righteous, and rejoice in the Lord;
shout for joy, all who are true of heart.   *Psalm 32:11*

Collect

Let us pray (for the faith to recognise
God's presence in our world):

God our Father,
open our eyes to see your hand at work
in the splendour of creation
and in the beauty of human life.
Touched by your hand our world is holy.
Help us to cherish the gifts that surround us,
to share your blessings with our brothers and sisters,
and to experience the joy of life in your presence;
through Jesus Christ our Lord.

Readings

2 Samuel 12:1-14   Psalm 32

Ephesians 3:14-21   John 6:1-15

Sunday 18 — Year B

(Sunday between 31 July and 6 August inclusive)

Sentence

Jesus said: I am the bread of life;
whoever comes to me shall not hunger,
and whoever believes in me shall never thirst. *John 6:35*

Collect

Heavenly Father,
you have placed within the hearts of all your children
a longing for your word and a hunger for your truth.
Grant that, believing in the One whom you have sent,
we may know him to be the true bread of heaven
and food of eternal life,
your Son, our Lord Jesus Christ,
to whom with you and the Holy Spirit be glory and honour
for ever and ever.

Readings

2 Samuel 12:15b-24   Psalm 34:11-22

Ephesians 4:1-6   John 6:24-35

Sunday 19 — Year B

(Sunday between 7 and 13 August inclusive)

Sentence

I am the living bread which came down from heaven,
says the Lord;
whoever eats this bread will live for ever. *John 6:51*

Collect

Let us pray (to be defended in doubt and difficulty):

Merciful Father,
whose Son laid down his life
that we might die to self and live in him:
grant us so perfect a communion with him
that, in all the doubts and dangers that assail us,
our faith may not be found wanting;
through Jesus Christ our Lord.

Readings

2 Samuel 18:1, 5, 9-15   Psalm 143:1-10

Ephesians 4:25 to 5:2   John 6:35, 41-51

Sunday 20 — Year B

(Sunday between 14 and 20 August inclusive)

Sentence

Jesus said: Those who eat my flesh and drink my blood
abide in me, and I in them.   *John 6:56*

Collect

Almighty and ever-living God,
you have given great and precious promises
to those who believe.
Grant us the perfect faith which overcomes all doubt;
through your Son, Jesus Christ our Lord.

Readings

2 Samuel 18:24-33   Psalm 102:1-12

Ephesians 5:15-20   John 6:51-58

Sunday 21 — Year B

(Sunday between 21 and 27 August inclusive)

Sentence

Lord, to whom shall we go?
You have the words of eternal life;
and we have believed, and have come to know,
that you are the Holy One of God.   *John 6:68, 69*

Collect

Let us pray (that our minds may be fixed on eternal truth):

Lord our God,
all truth is from you,
and you alone bring oneness of heart.
Give your people the joy of hearing your word
amid the din of human noise,
and of longing for your presence
more than for life itself.
May all the attractions of a changing world
point us to the peace of your kingdom,
a peace which this world does not give.
We ask this through Jesus Christ our Lord.

Readings

2 Samuel 23:1-7   Psalm 67

Ephesians 5:21-33   John 6:55-69

Sunday 22 — Year B

(Sunday between 28 August and 3 September inclusive)

Sentence

I lift up my eyes to the hills;
from where is my help to come?
My help comes from the Lord,
the maker of heaven and earth.   *Psalm 121:1, 2*

Collect

Almighty and everlasting God,
you are always more ready to hear than we to pray,
and constantly give more than either we desire or deserve.
Pour down upon us the abundance of your mercy,
forgiving us those things
of which our conscience is afraid,
and giving us those good things
which we are not worthy to ask,
except through the merits and mediation of Jesus Christ,
your Son, our Lord.

Readings

1 Kings 2:1-4, 10-12   Psalm 121

Ephesians 6:10-20   Mark 7:1-8, 14, 15, 21-23

Sunday 23 — Year B

(Sunday between 4 and 10 September inclusive)

Sentence

Every good endowment and every perfect gift is from above,
coming down from the Father of lights
with whom there is no variation or shadow due to change.

James 1:17

Collect

Let us pray (to our just and merciful God):

Lord our God,
in you mercy and justice meet.
With unparalleled love you have saved us from death
and drawn us into the circle of your life.
Open our eyes to the wonders this life sets before us,
that we may serve you, free from fear,
and address you as God our Father.
We ask this through Jesus Christ our Lord.

Readings

Proverbs 2:1-8   Psalm 119:129-136

James 1:17-27   Mark 7:31-37

Sunday 24 — Year B

(Sunday between 11 and 17 September inclusive)

Sentence

Those who trust in the Lord are like Mount Zion,
which cannot be moved, but stands fast for ever.
The hills stand about Jerusalem;
so does the Lord stand round about his people,
from this time forth for evermore.   *Psalm 125:1, 2*

Collect

Let us pray (for the peace
which is born of faith and hope):

Father in heaven, Creator of all,
look down upon your people in their moments of need,
for you alone are the source of our peace.
Bring us to the dignity which distinguishes the poor in spirit,
and show us how great is the call to serve,
that we may share in the peace of Christ
who offered his life in the service of all.
We ask this in the name of your Son, our Lord Jesus Christ.

Readings

Proverbs 22:1, 2, 8, 9   Psalm 125

James 2:1-5, 8-10, 14-17   Mark 8:27-38

Sunday 25 — Year B

(Sunday between 18 and 24 September inclusive)

Sentence

The Lord is my light and my salvation;
whom then shall I fear?
The Lord is the strength of my life;
of whom then shall I be afraid?   *Psalm 27:1*

Collect

God and Father of all,
you have willed that the last should be first,
and you have made a little child the measure of your kingdom.
Give us that wisdom which is from above,
that we may welcome the word of your Son
and understand that, in your sight,
the greatest of all is the one who serves.
We ask this through our Lord Jesus Christ, your Son,
who lives and reigns with you
in the unity of the Holy Spirit,
one God, for ever and ever.

Readings

Job 28:20-28	Psalm 27:1-6
James 3:13-18	Mark 9:30-37

Sunday 26 — Year B

(Sunday between 25 September and 1 October inclusive)

Sentence

O wait for the Lord's pleasure;
be strong, and he shall comfort your heart;
wait patiently for the Lord.   *Psalm 27:14*

Collect

Lord of all power and might,
the author and giver of all good things:
graft in our hearts the love of your name,
increase in us true religion,
nourish us in all goodness,
and keep us in your great mercy;
through Jesus Christ our Lord.

Readings

Job 42:1-6   Psalm 27:7-14

James 4:13-17; 5:7-11   Mark 9:38-50

Sunday 27 — Year B

(Sunday between 2 and 8 October inclusive)

Sentence

If we love one another, God abides in us
and his love is perfected in us.   *1 John 4:12*

Collect

Loving God,
you have made us in your image,
creating us male and female;
and you have given us the covenant of marriage
that we may fulfil one another in love.
Pour down your grace on all husbands and wives,
that, keeping the promise of faithfulness to each other,
they may continue to grow in their love
and reflect in their lives your love for us all;
through Jesus Christ our Lord.

Readings

Genesis 2:18-24	Psalm 128
Hebrews 1:1-4; 2:9-11	Mark 10:2-16

Sunday 28 — Year B

(Sunday between 9 and 15 October inclusive)

Sentence

Lord, you have been our refuge
from one generation to another.
Before the mountains were brought forth,
or the land and the earth were born,
from age to age you are God.   *Psalm 90:1, 2*

Collect

Let us pray (for God's forgiveness
and for the happiness it brings):

Father,
you show your almighty power
in your mercy and forgiveness.
Continue to fill us with your gifts of love.
Help us to hurry towards the eternal life you promised
and to share in the joys of your kingdom.
Grant this through our Lord Jesus Christ, your Son,
who lives and reigns with you and the Holy Spirit,
one God, for ever and ever.

Readings

Genesis 3:8-19   Psalm 90:1-12

Hebrews 4:1-3, 9-13   Mark 10:17-30

Sunday 29 — Year B

(Sunday between 16 and 22 October inclusive)

Sentence

The Son of man came not to be served but to serve,
and to give his life as a ransom for many.   *Mark 10:45*

Collect

God our Father,
you have revealed your love for us
in the cross of Christ.
Grant us grace to take up our cross each day,
that, in the company of our Saviour,
we may gladly do your will
and attain to life in all its fullness;
through Jesus Christ our Lord,
who lives and reigns with you and the Holy Spirit,
one God, for ever and ever.

Readings

Isaiah 53:7-12   Psalm 35:17-28

Hebrews 4:14-16   Mark 10:35-45

Sunday 30 — Year B

(Sunday between 23 and 29 October inclusive)

Sentence

Do not be ashamed of testifying to our Lord,
but take your share of suffering for the gospel
in the power of God, who saved us
and called us with a holy calling.   *2 Timothy 1:8, 9*

Collect

O God, light to the blind and joy to the troubled,
in your only-begotten Son
you have given us a high priest, just and compassionate
toward those who groan in oppression and sorrow.
Listen to our cry;
grant that all may recognise in him
the tenderness of your love,
and walk in the way that leads towards you.
We ask this through our Lord Jesus Christ, your Son,
who lives and reigns with you
in the unity of the Holy Spirit,
one God, for ever and ever.

Readings

Jeremiah 31:7-9   Psalm 126

Hebrews 5:1-6   Mark 10:46-52

Sunday 31 — Year B

Sentence

Blessed are the poor in spirit,
for theirs is the kingdom of heaven.

Matthew 5:3

Collect

Let us pray (to be faithful stewards of God's gifts):

Almighty Father,
whose hand is open
to fill all things living with plenteousness:
make us ever thankful for your goodness;
and grant that we, remembering the account
which we must one day give,
may be faithful stewards of your bounty;
through Jesus Christ our Lord.

Readings

Deuteronomy 6:1-9	Psalm 119:33-48
Hebrews 7:23-28	Mark 12:28-34

Sunday 32 — Year B

(Sunday between 6 and 12 November inclusive)

Sentence

Hallelujah!
Praise the Lord, O my soul!
I will praise the Lord as long as I live;
I will sing praises to my God while I have my being.

Psalm 146:1, 2

Collect

O God,
Father of the widow and the orphan,
welcoming refuge for strangers,
and justice for the oppressed:
uphold the hope of the poor
who place their trust in your love;
that the time may soon come when no one will lack
the bread and freedom which you provide,
and all will learn to share freely
after the example of him who has given his very self,
Jesus Christ, your Son, our Lord,
who lives and reigns with you and the Holy Spirit,
one God, for ever and ever.

Readings

1 Kings 17:8-16	Psalm 146
Hebrews 9:24-28	Mark 12:38-44

Sunday 33 — Year B

(Sunday between 13 and 19 November inclusive)

Sentence

The Lord is gracious and full of compassion,
slow to anger and of great kindness.   *Psalm 145:8*

Collect

Almighty and ever-living God,
before the earth was formed
and even after it ceases to be, you are God.
Break into our short span of life,
and let us see the signs of your final will and purpose;
through your Son, Jesus Christ our Lord.

Readings

Daniel 7:9-14   Psalm 145:8-13

Hebrews 10:11-18   Mark 13:24-32

The Festival of Christ the King
The Last Sunday after Pentecost — Year B

(Sunday between 20 and 26 November inclusive)

Sentence

I am the Alpha and the Omega, says the Lord God;
who is, and who was, and who is to come, the Almighty.

Revelation 1:8

Collect

Let us pray (that the kingdom of Christ
may live in our hearts and come to our world):
Father all-powerful, God of love,
you have raised our Lord Jesus Christ from death to life,
resplendent in glory as King of creation.
Open our hearts,
free all the world to rejoice in his peace,
to glory in his justice, to live in his love.
Bring all people together in Jesus Christ your Son,
whose kingdom is with you and the Holy Spirit,
one God, for ever and ever.

Readings

Jeremiah 23:1-6	Psalm 93
Revelation 1:4b-8	John 18:33-37

The Annunciation of Jesus to Mary
Years A, B, C   *25 March*

See Year A, page 223.

All Saints' Day — Year B   *1 November*

Sentence

I am the resurrection and the life, says the Lord;
whoever lives and believes in me shall never die.   *John 11:25, 26*

Collect

Almighty God,
whose people are knit together in one holy church,
the mystical body of your Son:
grant us grace to follow your blessed saints
in lives of faith and commitment,
and to know the inexpressible joy you have prepared
for those who love you;
through your Son, Jesus Christ our Lord,
who lives and reigns with you and the Holy Spirit,
one God, now and for ever.

Readings

Revelation 21:1-6a	Psalm 24
Colossians 1:9-14	John 11:32-44

First Sunday in Advent — Year C

Sentence

They will see the Son of man coming in a cloud
with power and great glory.
Now when these things begin to take place,
look up and raise your heads,
because your redemption is drawing near.   *Luke 21:27, 28*

Collect

Father, God of all holiness,
whose promises stand unshaken through all generations:
lift up the human race,
burdened and brought low by so much evil;
and open our hearts to renewed hope;
that we may look forward without fear or anguish
to the glorious return of Jesus Christ,
our Judge and our Saviour,
who lives and reigns with you
in the unity of the Holy Spirit,
one God, for ever and ever.

Readings

Jeremiah 33:14-16   Psalm 25:1-10

1 Thessalonians 3:9-13   Luke 21:25-36

Second Sunday in Advent — Year C

Sentence

Behold, I send my messenger
to prepare the way before me,
and the Lord whom you seek
will suddenly come to his temple.   *Malachi 3:1*

Collect

Merciful God,
who sent your messengers the prophets
to preach repentance and prepare the way for our salvation:
give us grace to heed their warnings and forsake our sins,
that we may greet with joy
the coming of Jesus Christ our Redeemer;
who lives and reigns with you and the Holy Spirit,
one God, now and for ever.

Readings

Malachi 3:1-4   Psalm 126

Philippians 1:3-11   Luke 3:1-6

Third Sunday in Advent — Year C

Sentence

Give thanks to the Lord, call upon his name;
make known his deeds among the nations,
proclaim that his name is exalted. *Isaiah 12:4*

Collect

O God, the fountain of all life and joy,
renew us by the power of your Holy Spirit,
that we may joyfully run in the way of your commandments
and carry to all the good news of our Saviour,
Jesus Christ,
who lives and reigns with you
in the unity of the Holy Spirit,
one God, for ever and ever.

Readings

Zephaniah 3:14-20   Isaiah 12:2-6

Philippians 4:4-9   Luke 3:7-18

Fourth Sunday in Advent — Year C

Sentence

Turn to me and be saved,
all the ends of the earth!
For I am God, and there is no other.   *Isaiah 45:22*

or

Mary said: I am the servant of the Lord;
let it be to me according to your word.   *Luke 1:38*

Collect

Let us pray (as Advent draws to a close
for the faith that opens our lives to the Spirit of God):

Father, all-powerful God,
your eternal Word took flesh on our earth
when the Virgin Mary placed her life
at the service of your plan.
Lift our minds in watchful hope
to hear the voice which announces his glory,
and open our hearts to receive the Spirit
who prepares us for his coming.
We ask this through Jesus Christ our Lord.

Readings

Micah 5:2-4   Psalm 80:1-7

Hebrews 10:5-10   Luke 1:39-55

Christmas — Years A, B, C   *24, 25 December*

See Year A, page 149.

First Sunday of Christmas — Year C

Sentence

Let the peace of Christ rule in your hearts;
let the word of Christ dwell in you richly.

Colossians 3:15, 16

Collect

Let us pray (that we may love one another
as God has loved us):

Grant, Lord,
that in all our dealings with one another
we may be subject to you, Father of all,
and follow the pattern of your Son Jesus Christ,
who, in obedience to your will,
gave up his life for us,
yet lives and reigns with you and the Holy Spirit,
one God, now and for ever.

Readings

1 Samuel 2:18-20, 26	Psalm 111
Colossians 3:12-17	Luke 2:41-52

The Naming of Jesus
Years A, B, C

1 January

See Year A, page 154.

Second Sunday of Christmas — Years A, B, C

See Year A, page 155.

The Epiphany of the Lord
Years A, B, C

6 January

See Year A, page 156.

First Sunday after Epiphany — Sunday 1 Year C

(The Baptism of Jesus)

Sentence

When Jesus had been baptised and was praying,
the heaven was opened,
and the Holy Spirit descended upon him as a dove,
and a voice came from heaven:
Thou art my beloved Son; with thee I am well pleased.

Luke 3:21, 22

Collect

Eternal Father,
who at the baptism of Jesus
revealed him to be your Son,
anointing him with the Holy Spirit:
keep your children, born of water and the Spirit,
faithful to their calling;
through Jesus Christ our Lord,
who lives and reigns with you and the Holy Spirit,
one God, now and for ever.

Readings

Isaiah 61:1-4	Psalm 29
Acts 8:14-17	Luke 3:15-17, 21, 22

Second Sunday after Epiphany — Sunday 2 Year C

Sentence

Jesus manifested his glory,
and his disciples believed in him.   *John 2:11*

Collect

Let us pray (for grace to be true to our calling):

Almighty God,
by whose grace alone we are accepted
and called to your service:
strengthen us by your Holy Spirit,
and make us worthy of our calling;
through Jesus Christ our Lord.

Readings

Isaiah 62:1-5	Psalm 36:5-10
1 Corinthians 12:1-11	John 2:1-11

Third Sunday after Epiphany — Sunday 3
Year C

Sentence

The Lord has anointed me to preach good news to the poor
and release to the captives. *Luke 4:18*

Collect

Father,
you have sent your anointed One as king and prophet
to announce to the poor the glad tidings of your reign.
Grant that his words may this day resound in the church,
build us up into one body,
and fashion us into instruments of liberation and salvation.
We ask this through our Lord Jesus Christ, your Son,
who lives and reigns with you
in the unity of the Holy Spirit,
one God, for ever and ever.

Readings

Nehemiah 8:1-4a, 5, 6, 8-10   Psalm 19:7-14

1 Corinthians 12:12-30   Luke 4:14-21

Fourth Sunday after Epiphany — Sunday 4
   Year C

Sentence

In you, O Lord, have I taken refuge;
let me never be ashamed.
In your righteousness, deliver me and set me free;
incline your ear to me and save me.   *Psalm 71:1, 2*

Collect

Living God,
in Christ you make all things new.
Transform the poverty of our nature
by the riches of your grace,
and in the renewal of our lives
make known your glory;
through Jesus Christ our Lord,
who is alive and reigns with you and the Holy Spirit,
one God, now and for ever.

Readings

Jeremiah 1:4-10	Psalm 71:1-6
1 Corinthians 13:1-13	Luke 4:21-30

Fifth Sunday after Epiphany — Sunday 5
Year C

Sentence

Holy, holy, holy is the Lord of hosts;
the whole earth is full of his glory.   *Isaiah 6:3*

Collect

Lord of hosts,
whose glory fills all heaven and earth:
you have entrusted to our unclean lips and fragile hands
the mission of proclaiming the gospel.
Strengthen us with your Spirit,
that your word may find a welcome
in hearts both open and generous,
and so bring forth abundant fruit
in every part of the world.
We ask this through our Lord Jesus Christ, your Son,
who lives and reigns with you
in the unity of the Holy Spirit,
one God, for ever and ever.

Readings

Isaiah 6:1-8 (9-13)   Psalm 138

1 Corinthians 15:1-11   Luke 5:1-11

Sixth Sunday after Epiphany — Sunday 6 Year C

Sentence

Rejoice and leap for joy,
for behold, your reward is great in heaven. *Luke 6:23*

Collect

Almighty and everliving God,
whose Son Jesus Christ healed the sick
and restored them to wholeness of life:
look with compassion on the anguish of the world,
and by your power make whole all peoples and nations;
through Jesus Christ our Lord,
who lives and reigns with you and the Holy Spirit,
one God, now and for ever.

Readings

Jeremiah 17:5-10	Psalm 1
1 Corinthians 15:12-20	Luke 6:17-26

Seventh Sunday after Epiphany — Sunday 7 Year C

Sentence

A new commandment I give to you,
that you love one another; even as I have loved you,
that you also love one another.   *John 13:34*

Collect

God of compassion,
keep before us the love you have revealed in your Son,
who prayed even for his enemies;
in our words and deeds
help us to be like him through whom we pray,
Jesus Christ our Lord.

Readings

Genesis 45:3-11, 15	Psalm 37:1-11
1 Corinthians 15:35-38, 42-50	Luke 6:27-38

Eighth Sunday after Epiphany — Sunday 8 Year C

Sentence

It is a good thing to give thanks to the Lord,
and to sing praises to your name, O Most High;
to tell of your loving-kindness early in the morning
and of your faithfulness in the night season. *Psalm 92:1, 2*

Collect

Almighty Father,
in Christ your Son you have adopted us
as your own dear children.
So guide us by your loving Spirit,
that we may fearlessly work for unity and peace,
and in all things give glory to your holy name;
through Jesus Christ our Lord,
who lives and reigns with you and the Holy Spirit,
one God, for ever and ever.

Readings

Isaiah 55:10-13

Psalm 92:1-4, 12-15

1 Corinthians 15:51-58

Luke 6:39-49

Last Sunday after Epiphany
Sunday before Ash Wednesday — Year C

(The Transfiguration of Jesus)

Sentence

A cloud came and overshadowed them;
and they were afraid as they entered the cloud.
And a voice came out of the cloud, saying:
This is my Son, my Chosen; listen to him!   *Luke 9:34, 35*

Collect

Let us pray (that we may be transfigured
into the likeness of Christ):

Almighty Father,
whose Son Jesus Christ was revealed in majesty
before he suffered death upon the cross:
give us grace to perceive his glory,
that we may be strengthened to suffer with him
and be changed into his likeness, from glory to glory:
who lives and reigns with you and the Holy Spirit,
one God, now and for ever.

Readings

Exodus 34:29-35	Psalm 99
2 Corinthians 3:12 to 4:2	Luke 9:28-36

Ash Wednesday — Years A, B, C

See Year A, page 167.

First Sunday in Lent — Year C

Sentence

If you confess with your lips that Jesus is Lord,
and believe in your heart
that God raised him from the dead,
you will be saved.   *Romans 10:9*

Collect

Lord our God,
listen to the voice of your church,
calling to you from the desert of this world.
Protect us with your strong hand and outstretched arm,
that, nourished by the bread of your word
and fortified by your Spirit,
we may conquer with fasting and prayer
the persistent seductions of the Evil One.
We ask this through our Lord Jesus Christ, your Son,
who lives and reigns with you
in the unity of the Holy Spirit,
one God, for ever and ever.

Readings

Deuteronomy 26:1-11	Psalm 91:9-16
Romans 10:8b-13	Luke 4:1-13

Second Sunday in Lent — Year C

Sentence

God is spirit, and those who worship him
must worship in spirit and truth.   *John 4:24*

Collect

Almighty God,
you know that we have no power in ourselves
to help ourselves.
Keep us both outwardly in our bodies
and inwardly in our souls,
that we may be defended from all adversities
which may happen to the body,
and from all evil thoughts
which may assault and hurt the soul;
through Jesus Christ our Lord,
who lives and reigns with you and the Holy Spirit,
one God, for ever and ever.

Readings

Genesis 15:1-12, 17,18   Psalm 127

Philippians 3:17 to 4:1   Luke 13:31-35

Third Sunday in Lent — Year C

Sentence

Bless the Lord, O my soul,
and all that is within me, bless his holy name.
As the heavens are high above the earth,
so is his mercy great upon those who fear him.
As far as the east is from the west,
so far has he removed our sins from us. *Psalm 103:1, 11, 12*

Collect

Holy and merciful Father,
you never leave your children abandoned
but always reveal your name to them.
Break through the hardness of our minds and hearts,
so that we may learn to receive your teachings
with childlike simplicity,
and bear the fruit of true and continual conversion.
We ask this through our Lord Jesus Christ, your Son,
who lives and reigns with you
in the unity of the Holy Spirit,
one God, for ever and ever.

Readings

Exodus 3:1-15   Psalm 103:1-13

1 Corinthians 10:1-13   Luke 13:1-9

Fourth Sunday in Lent — Year C

Sentence

I will arise and go to my father, and I will say to him:
Father, I have sinned against heaven and before you. *Luke 15:18*

Collect

Gracious Father,
you are truly compassionate to all your children,
for you remember that we are but dust.
So fill us with your love,
that, rising above our weaknesses,
we may always remain true to Christ;
who lives and reigns with you and the Holy Spirit,
one God, for ever and ever.

Readings

Joshua 5:9-12   Psalm 34:1-10

2 Corinthians 5:16-21   Luke 15:1-3, 11-32

Fifth Sunday in Lent — Year C

Sentence

One thing I do; forgetting what lies behind
and straining forward to what lies ahead,
I press on toward the goal for the prize
of the upward call of God in Christ Jesus.   *Philippians 3:13, 14*

Collect

Most generous God,
no human words or costly gifts
can ever express our thanks and praise
for all that you have done for us through Christ your Son.
Grant that we may gladly give you
the one precious gift that we have to bring,
the offering of our loyalty and love;
and enable us to walk in love for others,
as Christ loved us and gave himself up for us,
a fragrant offering and sacrifice to you.
We ask this through your Son, our Lord Jesus Christ.

Readings

Isaiah 43:16-21   Psalm 126

Philippians 3:8-14   John 12:1-8

Sixth Sunday in Lent — Year C

Sentence

(when observed as The Sunday of the Passion: Passion Sunday)

Behold my servant, whom I uphold,
my chosen, in whom my soul delights;
I have put my spirit upon him;
he will bring forth justice to the nations. *Isaiah 42:1*

(when observed as Palm Sunday)

Lift up your heads, O gates;
lift them high, O overlasting doors;
and the King of glory shall come in. *Psalm 24:7*

Collect

(when observed as The Sunday of the Passion: Passion Sunday)

Father,
your Son, our Lord Jesus Christ,
loved the world so much
that he went to the cross for our sake.
So strengthen us with your grace,
that we, for whom Christ died,
may show forth the same selfless love
and for ever walk in his ways;
who lives and reigns with you and the Holy Spirit,
one God, for ever and ever.

It is right to praise you, almighty God,
for the acts of love by which you have redeemed us
through your Son Jesus Christ our Lord.
The Hebrews acclaimed Jesus as Messiah and King,
with palm branches in their hands, crying:
Hosanna in the highest!
May we also, carrying these emblems, go forth to meet Christ
and follow him in the way that leads to eternal life;
who lives and reigns in glory with you and the Holy Spirit,
now and for ever.

Readings

(when observed as The Sunday of the Passion: Passion Sunday)

Isaiah 50:4-9a	Psalm 31:9-16
Philippians 2:5-11	Luke 22:14 to 23:56 *or* 23:1-49

(when observed as Palm Sunday)

Isaiah 50:4-9a	Psalm 118:19-29
Philippians 2:5-11	Luke 19:28-40

Monday in Holy Week — Years A, B, C

See Year A, page 176.

Tuesday in Holy Week — Years A, B, C

See Year A, page 177.

Wednesday in Holy Week — Years A, B, C

See Year A, page 178.

Holy Thursday — Year C

Sentence

Behold, the days are coming, says the Lord,
when I will make a new covenant
with the house of Israel and the house of Judah.
I will put my law within them,
and I will write it upon their hearts.   *Jeremiah 31:31, 33b*

Collect

Holy God, source of all love,
on the night of his betrayal
Jesus gave his disciples a new commandment:
to love one another as he had loved them.
By your Holy Spirit,
write this commandment in our hearts;
through your Son, Jesus Christ our Lord,
who lives and reigns with you and the Holy Spirit,
one God, now and for ever.

Readings

Jeremiah 31:31-34	Psalm 116:12-19
Hebrews 10:16-25	Luke 22:7-20

Good Friday — Years A, B, C

See Year A, page 180.

Holy Saturday — Years A, B, C

See Year A, page 182.

Easter Vigil — Years A, B, C

See Year A, page 183.

Easter Day — Year C

Sentence

Christ has been raised from the dead,
the firstfruits of those who have fallen asleep.
For as in Adam all die,
so also in Christ shall all be made alive.   *1 Corinthians 15:20, 22*

Collect

Lord of life and power,
through the mighty resurrection of your Son
you have overcome the old order of sin and death
and have made all things new in him.
May we, being dead to sin
and alive to you in Jesus Christ,
reign with him in glory,
who, with you and the Holy Spirit ever lives,
one God, from all eternity.

Readings

Acts 10:34-43 *or*   Psalm 118:14-24
Isaiah 65:17-25

1 Corinthians 15:19-26 *or*   John 20:1-18 *or*
Acts 10:34-43   Luke 24:1-12

If the Old Testament passage is chosen for the first reading, the Acts
passage is used as the second reading in order to initiate the sequential
reading of Acts during the fifty days of Easter.

Evening of Easter Day — Years A, B, C

See Year A, page 185.

Second Sunday of Easter — Year C

Sentence

Jesus came and stood among them
and said to them: Peace be with you.   *John 20:19b*

Collect

Father,
you gather us together on this day
which you have made your own
that we may celebrate Jesus Christ,
the First and the Last,
the living One who has conquered death.
Breathe on us your life-giving Spirit,
and send us out into all the world;
that we may boldly announce the forgiveness of sins
through faith in our risen Lord,
who lives and reigns with you and the Holy Spirit,
one God, for ever and ever.

Readings

Acts 5:27-32   Psalm 2

Revelation 1:4-8   John 20:19-31

Third Sunday of Easter — Year C

Sentence

Worthy is the Lamb who was slain,
to receive power and wealth and wisdom and might
and honour and glory and blessing.   *Revelation 5:12*

Collect

Let us pray (that we may submit ourselves
to Christ's direction):

God of peace,
who brought again from the dead our Lord Jesus,
that great shepherd of the sheep,
by the blood of the everlasting covenant:
make us perfect in every good thing to do your will,
and work in us that which is well-pleasing in your sight;
through Jesus Christ our Lord.

Readings

Acts 9:1-20   Psalm 30:4-12

Revelation 5:11-14   John 21:1-19 *or*
                                     21:15-19

Fourth Sunday of Easter — Year C

Sentence

My sheep hear my voice, and I know them,
and they follow me; and I give them eternal life.   *John 10:27, 28*

or

Blessing and glory and wisdom and thanksgiving
and honour and power and might
be to our God for ever and ever.   *Revelation 7:12*

Collect

O God, the fountain of joy and peace,
you have subjected to the royal power of your Son
the destinies of all peoples and nations.
Sustain us by the power of your Spirit,
and grant that, in the midst of all life's varied changes,
we may never be separated from our Good Shepherd,
who guides us to the springs of life,
Jesus Christ, who lives and reigns with you
in the unity of the Holy Spirit,
one God, for ever and ever.

Readings

Acts 13:15, 16, 26-33   Psalm 23

Revelation 7:9-17   John 10:22-30

Fifth Sunday of Easter — Year C

Sentence

A new commandment I give to you,
that you love one another as I have loved you.   *John 13:34*

Collect

Almighty Father,
whose Son, our Lord Jesus Christ,
is the light of the world:
set us on fire with the Spirit of power,
that, in everything we think and say and do,
we may proclaim the wonder of Christ's resurrection.
He lives and reigns with you and the Holy Spirit,
one God, for ever and ever.

Readings

Acts 14:8-18   Psalm 145:13b-21

Revelation 21:1-6   John 13:31-35

Sixth Sunday of Easter — Year C

Sentence

If you love me, you will keep my word,
and my Father will love you,
and we will come to you and make our home with you.

Based on John 14:23

Collect

O God,
you have promised to make your dwelling place
within the hearts of all who hear your words
and put them into practice.
Send your Spirit to bring to our mind
all that your Son did and taught,
and empower us to bear witness to him
in our own words and deeds.
We ask this through our Lord Jesus Christ, your Son,
who lives and reigns with you
in the unity of the Holy Spirit,
one God for ever and ever.

Readings

Acts 15:1, 2, 22-29   Psalm 67

Revelation 21:10, 22-27   John 14:23-29

Ascension Day — Years A, B, C

See Year A, page 191.

Seventh Sunday of Easter — Year C

Sentence

The Lord is king; let the earth rejoice;
let the multitude of the isles be glad.
The heavens declare his righteousness,
and all the peoples see his glory.   *Psalm 97:1, 6*

or

I do not pray for my disciples only,
but also for those who are to believe in me
through their word, that they may all be one.   *John 17:20, 21a*

Collect

God, our creator and redeemer,
your Son Jesus prayed that his followers might be one.
Make all christians one with him,
as he is one with you,
so that in peace and concord
we may carry to the world the message of your love;
through Jesus Christ our Lord,
who lives and reigns with you and the Holy Spirit,
one God, now and for ever.

Readings

Acts 16:16-34	Psalm 97
Revelation 22:12-14, 16, 17, 20	John 17:20-26

The Day of Pentecost — Year C

Sentence

Jesus said: I will pray the Father,
and he will give you another Counsellor,
to be with you for ever,
even the Spirit of truth.

John 14:16, 17

or

Come, Holy Spirit, fill the hearts of your faithful people,
and kindle in us the fire of your love.

Collect

Almighty and everliving God,
who fulfilled the promises of Easter
by sending us your Holy Spirit,
and opening to every race and nation
the way of life eternal:
keep us in the unity of your Spirit,
that every tongue may tell of your glory;
through Jesus Christ our Lord,
who lives and reigns with you and the Holy Spirit,
one God, now and for ever.

Readings

Acts 2:1-21 *or*   Psalm 104:24-34
Genesis 11:1-9

Romans 8:14-17 *or*   John 14:8-17, 25-27
Acts 2:1-21

> If the Old Testament passage is chosen for the first reading, the Acts
> passage is used as the second reading.

Trinity Sunday — Year C

Sentence

Holy, holy, holy is the Lord of hosts;
the whole earth is full of his glory.   *Isaiah 6:3*

or

God's love has been poured into our hearts
through the Holy Spirit who has been given to us.

                                                  Romans 5:5b

Collect

Almighty and everlasting God,
you have given to your servants grace,
by the confession of a true faith,
to acknowledge the glory of the eternal Trinity,
and in the power of your divine Majesty
to worship the Unity.
Keep us steadfast in this faith and worship,
and bring us at last to see you
in your one and eternal glory, O Father;
for you live and reign with the Son and the Holy Spirit,
one God, for ever and ever.

Readings

Proverbs 8:22-31   Psalm 8

Romans 5:1-5   John 16:12-15

Sunday 9 — Year C

(Sunday between 29 May and 4 June inclusive, if after Trinity Sunday)

* If there is a very early Easter and a Sunday between 24 and 28 May inclusive follows Trinity Sunday, use the resources for Sunday 8.

Sentence

Be joyful in the Lord, all you lands;
serve the Lord with gladness
and come before his presence with a song.   *Psalm 100:1*

Collect

Let us pray (for the confidence born of faith):

God our Father,
teach us to cherish the gifts that surround us.
Increase our faith in you,
and bring our trust to its promised fulfilment
in the joy of your kingdom;
through Jesus Christ our Lord.

Readings

1 Kings 8:22, 23, 41-43	Psalm 100
Galatians 1:1-10	Luke 7:1-10

Sunday 10 — Year C

(Sunday between 5 and 11 June inclusive, if after Trinity Sunday)

Sentence

Hallelujah!
Give praise, you servants of the Lord;
praise the name of the Lord. *Psalm 113:1*

Collect

O God, the consoler of the afflicted,
you illumine the mystery of suffering and death
by the light that shines from the face of Christ.
Grant that, in all the trials of our earthly pilgrimage,
we may remain united to your Son in his passion,
so that there may be revealed in us
the power of his resurrection.
He lives and reigns with you and the Holy Spirit,
one God, for ever and ever.

Readings

1 Kings 17:17-24	Psalm 113
Galatians 1:11-24	Luke 7:11-17

Sunday 11 — Year C

(Sunday between 12 and 18 June inclusive, if after Trinity Sunday)

Sentence

I have been crucified with Christ;
it is no longer I who live, but Christ who lives in me;
and the life I now live in the flesh
I live by faith in the Son of God,
who loved me and gave himself for me.   *Galatians 2:20*

Collect

Let us pray (to the Father,
whose love gives us strength to follow his Son):

God our Father,
we rejoice in the faith that draws us together,
aware that selfishness can drive us apart.
Let your encouragement be our constant strength.
Keep us one in the love that has sealed our lives,
and help us to live the gospel we profess
as one family, united in Jesus Christ our Lord.

Readings

1 Kings 19:1-8	Psalm 42
Galatians 2:15-21	Luke 7:36 to 8:3

Sunday 12 — Year C

(Sunday between 19 and 25 June inclusive, if after Trinity Sunday)

Sentence

Send out your light and your truth,
that they may lead me,
and bring me to your holy hill and to your dwelling.

Psalm 43:3

Collect

Father,
fashion us into disciples
whose hope springs from the love of our Master,
exalted on the throne of the cross.
May the assurance he gives empower us
to conquer the temptations that alarm us within,
and the fears that assail us from without;
that we may journey with courage along the way of Calvary
to the true and eternal life that awaits us.
We ask this through our Lord Jesus Christ.

Readings

1 Kings 19:9-14	Psalm 43
Galatians 3:23-29	Luke 9:18-24

Sunday 13 — Year C

(Sunday between 26 June and 2 July inclusive)

Sentence

Be imitators of God, as beloved children.
And walk in love, as Christ loved us,
and gave himself up for us.   *Galatians 5:1, 2*

Collect

O God, the protector of all who trust in you,
without whom nothing is strong, nothing is holy:
increase and multiply upon us your mercy;
that, with you as our ruler and guide,
we may so pass through things temporal
that we lose not the things eternal;
through Jesus Christ our Lord,
who lives and reigns with you and the Holy Spirit,
one God, for ever and ever.

Readings

1 Kings 19:15-21   Psalm 44:1-8

Galatians 5:1, 13-25   Luke 9:51-62

Sunday 14 — Year C

(Sunday between 3 and 9 July inclusive)

Sentence

The harvest is plentiful, but the labourers are few;
pray therefore the Lord of the harvest
to send out labourers into his harvest. *Luke 10:2*

Collect

Father,
in the resurrection of your Son
death gives birth to new life;
the suffering he endured restores hope to a fallen world.
Let sin never ensnare us
with empty promises of passing joy.
Keep us one with you always,
so that our joy may be holy
and our love may give strength to others.
We ask this through your Son, our Lord Jesus Christ.

Readings

1 Kings 21:1-3, 17-21   Psalm 5:1-8

Galatians 6:7-18   Luke 10:1-12, 17-20

Sunday 15 — Year C

(Sunday between 10 and 16 July inclusive)

Sentence

You shall love the Lord your God with all your heart,
and with all your soul, and with all your strength,
and with all your mind; and your neighbour as yourself.

Luke 10:27

Collect

Merciful Father,
in the great commandment of love
you have given us the summary and spirit of the whole law.
Make our hearts attentive
to the sufferings and anxieties of our brothers and sisters,
and help us to be generous in response and service,
that we may become like Christ,
the Good Samaritan to the world,
the Lord who lives and reigns with you and the Holy Spirit,
one God, for ever and ever.

Readings

2 Kings 2:1, 6-14   Psalm 139: 1-12

Colossians 1:1-14   Luke 10:25-37

Sunday 16 — Year C

(Sunday between 17 and 23 July inclusive)

Sentence

God chose to make known how great among the Gentiles
are the riches of the glory of this mystery,
which is Christ in you, the hope of glory.   *Colossians 1:27*

Collect

Almighty God,
your Son has opened for us
a new and living way into your presence.
Give us pure hearts and constant wills
to worship you in spirit and in truth;
through Jesus Christ our Lord,
who lives and reigns with you and the Holy Spirit,
one God, now and for ever.

Readings

2 Kings 4:8-17   Psalm 139:13-18

Colossians 1:21-29   Luke 10:38-42

Sunday 17 — Year C

(Sunday between 24 and 30 July inclusive)

Sentence

Ask, and it will be given you;
seek, and you will find;
knock, and it will be opened to you.   *Luke 11:9*

Collect

Almighty God,
your Son Jesus Christ fed the hungry
with the bread of his life
and the word of his kingdom.
Renew your people with your heavenly grace,
and in all our weakness
sustain us by Christ the true and living bread,
who lives and reigns with you and the Holy Spirit,
one God, now and for ever.

Readings

2 Kings 5:1-15   Psalm 21:1-7

Colossians 2:6-15   Luke 11:1-13

Sunday 18 — Year C

(Sunday between 31 July and 6 August inclusive)

Sentence

If you have been raised with Christ,
seek the things that are above, where Christ is,
seated at the right hand of God.   *Colossians 3:1*

Collect

Father,
you call your children to walk in the light of Christ.
Free us from darkness,
that we may be illumined by the radiance of your truth;
through Jesus Christ our Lord,
who lives and reigns with you and the Holy Spirit,
one God, for ever and ever.

Readings

2 Kings 13:14-20a   Psalm 28

Colossians 3:1-11   Luke 12:13-21

Sunday 19 — Year C

(Sunday between 7 and 13 August inclusive)

Sentence

Blessed are those servants
whom the master finds awake when he comes.
You also must be ready;
for the Son of man is coming at an hour you do not expect.

Luke 12:37a, 40

Collect

Kindle in our hearts, O Father,
the same faith that impelled Abraham
to go forth from his homeland
and live as a pilgrim upon earth.
Never allow our lamps to be extinguished,
but keep us watchful for your coming,
that we may be welcomed by you
into the joy of our eternal home.
We ask this through your Son, our Lord Jesus Christ.

Readings

Jeremiah 18:1-11	Psalm 14
Hebrews 11:1-3, 8-19	Luke 12:32-40

Sunday 20 — Year C

(Sunday between 14 and 20 August inclusive)

Sentence

Since we are surrounded by so great a cloud of witnesses,
let us also lay aside every weight
and sin which clings so closely,
and let us run with perseverance the race that is set before us,
looking to Jesus, the pioneer and perfecter of our faith.

Hebrews 12:1, 2b

Collect

Holy God,
who in your great love for the world
gave your only Son to die for us all:
have mercy on those who are enemies of the cross of Christ,
actively opposing him by word or deed,
or persecuting his disciples.
And to those who endure suffering in this present time
for the sake of Christ and his gospel,
give the sure confidence of the victory of faith
and the knowledge of the glory that shall be revealed;
through Jesus Christ our Lord.

Readings

Jeremiah 20:7-13	Psalm 10:12-18
Hebrews 12:1, 2, 12-17	Luke 12:49-56

Sunday 21 — Year C

(Sunday between 21 and 27 August inclusive)

Sentence

Strive to enter by the narrow door,
for many will seek to enter and will not be able.   *Luke 13:24*

Collect

Lord God,
you know us to be set in the midst of so many great dangers
that by reason of the frailty of our nature
we cannot always stand upright.
Grant us such strength and protection
as may support us in all dangers
and carry us through all temptations;
through Jesus Christ our Lord.

Readings

Jeremiah 28:1-9	Psalm 84
Hebrews 12:18-29	Luke 13:22-30

Sunday 22 — Year C

(Sunday between 28 August and 3 September inclusive)

Sentence

Jesus Christ is the same yesterday and today,
and for ever.   *Hebrews 13:8*

Collect

O God,
you call the poor and the sinful to take their place
in the festive assembly of the new covenant.
May your church always honour the presence of the Lord
in the humble and the suffering,
and may we learn to recognise each other
as brothers and sisters,
gathered together around your table.
We ask this through our Lord Jesus Christ, your Son,
who lives and reigns with you
in the unity of the Holy Spirit,
one God, for ever and ever.

Readings

Ezekiel 18:1-9, 25-29   Psalm 15

Hebrews 13:1-8   Luke 14:1, 7-14

Sunday 23 — Year C

(Sunday between 4 and 10 September inclusive)

Sentence

As I live, says the Lord God,
I have no pleasure in the death of the wicked,
but rather that they turn from their way and live.   *Ezekiel 33:11*

Collect

Lord of the ages,
you have called your church
to keep watch in the life of the world
and to discern the signs of the times.
Grant us the wisdom which your Spirit bestows,
that with courage we may proclaim your prophetic word,
and as faithful disciples and witnesses of the cross
may finish the work you have given us to do;
through Jesus Christ our Lord.

Readings

Ezekiel 33:1-11   Psalm 94:12-22

Philemon 1-20   Luke 14:25-33

Sunday 24 — Year C

(Sunday between 11 and 17 September inclusive)

Sentence

The saying is sure and worthy of full acceptance,
that Christ Jesus came into the world to save sinners.

1 Timothy 1:15

Collect

Gracious Father,
by whose mercy we are redeemed and made worthy:
grant us ever to remember
that our righteousness consists
not in ourselves
but in the merits of your Son Jesus Christ,
who lives and reigns with you and the Holy Spirit,
one God, now and for ever.

Readings

Hosea 4:1-3, 5:15 to 6:6   Psalm 77:11-20

1 Timothy 1:12-17   Luke 15:1-10

Sunday 25 — Year C

(Sunday between 18 and 24 September inclusive)

Sentence

Give thanks to the Lord, for he is good,
and his mercy endures for ever. *Psalm 107:1*

Collect

Almighty God,
without you we are not able to please you.
Mercifully grant that your Holy Spirit
may in all things direct and rule our hearts;
through Jesus Christ our Lord,
who is alive and reigns with you and the Holy Spirit,
one God, now and for ever.

Readings

Hosea 11:1-11   Psalm 107:1-9

1 Timothy 2:1-7   Luke 16:1-13

Sunday 26 — Year C

(Sunday between 25 September and 1 October inclusive)

Sentence

Fight the good fight of faith;
take hold of the eternal life to which you were called
when you made the good confession
in the presence of many witnesses. *1 Timothy 6:12*

Collect

Father,
you graciously strengthen and replenish
all who wait upon you.
Grant us your Holy Spirit,
that, by gladly serving others,
we may always be true to Christ,
our Lord and our Redeemer.
He lives and reigns with you and the Holy Spirit,
one God, for ever and ever.

Readings

Joel 2:23-30

Psalm 107:1, 33-43

1 Timothy 6:6-19

Luke 16:19-31

Sunday 27 — Year C

(Sunday between 2 and 8 October inclusive)

Sentence

God did not give us a spirit of timidity,
but a spirit of power and love and self-control.   *2 Timothy 1:7*

Collect

Faithful God,
have mercy on us your unworthy servants,
and increase our faith;
that, trusting your power to work in us and through us,
we may never be afraid of testifying to our Lord,
but may obediently serve him all our days.
We ask this through your Son, our Lord Jesus Christ.

Readings

Amos 5:6, 7, 10-15   Psalm 101

2 Timothy 1:1-14   Luke 17:5-10

Sunday 28 — Year C

(Sunday between 9 and 15 October inclusive)

Sentence

Give thanks in all circumstances,
for this is the will of God in Christ Jesus for you.

1 Thessalonians 5:18

Collect

Father in heaven,
the hand of your loving kindness
powerfully yet gently guides all the moments of our day.
Go before us in the pilgrimage of life,
anticipate our needs and prevent our falling.
Send your Spirit to unite us in faith,
that, sharing in your service,
we may rejoice in your presence;
through Jesus Christ our Lord.

Readings

Micah 1:2; 2:1-10   Psalm 26

2 Timothy 2:8-15   Luke 17:11-19

Sunday 29 — Year C

(Sunday between 16 and 22 October inclusive)

Sentence

All Scripture is inspired by God
and profitable for teaching, for reproof, for correction,
and for training in righteousness.   *2 Timothy 3:16*

Collect

Almighty and everliving God,
increase in us your gift of faith,
that, forsaking what lies behind
and reaching out to what is before,
we may run the way of your commandments
and win the crown of everlasting joy;
through Jesus Christ our Lord,
who lives and reigns with you and the Holy Spirit,
one God, for ever and ever.

Readings

Habakkuk 1:1-3; 2:1-4   Psalm 119:137-144

2 Timothy 3:14 to 4:5   Luke 18:1-8

Sunday 30 — Year C

(Sunday between 23 and 29 October inclusive)

Sentence

You, O Lord, are a shield about me;
you are my glory, the one who lifts up my head.
I call aloud upon the Lord,
and he answers me from his holy hill.   *Psalm 3:3, 4*

Collect

Lord God of justice,
you know no favourites and show no partiality;
but you have given us assurance
that the prayers of the lowly pierce the clouds,
their petitions reach the heavens.
Look upon us who come before you
as did the penitent tax collector,
and grant that we may open ourselves
with confidence in your mercy,
and be justified by your grace.
We ask this through your Son, our Lord Jesus Christ.

Readings

Zephaniah 3:1-9   Psalm 3

2 Timothy 4:6-8, 16-18   Luke 18:9-14

Sunday 31 — Year C

(Sunday between 30 October and 5 November inclusive)

Sentence

You are to be praised, O God, in Zion;
to you shall vows be performed in Jerusalem.
To you that hear prayer shall all flesh come. *Psalm 65:1, 2*

Collect

Merciful God,
righteous judge of all,
we bless you that the Son of man came
to seek and to save those who are lost.
Grant that, like Zacchaeus of Jericho,
we may eagerly seek the Saviour,
joyfully welcome him into our homes and lives,
and gladly do what is pleasing in his sight.
We ask this through your Son, our Lord Jesus Christ.

Readings

Haggai 2:1-9   Psalm 65:1-8

2 Thessalonians 1:5-12   Luke 19:1-10

Sunday 32 — Year C

(Sunday between 6 and 12 November inclusive)

Sentence

May our Lord Jesus Christ himself, and God our Father,
who loved us and gave us eternal comfort
and good hope through grace,
comfort your hearts
and establish them in every good work and word.

2 Thessalonians 2:16, 17

Collect

Let us pray (for health of mind and body):

God of power and mercy,
protect us from all harm.
Give us freedom of spirit
and health in mind and body
to do your work on earth.
We ask this through our Lord Jesus Christ, your Son,
who lives and reigns with you and the Holy Spirit,
one God, for ever and ever.

Readings

Zechariah 7:1-10	Psalm 9:11-20
2 Thessalonians 2:13 to 3:5	Luke 20:27-38

Sunday 33 — Year C

(Sunday between 13 and 19 November inclusive)

Sentence

Look up and raise your heads,
because your redemption is drawing near.   *Luke 21:28b*

Collect

Almighty God,
whose sovereign purpose none can make void:
give us faith to be steadfast
amid the tumults of this world,
knowing that your kingdom shall come
and your will be done,
to your eternal glory;
through Jesus Christ our Lord,
who lives and reigns with you and the Holy Spirit,
one God, now and for ever.

Readings

Malachi 4:1-6   Psalm 82

2 Thessalonians 3:6-13   Luke 21:5-19

The Festival of Christ the King
The Last Sunday after Pentecost — Year C

(Sunday between 20 and 26 November inclusive)

Sentence

Come, let us sing to the Lord;
let us shout for joy to the rock of our salvation.
For the Lord is a great God,
and a great king above all gods.   *Psalm 95:1, 3*

Collect

Almighty and everlasting God,
whose will it is to restore all things
in your well-beloved Son, our Lord and King:
grant that the peoples of the earth,
now divided and enslaved by sin,
may be freed and brought together
under his gentle and loving rule;
who lives and reigns with you and the Holy Spirit,
one God, now and for ever.

Readings

2 Samuel 5:1-5	Psalm 95
Colossians 1:11-20	John 12:9-19

The Annunciation of Jesus to Mary
Years A, B, C

25 March

See year A, page 223.

All Saints' Day — Year C

1 November

Sentence

Since we believe that Jesus died and rose again,
even so, through Jesus, God will bring with him
those who have fallen asleep.   *1 Thessalonians 4:14*

Collect

We praise you, heavenly Father,
that you have knit together your chosen people
in one communion and fellowship
in the mystical body of your Son, Christ our Lord.
Give us grace so to follow your blessed saints
in all virtuous and godly living,
that we may come to those inexpressible joys
that you have prepared for those who love you;
through Jesus Christ our Lord.

Readings

Daniel 7:1-3, 15-18   Psalm 149

Ephesians 1:11-23   Luke 6:20-36

A Calendar of
Other Commemorations

The church also celebrates the lives of particular people or particular events in christian history. In some denominations, this list of commemorations is called a *Calendar of Saints' Days* or a *Sanctoral Cycle*. Sometimes there is a table of *Greater Holy Days* when the disciples of Jesus and other well-known people from the New Testament are commemorated. Next there is a table of *Lesser Festivals and Commemorations* when less significant names in the New Testament and famous people in the story of the church through the centuries are recalled.

This *Calendar of Other Commemorations* is a single table; it calls to mind a representative group of people from the communion of saints, that great company whom no one can number, who have been the servants of Christ in their day and generation. It makes no attempt to be all-inclusive, and has limited resemblance to similar calendars prepared by other denominations. This calendar includes some saints' days which are of great antiquity and wide observance. But it also includes a representative list of the names of men and women across the centuries, from East and West. Some of the names give a particular emphasis to our christian heritage in Australia and the Pacific. Synods and presbyteries, parishes and congregations are encouraged to add to this calendar the names of significant christians and of important events.

This calendar may provide helpful resources for congregations which hold services during the week, or in Bible study, fellowship, or house groups. It may stimulate ideas for christian education programs, for the work of the Sunday School, and particularly for an address to young people during the service of the Lord's Day. In due course, biographical notes and other resources relating to this calendar will be prepared.

Each name listed in these ninety-five commemorations is placed in one of nine groupings. At the end of the calendar, appropriate Bible readings and collects are offered.

January	2	Basil and Gregory of Nyssa and Gregory of Nazianzus	*christian thinkers*
	13	George Fox	*renewer of society*
	17	Antony of Egypt	*reformer of the church*
	21	Agnes of Rome	*martyr*
	24	Timothy and Titus	*apostles*
	27	John Chrysostom	*faithful servant*
	28	Thomas Aquinas	*christian thinker*
February	2	Simeon and Anna	*witnesses to Jesus*
	3	First christian service in Australia	*christian pioneers*
	5	Herbert Davies and missionaries in Korea and Japan	*christian pioneers*
	12	Friedrich Schleiermacher	*christian thinker*
	13	Priscilla, Dorcas and Phoebe	*faithful servants*
	14	Cyril and Methodius	*christian pioneers*
	18	Martin Luther	*reformer of the church*
	27	George Herbert	*faithful servant*
	28	Martin Bucer	*reformer of the church*
March	7	Perpetua and Felicity	*martyrs*
	17	Patrick and Ninian	*christian pioneers*
	18	Joseph of Arimathea	*witness to Jesus*
	19	Joseph of Nazareth	*witness to Jesus*
	20	Cuthbert, Aidan and Bede	*christian pioneers*
	24	Paul Couturier	*reformer of the church*
	26	Caroline Chisholm	*renewer of society*
April	4	Martin Luther King Jnr	*martyr*
	9	Dietrich Bonhoeffer	*christian thinker*
	18	Kentigern	*christian pioneer*
	22	Toyohiko Kagawa	*renewer of society*

	24	Oscar Romero	*martyr*
	29	Catherine of Siena	*faithful servant*
May	2	Athanasius	*christian thinker*
	3	Philip and James	*apostles*
	4	Monica, mother of Augustine of Hippo	*faithful servant*
	5	John Flynn	*christian pioneer*
	8	Julian of Norwich	*person of prayer*
	14	Matthias, Simon and Jude	*apostles*
	24	John and Charles Wesley	*reformers of the church*
	27	John Calvin	*reformer of the church*
June	3	Pope John XXIII	*reformer of the church*
	9	Columba of Iona	*christian pioneer*
	10	Albrecht Ritschl and Adolf von Harnack	*christian thinkers*
	11	Barnabas	*apostle*
	15	Evelyn Underhill	*person of prayer*
	24	John the Baptist	*witness to Jesus*
	29	Peter and Paul	*apostles*
July	3	Thomas	*apostle*
	5	Visser 't Hooft	*reformer of the church*
	6	Jan Hus and Peter Waldo	*reformers of the church*
	11	Benedict of Nursia	*person of prayer*
	12	Desiderius Erasmus	*reformer of the church*
	17	D. T. Niles	*faithful servant*
	18	Macrina of Nyssa	*person of prayer*
	21	Mary Magdalene	*witness to Jesus*
	25	James the Great	*apostle*
	29	Mary and Martha of Bethany	*witnesses to Jesus*
	30	William Wilberforce	*renewer of society*
	31	Ignatius Loyola	*person of prayer*

August	13	Florence Nightingale
		and Edith Cavell	*renewers of society*
	15	Mary, mother of Jesus	*witness to Jesus*
	18	Helena, mother of
		Constantine	*faithful servant*
	20	Bernard of Clairvaux	*person of prayer*
	24	Bartholomew	*apostle*
	28	Augustine of Hippo	*christian thinker*
	31	John Bunyan	*faithful servant*
September	1	George Brown and John
		Thomas	*christian pioneers*
	4	Albert Schweitzer	*christian pioneer*
	5	Robert Browne	*reformer of the church*
	17	Hildegaard of Bingen	*person of prayer*
	18	Dag Hammarsjkold	*faithful servant*
	20	John.Hunt and Pacific Martyrs	*martyrs*
	21	Lazarus Lamilami	*faithful servant*
October	4	Clare and Francis of Assisi	*faithful servants*
	6	William Tyndale	*reformer of the church*
	11	Ulrich Zwingli	*reformer of the church*
	12	Elizabeth Fry	*renewer of society*
	15	Teresa of Avila
		and John of the Cross	*people of prayer*
	18	Matthew, Mark, Luke
		and John	*witnesses to Jesus*
	23	James, brother of Jesus	*apostle*
	31	Reformation Day	*reformers of the church*

November	1	All Saints	*faithful servants*
	4	Soren Kierkegaard	*christian thinker*
	16	Margaret of Scotland	*faithful servant*
	17	Hilda of Whitby	*faithful servant*
	20	John Williams and	
		Thomas Baker	*christian pioneers*
	24	John Knox	*reformer of the church*
	25	Isaac Watts, G. F. Handel	
		and J. S. Bach	*faithful servants*
	29	Dorothy Day	*faithful servant*
	30	Andrew	*apostle*
December	1	Charles de Foucauld	*person of prayer*
	8	Richard Baxter	*faithful servant*
	9	Karl Barth	*christian thinker*
	10	Thomas Merton	*person of prayer*
	14	John Geddie and John Paton	*christian pioneers*
	26	Stephen	*martyr*
	28	The Innocents	*martyrs*
	31	Josephine Butler	*renewer of society*

Readings and Collects for Other Commemorations

APOSTLES

Isaiah 62:1-7	I will not keep silent	Psalm 48
Joshua 1:1-9	The Lord your God is with you	Psalm 44:1-8
Isaiah 49:1-6	The Lord called me from the womb	Psalm 139
Ezekiel 3:16-21	You are a watchman for Israel	Psalm 18:19-27
Isaiah 49:7-13	The Holy One of Israel has chosen you	Psalm 122
Isaiah 6:1-8	Here am I, send me	Psalm 46

Acts 1:1-8	You will be my witnesses
Romans 10:11-17	Faith comes from what is heard
1 Corinthians 12:14-28	God has appointed apostles in the church
Philippians 1:1-11	I thank God for you
1 Thessalonians 2:2b-8	We have courage to declare the gospel
1 Timothy 4:6-8, 17, 18	Be a good minister of Jesus Christ

Luke 24:44-53	You are witnesses of these things
Mark 3:13-19	The call of the disciples
Luke 5:1-11	You will be fishers of men
John 17:11, 17-23	Father, keep them in thy name
Luke 10:1-20	The mission of the seventy
Mark 8:27-38	Those who lose their life will save it

The following readings may be used as alternatives to the above:

John 1:35-42	Andrew	Acts 11:19-26	Barnabas
John 1:45-51	Bartholomew	Acts 11:27 to 12:3	James the Great
John 14:6-14	Philip	Acts 21:15-25	James, brother of Jesus
John 20:24-29	Thomas	2 Corinthians 7:5-7, 13-16	Titus
John 21:15-19	Peter	Galatians 2:1-10	Paul
Acts 1:15-26	Matthias	2 Timothy 1:1-8	Timothy

Almighty God,
you have built your church
on the foundation of the apostles and prophets,
Jesus Christ himself being the chief cornerstone.
Grant us so to embrace and hold fast the faith
which has been handed on through the ages,
that we too may grow into a holy temple in the Lord;
who lives and reigns with you and the Holy Spirit,
one God, for ever and ever.

Holy and mighty God,
we thank you for the glorious company of the apostles
as we remember today your servant N.
Grant that your church,
inspired by the teaching and example of all the apostles,
and made one by the Holy Spirit,
may always stand firm upon the one foundation,
Jesus Christ our Lord;
who lives and reigns with you and the Holy Spirit,
one God, now and for ever.

CHRISTIAN PIONEERS

Isaiah 62:1-7	The nations shall see your vindication	Psalm 67
Isaiah 49:1-12	These shall come from afar	Psalm 111
Isaiah 52:7-10	How beautiful upon the mountains	Psalm 119:105-112
1 John 4:1-6	Tests the spirits	
Galatians 1:11-24	The gospel I preached is from Christ	
1 John 1:1 to 2:2	God is light	
Matthew 28:16-20	Make disciples of all nations	
Mark 12:41-44	She contributed out of her poverty	
John 1:35-51	The call of the disciples	

Everlasting God,
whose servant N carried the good news of your Son
to a distant place on earth:
grant that we who commemorate his/her service
may know the hope of the gospel in our hearts
and manifest its light in all our ways;
through Jesus Christ our Lord.

God of grace and might,
we praise you for your servant N,
to whom you gave gifts to make the good news known.
Raise up, we pray, in every country
heralds and evangelists of your kingdom,
so that the world may know the unsearchable riches
of our Saviour, Jesus Christ our Lord.

A local pioneer/founder

Jeremiah 31:10-14	Hear the word of the Lord	Psalm 84
Ezekiel 34:11-16	I will shepherd my sheep	Psalm 23
Exodus 3:1-15	The call of Moses	Psalm 113

Revelation 22:1, 2, 14-21	For the healing of the nations
Ephesians 4:1-13	Lead a life worthy of your calling
Romans 12:1-21	Present your bodies as a living sacrifice
Matthew 9:35 to 10:4	The Lord of the harvest
Luke 10:38-42	Mary and Martha
Luke 21:10-19	By your endurance you shall gain life

God of grace,
we thank you for the life and witness of N
through whom you began the work of the gospel
in this congregation and community.
Raise up, we pray, in every generation
heralds and teachers of your truth,
that all may hear the good news of salvation
which is freely offered through Christ our Lord,
who lives and reigns with you and the Holy Spirit,
one God, through the ages of ages.

Everliving God,
you are constantly raising up in your church
faithful leaders of your people.
Today we recall the work and witness of your servant N
in this congregation.
May his/her example be a source of joy to our spirit
and an inspiration to our faith.
Encouraged by the example of all your faithful people
who have gone before us,
may we continue to grow into the full stature
of our Lord and Saviour Jesus Christ,
who lives and reigns with you and the Holy Spirit,
one God, for ever and ever.

CHRISTIAN THINKERS

Proverbs 3:11-20	Happy are they who find wisdom	Psalm 119:97-104
Jeremiah 1:4-9	I have put my words in your mouth	Psalm 96
Ezekiel 3:16-21	You are a watchman over Israel	Psalm 19:1-10
1 Corinthians 1:1-9	Enriched in Christ with all knowledge	
1 Corinthians 2:1-13	I know nothing except Christ crucified	
Hebrews 12:22-29	You have come to the heavenly Jerusalem	
Matthew 11:25-30	I thank you for revealing these things to babes	
John 14:1-7	I am the way, the truth and the life	
Luke 9:57-62	Readiness for the kingdom of God	

Almighty God,
who through the teaching of your servant N
enlightened and enabled all your church
to understand the truth of Jesus Christ:
raise up among us teachers of your word,
that, set free by truth from unbelief,
we may come to know our great salvation;
through Jesus Christ our Lord,
who lives and reigns with you and the Holy Spirit,
one God, now and for ever.

O God of truth,
your Holy Spirit gives to one the word of wisdom,
to another the word of knowledge,
and to another the word of faith.
We praise you for the gifts of grace
imparted to your servant N;
and we pray that by his/her teaching
your church may be led to a fuller knowledge
of the truth we have seen in your Son,
Jesus Christ our Lord.

FAITHFUL SERVANTS

Daniel 7:9-17	The saints shall receive the kingdom	Psalm 149
Exodus 3:1-6, 9-12	I AM has sent me to you	Psalm 27
1 Kings 19:16, 19-21	Elisha shall be appointed prophet	Psalm 38
1 Samuel 3:1-10	Speak, for your servant hears	Psalm 43
Isaiah 58:6-11	The Lord shall hear your cry	Psalm 1
Micah 6:6-8	What the Lord requires	Psalm 9:1-10

1 John 3:1-3	See what love the Father has
Colossians 1:9-14	Lead a life worthy of God
Ephesians 1:11-23	You are sealed by the Spirit
1 Corinthians 1: 26-31	God is the source of your life in Christ
Acts 9:36-42	Tabitha saw Peter and sat up
Hebrews 12:18-24	You have come to the heavenly Jerusalem

Matthew 5:1-12	Blessed are the poor in spirit
John 11:32-44	Mary fell at Jesus' feet
John 15:1-8	I am the true vine
Mark 10:17-27	All things are possible with God
Matthew 10:16-33	Sheep in the midst of wolves
Matthew 5:13-16	You are the salt of the earth

The following may be used as an alternative first reading on 1 November and during the Easter season:

Revelation 7:9-17	A great multitude stood before the throne	Psalm 34:1-10
Revelation 21:1-6a	I am the beginning and the end	Psalm 24:1-6

Almighty God,
who gave to your servant N boldness
to confess the name of our Saviour Jesus Christ
before the rulers of this world:
grant us, who remember him/her with thanksgiving,
to be faithful to you in our witness day by day,
and at last to receive with him/her the crown of life;
through Jesus Christ our Lord,
who lives and reigns with you and the Holy Spirit,
one God, for ever and ever.

Faithful God,
whose will it is to be glorified in your saints,
and who raised up your servant N
to be a light in the world:
shine, we pray, in our hearts,
that we also in our generation may remain faithful to you,
and proclaim your praise with our lips and in our lives;
for you have called us out of darkness
into your marvellous light through your Son,
Jesus Christ our Lord.

MARTYRS

Jeremiah 20:7-10	God's word has become a reproach	Psalm 18:1-6, 16-19
Jeremiah 15:15-20	Lord, remember me and visit me	Psalm 124
Jeremiah 31:15-20	A voice of weeping is heard in Ramah	Psalm 31:1-8

Revelation 7:13-17	They have washed their robes
1 Peter 4:12-19	Do not be surprised at the fiery ordeal
2 Corinthians 4:7-15	We have this treasure in earthen vessels

Luke 12:2-12	Do not fear those who kill the body
Mark 8:34-38	Those who lose their life will save it
John 15:18-21	They will persecute you

The following readings may be used as alternatives to the above:

Matthew 2:13-18	The Innocents
Mark 6:17-29	John the Baptist
Acts 6:8-10; 7:54-60	Stephen

Almighty God,
who gave your servant N courage to confess Jesus Christ
and to die for this faith:
may we always be ready
to give a reason for the hope that is in us,
and to suffer gladly for his sake;
through Jesus Christ our Lord,
who lives and reigns with you and the Holy Spirit,
one God, now and for ever.

Gracious Lord,
in every age you have sent men and women
who have given their lives for the message of your love.
Inspire us with the memory of those martyrs for the gospel,
like your servant N,
whose faithfulness led them in the way of the cross,
and give us courage to bear true witness with our lives
to your Son's victory over sin and death;
through Jesus Christ our Lord.

PEOPLE OF PRAYER

Isaiah 61:10 to 62:5	I will greatly rejoice in the Lord	Psalm 80:1-7
1 Kings 19:9-12	The still small voice	Psalm 131
Isaiah 66:10-14	Your heart shall rejoice	Psalm 16:1-8

2 Corinthians 6:1-10	Now is the day of salvation
Romans 8:22-27	The Spirit helps us in our weakness
Hebrews 4:14-16; 7:23-28	We have a great high priest

Mark 1:32-39	Jesus went out to a lonely place and prayed
Matthew 6:25-33	Seek first the kingdom of God
Luke 11:1-10	Lord, teach us to pray

Almighty God,
you have brought forth in your church
the love and devotion of many people.
We give thanks for your servant N
whom we commemorate today.
Inspire us by his/her example,
and keep us faithful in prayer,
that we in our generation may rejoice with him/her
in the vision of your glory;
through Jesus Christ our Lord.

Holy God,
by whose grace N, kindled with the fire of your love,
became a burning and shining light in the church:
inflame us with the same spirit of discipline and devotion,
that we may know our union with you through prayer,
and always walk as children of the light;
through Jesus Christ our Lord,
who lives and reigns with you and the Holy Spirit
in glory for ever.

REFORMERS OF THE CHURCH

Exodus 33:12-17	My presence will go with you	Psalm 46
Isaiah 51:1-11	Listen to me, my people	Psalm 115
Amos 4:4-13	And yet you did not return to me	Psalm 130

1 Peter 2:1-10	Come to Christ, the living stone
Romans 3:21-26	The righteousness of God has been manifested
Romans 5:1-11	We are justified by grace through faith

Matthew 23:1-8, 11, 12	Those who humble themselves will be exalted
John 8:31-38	The truth will set you free
John 2:13-22	The cleansing of the temple

Almighty God,
you raised up your servant N
to proclaim anew the gift of salvation
and the life of holiness.
Pour out the Holy Spirit in our day,
and revive your work among us;
that, inspired by the one true faith,
and upheld by grace in word and sacrament,
we and all your people may be made one
in the unity of your church on earth,
even as in heaven we are made one in you;
through Jesus Christ our Lord.

Renewing God,
we praise you for the men and women you have sent
to recall the church to its mission
and to reform its life, such as your servant N.
Raise up in our own day
teachers and prophets inspired by the Holy Spirit,
whose voice will give strength to your church
and proclaim the reality of your kingdom;
through your Son, Jesus Christ our Lord.

RENEWERS OF SOCIETY

Isaiah 5:11-24	Woe to those who call evil good	Psalm 22:22-31
Zechariah 8:3-12, 16, 17	These are the good things that you shall do	Psalm 72:1-4, 12-14
Amos 5:10-15	Seek good and not evil	Psalm 146
Romans 12:9-21	Let love be genuine	
Acts 3:1-10	I give you what I have	
James 2:1-5	Show no partiality	
Matthew 25:31-46	The judgment of the nations	
Mark 12:13-17	Render to Caesar the things that are Caesar's	
Luke 6:27-36	Love your enemies	

Loving God,
your Son came among us to serve and not to be served,
and to give his life for the world.
Lead us by his love to serve all those
to whom the world offers no comfort and little help.
Through us give hope to the hopeless,
love to the unloved,
peace to the troubled,
and rest to the weary;
through your Son, Jesus Christ our Lord.

Holy and righteous God,
you created us in your image.
Grant us grace to contend fearlessly against evil
and to make no peace with oppression.
Help us, like your servant N, to use our freedom
to bring justice among people and nations,
to the glory of your name;
through your Son, Jesus Christ our Lord.

WITNESSES TO JESUS

Malachi 3:1-4	I send my messenger before me	Psalm 139:1-3, 13-17
Malachi 4:1-6	The day of the Lord is coming	Psalm 141
Isaiah 40:1-11	Comfort, comfort my people	Psalm 85:7-13

Acts 13:22-26	The message of salvation
Acts 19:1-9	Baptism in the name of the Lord Jesus
Revelation 7:13-17	The Lamb will be their shepherd

Luke 1:57-66, 80	Elizabeth gave birth to a son
Luke 3:7-19	He will baptise you with the Holy Spirit
Matthew 6:17-29	Do not be anxious about your life

The following readings may be used as alternatives to the above:

Matthew 2:13-23	Joseph of Nazareth	John 1:19-28	John the Baptist
Luke 1:46-55	Mary, mother of Jesus	John 19:38-42	Joseph of Arimathea
Luke 2:22-38	Simeon and Anna	John 20:1, 2, 11-18	Mary Magdalene
Luke 10:38-42	Mary and Martha	John 20:30, 31	Matthew, Mark, Luke and John

Faithful God,
you gave to your servant N
grace and strength to bear witness to the truth.
Grant that we, mindful of his/her victory of faith,
may glorify in life and death the name of Jesus Christ,
who lives and reigns with you and the Holy Spirit,
one God, for ever and ever.

Lord God,
you have surrounded us with a great cloud of witnesses.
Grant that we, encouraged by the example of your servant N,
and looking to Jesus,
the author and finisher of our faith,
may persevere in the course that is set before us.

May we be living signs of the gospel,
and at last, with all your saints,
share in your eternal joy;
through your Son, Jesus Christ our Lord.

Readings for Other Occasions and Themes

FIRST READING	PSALM	SECOND READING	GOSPEL

New Year's Day 1 January

Deuteronomy 8:1-10	90:1-12	Revelation 21:1-6a	Matthew 25:31-46
Ecclesiastes 3:1-13	8	Colossians 2:1-7	Matthew 9:14-17
Isaiah 49:1-10	90:1-12	Ephesians 3:1-10	Luke 14:16-24

Australia Day 26 January

Deuteronomy 1:5-11	33:12-22	1 Thessalonians 5:12-24	Matthew 5:1-12
Jeremiah 29:4-14	20	Romans 13:1-8	Mark 12:13-17
Deuteronomy 28:1-9	145:1-7	Hebrews 11:8-16	John 8:31-36

Victims of injustice 21 March

Isaiah 42:1-7	130	1 Timothy 6:6-16	Luke 3:7-14
Amos 5:10-15	126	Acts 11:1-12a	Luke 4:16-21
Deuteronomy 24:9-18	34:11-18	Revelation 21:1-5a	Matthew 20:20-28

Anzac Day 25 April

2 Samuel 22:2-20	118:1-9	Ephesians 6:10-20	Matthew 5:38-48
Isaiah 42:10-17	76	Romans 8:31-35, 37-39	John 15:9-17
Proverbs 3:13-27	46	1 Peter 3:13-18	John 10:1-21

Inauguration of the Uniting Church in Australia 22 June

Ezekiel 37:15-28	122	Hebrews 13:1-8	John 17:20-26
2 Chronicles 30:1-9	127	Ephesians 2:19-22	John 17:1-11
Deuteronomy 30:1-10	100	1 Corinthians 3:10-17	John 15:1-8

Victims of the nuclear age 6 August

Exodus 34:29-35	40:1-9	2 Peter 1:13-21	Matthew 17:1-9
Isaiah 9:1-7	78:1-7	Romans 8:18-27	Mark 9:2-10
Ezekiel 34:25-31	89:1-11	2 Corinthians 6:2-10	Luke 9:28-36

Victims of the holocaust 9 November

Esther 3:7 to 4:3	74:1-8, 17, 18	Hebrews 4:1-13	Matthew 2:13-18

Remembrance day of peace 11 November

Micah 4:1-4	133	Colossians 3:12-17	Matthew 5:1-9
Isaiah 52:7-12	72:1-7	James 4:1-10	John 20:19-28
Leviticus 26:6, 9-12	29	Colossians 1:15-20	Matthew 4:1-11

FIRST READING	PSALM	SECOND READING	GOSPEL
Mission of the church			
Isaiah 22:1-5	67	Acts 11:19-26	Matthew 28:16-20
Isaiah 55:1-5	98	Acts 26:19-23	Luke 24:44-53
Isaiah 49:1-9a	96:1-9	Romans 10:9-18	Luke 10:1-9
Unity of the church			
Jeremiah 33:6-9a	122	Ephesians 4:1-6	Matthew 18:19-22
Isaiah 35:1-10	133	1 Corinthians 3:1-11	John 17:15-23
Ezekiel 37:15-22, 26-28	118:21-29	1 Corinthians 1:10-13	John 10:11-16
The Holy Spirit			
Joel 2:23a, 26-29	22:22-31	Acts 2:1-4	John 14:23-26
Ezekiel 36:24-28	96:1-9	Acts 1:3-8	Mark 1:4-11
Isaiah 61:1-4	139:1-10	Romans 8:12-17	Luke 11:9-13
Holy Scripture			
2 Kings 22:3-13	119:105-112	2 Timothy 2:8-15	John 5:36-47
2 Kings 23:1-3	20	Romans 10:1-11	Mark 12:18-27
Exodus 34:27-35	19	2 Timothy 3:14 to 4:5	Luke 24:30-48
Christian initiation			
Exodus 14:15-25	51:1, 2, 10-19	Romans 6:3-11	Matthew 28:16-20
Genesis 6:11-22	139:1-14	2 Corinthians 5:14-19	John 3:3-8
Jeremiah 31:31-34	139:13-24	Romans 5:1-5	Mark 1:9-11
The Eucharist			
Isaiah 25:6-9	34:1-10	1 Corinthians 11:23-26	Matthew 15:32-39
1 Kings 19:4-8	147:12-20	Acts 10:34a, 37-43	Luke 22:14-22a
Exodus 16:2-4, 12-15	116:12-18	Acts 2:42-47	Luke 19:1-10
Dedication or anniversary of a church			
Isaiah 56:1, 6, 7	23	1 Corinthians 3:9-17	Matthew 21:12-17
2 Chronicles 7:11-16	84	1 Peter 2:1-9	John 10:22-30
1 Kings 8:22-30	122	Hebrews 10:19-25	John 4:19-24
Meeting of a church council			
Micah 6:6-8	19:7-14	Philippians 2:1-11	John 15:1-11
Proverbs 24:3-6	19:1-6	2 Corinthians 4:1-10	John 16:7-15
Numbers 9:15-23	97	Acts 15:22-29	Luke 14:27-33

FIRST READING	PSALM	SECOND READING	GOSPEL

Repentance and reconciliation

Ezekiel 11:14-20	27	Romans 5:6-11	Luke 6:31-38
Isaiah 53:1-6	51	Colossians 3:8-10, 12-17	John 20:19-23
Nehemiah 1:4-11a	6	1 John 1:5 to 2:2	Luke 15:11-32

Christian education

Deuteronomy 6:4-9, 20-25	78:1-7	Acts 17:16-31	Matthew 11:25-30
Jonah 28:12-28	19:7-14	1 Timothy 4:10-16	Mark 10:13-19
Proverbs 3:13-17	27	2 Timothy 3:14 to 4:5	Luke 2:41-52

Family life

Deuteronomy 6:1-9	127	Colossians 3:12-24	Matthew 8:5-17
Proverbs 31:10-31	128	1 Peter 3:1-9	Mark 10:2-16
Isaiah 54:1-8	67	Ephesians 5:25 to 6:4	Mark 3:31-35

Marriage

Song of Solomon 1:2-4, 10-17	67	1 John 4:7-12	John 2:1-11
Song of Solomon 2:10-17	128	Romans 12:1, 2, 9-13	Matthew 7:21, 24-27
Song of Solomon 5:10-16	113	Ephesians 3:14-21	Mark 10:6-9

Death

Joshua 23:1-8	130	1 Corinthians 15:12-29	Matthew 27:45-54
Isaiah 25:6-9	146	1 Corinthians 15:35-49	Mark 15:33-39
Job 19:1, 23-27	121	1 Corinthians 15:51-57	Luke 23:39-46

Any need or trouble

Lamentations 3:17-26	85	Romans 8:18-30	Matthew 7:7-11
Genesis 9:8-17	86:1-7	Revelation 21:1-7	Mark 4:35-41
Job 1:13-21	49:1-9, 16-20	James 1:2-4, 12	Luke 18:1-8

Justice and peace

Deuteronomy 4:9-14	85	2 Corinthians 8:1-15	Matthew 25:31-46
Jeremiah 6:9-15	23	Ephesians 2:13-18	Luke 19:1-10
Amos 5:18-24	146	James 2:1-4, 8, 14-17	Matthew 10:34-42

FIRST READING	PSALM	SECOND READING	GOSPEL
Stewardship			
Micah 6:6-8	112	Romans 12:1, 2	Matthew 6:19-24
1 Chronicles 29:1-13	147:1-11	2 Corinthians 8:1-9	Mark 10:17-27
Deuteronomy 12:5-11	96	2 Corinthians 9:6-15	Luke 12:1-4
Harvest thanksgiving			
Deuteronomy 8:1-10	65	2 Corinthians 9:6-15	Matthew 13:1-9
Genesis 8:15-22	104:10-16, 24-27	Acts 14:13-17	John 6:26-35
Deuteronomy 8:11-20	67	1 Corinthians 3:6-10	Luke 13:6-9
Natural resources and the integrity of creation			
Genesis 1:11-12	24	2 Corinthians 9:6-11	Luke 12:13-21
Isaiah 55:6-13	126	2 Corinthians 8:1-5, 9-15	Mark 6:34-44
Joel 2:21-24, 26, 27	104:24-34	Romans 8:18-25	Luke 14:12-14
Daily work			
Genesis 1:26 to 2:3	90:2-4, 12-14, 16	Colossians 3:14-17	Matthew 25: 14-30
Genesis 2:4b-9, 15	127	2 Thessalonians 3:6-12	Mark 6:31-34
Genesis 29:15-20	107:1-9	1 Corinthians 3:10-14	Matthew 6:19-24
Industrial relations			
Amos 5:11-15	107:1-9	Colossians 3:22-25	John 6:5-14, 26, 27
Agricultural work			
Genesis 1:11-12	104:1-4, 14, 15	1 Corinthians 9:8-11	John 15:1-11
Sowing of a crop			
Joel 2:21-27	90:2-4, 14-17	1 Timothy 6:6-11, 17-19	Mark 4:26-29
First fruits of a crop			
Deuteronomy 26:1-11	Habakkuk 3: 3-11, 17, 18	James 1:16-18	Luke 10:1-9

Principal Liturgical Dates
to 2013 A.D.

unless other provision is made by an international and ecumenical council of the church

YEAR	ASH WEDNESDAY	EASTER DAY	PENTECOST	ADVENT SUNDAY
1989	8 February	26 March	14 May	3 December
1990	28 February	15 April	3 June	2 December
1991	13 February	31 March	19 May	1 December
1992	4 March	19 April	7 June	29 November
1993	24 February	11 April	30 May	28 November
1994	16 February	3 April	22 May	27 November
1995	1 March	16 April	4 May	3 December
1996	21 February	7 April	26 May	1 December
1997	12 February	30 March	18 May	30 November
1998	25 February	12 April	31 May	29 November
1999	17 February	4 April	23 May	28 November
2000	8 March	23 April	11 June	3 December
2001	28 February	15 April	3 June	2 December
2002	13 February	31 March	19 May	1 December
2003	5 March	20 April	8 June	30 November
2004	25 February	11 April	30 May	28 November
2005	9 February	27 March	15 May	27 November
2006	1 March	16 April	4 June	3 December
2007	21 February	8 April	27 May	2 December
2008	6 February	23 March	11 May	30 November
2009	25 February	12 April	31 May	29 November
2010	17 February	4 April	23 May	28 November
2011	9 March	24 April	12 June	27 November
2012	22 February	8 April	27 May	2 December
2013	13 February	31 March	19 May	1 December

Pastoral Services

The Marriage Service

NOTES

The christian celebration of marriage is an act of worship, an expression of the church's offering of the whole of life to God. It is a pastoral occasion in which the community of faith shares in the joy of bridegroom and bride. It is also an evangelical occasion in which all those who have come to witness the marriage may be challenged by the implications of the christian faith.

Normally a marriage is to be celebrated in a church. In exceptional circumstances, at the discretion of the minister, a marriage may be celebrated in a place other than a church building. Care should be taken that the suggested venue will not detract from the solemnity of the occasion. The minister also should make it clear to the couple that a non-ecclesiastical setting does not mean that the christian character of The Marriage Service is to be weakened or changed.

i There are at least three ways in which the bridegroom and bride and their attendants may be assembled prior to the beginning of the service.

   (a) The minister meets the bridegroom and his attendants in the vestry; they enter the church at the appointed time, and the minister asks them to sit at the front of the church until the bride, her escort and her attendants are ready to enter. The minister then either moves to the door of the church to await the arrival of the bride, or waits for the bride elsewhere in the church.

   (b) The minister meets the bridegroom and his attendants in the vestry; they enter the church at the appointed time and move to the door of the church to await the arrival of the bride. The bridegroom and bride enter the church together, accompanied by their attendants. (This procedure may be preferred where, for example, the bride does not wish to be 'presented' by a representative of her family, or the bridegroom or bride have been previously married.) The minister then accompanies the bridegroom and bride down the aisle or waits for them in the sanctuary area.

   (c) The bride and bridegroom arrive together at the main door and proceed down the aisle together.

ii   If entering with the wedding party, the minister and any other ministers participating in the service should lead the procession. The couple should decide in what order other people are to be placed in the procession. There are at least two ways for this:

        (a) The minister(s), any junior attendants, the bride (with her escort or with the bridegroom), the adult attendants.

        (b) The minister(s), any junior attendants, the adult attendants, the bride (with her escort or with the bridegroom).

iii   Consideration should be given to the entire bridal party being seated for the reading of Scripture and the sermon. The bridal party may sit in the front pew(s) of the church. Alternatively, if there is sufficient space in the chancel, two chairs may be placed appropriately for the use of the bride and bridegroom, and the attendants sit in the front pew(s). The practice of seating the bridal party creates a more relaxed atmosphere and often provides the minister with improved visual contact with the whole congregation.

iv   The participation in leadership of the service by lay people, particularly family members, attendants or close friends, is to be encouraged. The reading of Scripture and the Prayers lend themselves to this purpose.

v   If both the bridegroom and bride are regular communicants, they may desire the inclusion of holy communion in their wedding service. Because holy communion is the celebration of the community of faith, it should be open to all people present who would normally communicate.

vi   This order provides many opportunities for the congregation to participate in the worship. To ensure such full participation, permission is given to couples to reproduce the Affirmation by the People (10), the Acclamations (14), The Peace (16), one of the forms of The Lord's Prayer (18) and appropriate parts of the service of holy communion (19), if needed, in their own personalised order of service.

vii   The Signing of the Marriage Certificates may be done in the presence of the congregation or in the vestry.

viii The couple should be encouraged to prepare for and plan their marriage in the spirit of simplicity. Expensive dressing, an over-abundance of flowers and an unnecessarily large bridal party can easily detract from the simple joy of a bridegroom and bride pledging their love and fidelity to each other, before God and in the presence of their families and close friends.

ix At the first interview with the minister, the couple should be given a copy of The Marriage Service and be asked to study it before discussion of the service at a subsequent interview. The various options in the Declaration of Intent (8), the Affirmation by the Families (9), the Vows (11), and the Prayers (17) should be pointed out. The couple should be invited to select appropriate Scripture readings and hymns. The question of whether they wish to learn, read or repeat their vows should be decided. As a general rule, a rehearsal of The Marriage Service, close to the day of the celebration, is helpful for the bridegroom and bride, as well as for their attendants and those sharing in the leadership of the service.

x Hymns, songs and music should be chosen to express praise and thanksgiving to God, and to celebrate God's love for us, our love for God, our love for one another, or the love of husband and wife. Appropriate hymns from *The Australian Hymn Book* include:

All creatures of our God and King	3
All people that on earth do dwell	10
Come down, O Love divine	310
Come, gracious Spirit, heavenly dove	311
Eternal Ruler of the ceaseless round	513
Father, hear the prayer we offer	510
For the beauty of the earth	77
From all who dwell below the skies	42
God be in my head	456
Happy the home that welcomes you, Lord Jesus	495
In heavenly love abiding	504
Jesus, united by thy grace	365
Lead us, heavenly Father, lead us	492
Lord of all hopefulness	546
Lord divine, all loves excelling	148
May the mind of Christ my Saviour	537

Now thank we all our God	14
O God, from whom mankind derives its name	566
O Holy Spirit, Lord of grace	312
O Jesus, King most wonderful	125
O perfect Love, all human thought transcending	526
Our God, be gracious unto us	117
Praise, my soul, the king of heaven	68
Praise to the Lord, the Almighty	28
The Lord's my shepherd, I'll not want	16

xi   In the Greeting (1), the full names of the bridegroom and bride should be used. At all other places in the service, only the christian name is used, indicated by N.

xii   The Declaration of Purpose (4) should not be altered by the minister in any way or for any reason. The fact that the bride or bridegroom may have been previously married, that they are beyond child-bearing age, or that they do not intend to have children is not sufficient reason for amendment. The Declaration of Purpose is a brief statement of the christian understanding of marriage, and is addressed not only to the bridegroom and bride but also to all who are present to witness their marriage.

xiii   The Affirmation by the Families (9) provides an opportunity for members of the families involved in the marriage to indicate publicly that they are pleased that the marriage is taking place. There are three alternatives provided, catering for different circumstances and needs. The traditional custom of 'giving away' the bride, reflecting as it does the Old Testament image of God creating Eve and presenting her to Adam as his wife, is unhelpful today; it keeps alive the view that a woman is the property of her father until in marriage she becomes the property of her husband. The minister should discuss with the couple the participation of their families in the service.

xiv   Ministers should exercise extreme caution in admitting to the order of service any alternative form of vow suggested by the couple. In the Vows (11), there are four options, one in traditional and three in contemporary idiom. It is questionable whether some vows used by couples in recent years have been either legally or theologically acceptable. For example, the use of the phrase 'As long as love shall last' falls short of the christian understanding of marriage.

xv Symbolic actions may also be included in the service. In the Proclamation of the Marriage (13), the minister may take one end of the stole or scarf he/she is wearing and bind it around the couple's joined hands, before saying: 'Before God and in the presence of us all . . .' This is symbolic of the couple's love for each other being surrounded and strengthened by the love of God. Alternatively, the couple's joined hands may be bound with the stole or scarf for the Blessing (15), provided the couple remain standing for this section. If the husband and wife kneel for the Blessing, the minister may lay hands upon their heads. This is symbolic of the blessing of God being upon them, as in confirmation.

xvi One or more passages of Scripture shall be read (5). The following are suggested readings which may be appropriate:

OLD TESTAMENT

Genesis 1:26-28	Male and female he created them
Genesis 2:4-9, 15-24	A man cleaves to his wife and they become one flesh
Ruth 1:16-17	Entreat me not to leave you
Psalm 67	May God be merciful to us and bless us
Psalm 100	Be joyful in the Lord, all you lands
Psalm 128	Happy are they all who fear the Lord
Song of Solomon 2:10-13, 8:6-7	Many waters cannot quench love

EPISTLE

1 Corinthians 13:1-13	Love is patient and kind
Ephesians 3:14-21	The Father, from whom every family is named
Colossians 3:12-17	Love which binds everything together
1 John 4:7-16	Let us love one another, for love is of God

GOSPEL

Matthew 5:1-10	The Beatitudes
Matthew 5:13-16	You are the light . . . let your light shine
Matthew 7:21-29	Hearing and doing
Matthew 22:35-40	This is the great and first commandment
John 2:1-11	The marriage at Cana in Galilee
John 15:1-8	Abide in me, and I in you
John 15:9-17	This I command you, to love one another.

xvii   Not infrequently, ministers are requested to include in the service readings from sources other than Scripture. This may be permitted, at the discretion of the minister, providing that at least one portion of Scripture, preferably a gospel reading, is also included.

xviii   The Sermon (6) gives the minister the opportunity to personalise The Marriage Service for the particular couple, and to witness to the church's understanding of marriage.

xix   Where both the bridegroom and bride are actively involved in the life of the church, but one belongs to another Uniting Church parish or another denomination of the Church catholic, the minister is encouraged to indicate to the couple his/her willingness to share the conduct of the service with another parish minister, priest or pastor. Unless there are exceptional circumstances, the minister in whose church the marriage is to be celebrated shall be the 'authorised celebrant', be responsible for the registration of the legal certificates and record the marriage as having been celebrated according to the rites of the Uniting Church in Australia. The authorised celebrant, at the very least, shall conduct sections 8-13 inclusive.

xx   Where one person is a christian and the other is an active member of a non-christian religion or an unbeliever, the minister should exercise pastoral sensitivity while being faithful to the church's christian understanding of God. The trinitarian formulae in the Proclamation of the Marriage (13), the Acclamations (14), the Blessing of the couple (15) and the Blessing of the congregation (21) should not be modified.

xxi   Where a couple has already been married, either in a civil ceremony or in another form of religious ceremony, they may request the minister to give them a blessing on their marriage. The form of The Marriage Service can be used for this purpose, except that some parts of the text may need slight amendment, according to the individual circumstances. However, sections 8 to 13 inclusive should be omitted on all such occasions. The minister should note the requirements of the *Marriage Act,* Section 113 (5) & (6).

The Marriage Service

The Gathering of the Community

The people stand as the wedding party enters the church.

If a member or friend of the bride's family escorts her into the church, that person brings her to where the bridegroom is standing and then takes a seat in the congregation.

The persons to be married stand together before the minister, the bridegroom standing at the right hand of the bride, in the presence of two appointed witnesses and the congregation.

1 GREETING

(See People's Book, p. 81.)

The minister says:

Grace to you and peace
from God our Father and the Lord Jesus Christ.

Romans 1:7

Amen.

or

The Lord be with you.
And also with you.

We have come together in the presence of God
to witness the marriage of
NNN
and NNN,
to surround them with our prayers,
and to share in their joy.

The minister may welcome the people.

2   SCRIPTURE SENTENCES

The minister calls the people to worship with one or more
Scripture sentence(s), such as:

Come, let us sing to the Lord;
let us come before his presence with thanksgiving.

Psalm 95:1-2

Give thanks to the Lord, for he is good;
his mercy endures for ever.

Psalm 118:1

This is the day which the Lord has made;
let us rejoice and be glad in it.

Psalm 118:24

God is love,
and those who live in love live in God,
and God lives in them.

1 John 4:16

3   HYMN

A hymn or song may be sung.

4   DECLARATION OF PURPOSE

The minister says:

Marriage is appointed by God.
The church believes that marriage
is a gift of God in creation
and a means of grace in which man and woman
become one in heart, mind and body.

Marriage is the sacred and life-long union
of a man and a woman
who give themselves to each other in love and trust.
It signifies the mystery of the union
between Christ and the church.

Marriage is given that husband and wife
may enrich and encourage each other
in every part of their life together.

Marriage is given that with delight and tenderness
they may know each other in love,
and through their physical union
may strengthen the union of their lives.

Marriage is given that children may be born
and brought up in security and love,
that home and family life may be strengthened,
and that society may stand upon firm foundations.

Marriage is a way of life which all people should honour;
it is not to be entered into lightly or selfishly,
but responsibly and in the love of God.

N and N are now to begin this way of life
which God has created and Christ has blessed.
Therefore, on this their wedding day, we pray for them,
asking that they may fulfil God's purpose
for the whole of their lives.

The bride and bridegroom and their attendants may sit.

The Service of the Word

5   SCRIPTURE READINGS

A prayer for illumination may be offered.

One or more passages of Scripture shall be read.

The following may be used after the final reading:

This is the word of the Lord.
Thanks be to God.

A Bible may be presented to the couple here or after the sermon.

The minister may say:

Take this Bible.
May the gospel of Christ inspire you
as you build your home and marriage.

6   SERMON

The Marriage

7   PRAYER

*The minister calls the people to prayer and uses one of the
following prayers or offers free prayer:*

Gracious God,
your generous love surrounds us,
and everything we enjoy comes from you.

In your great love
you have given us the gift of marriage.
Bless N and N as they pledge their lives to each other;
that their love may continue to grow
and be the true reflection of your love for us all;
through Jesus Christ our Lord.
Amen.

or

Father,
you have made the covenant of marriage a holy mystery,
a symbol of Christ's love for the church.
Hear our prayers for N and N.
With faith in you and in each other,
they pledge their love today.
May their lives always bear witness
to the reality of that love.
We ask this through your Son,
our Lord Jesus Christ.
Amen.

or

Living God,
you are always faithful in your love for us.
Look mercifully upon N and N
who have come seeking your blessing.
Let the Holy Spirit rest upon them,
so that with steadfast love
they may honour the promises they make this day;
through Jesus Christ our Saviour.
Amen.

8   DECLARATION OF INTENT

The bride and bridegroom stand.

The minister may ask them:

N and N,
do you believe that God has blessed and guided you,
and now calls you into marriage?

The bridegroom and bride each answer:

I do.

The minister shall ask the bridegroom:

N, will you give yourself to N to be her husband,
to live together in the covenant of marriage?
Will you love her, comfort her,
honour and protect her,
and, forsaking all others, be faithful to her,
as long as you both shall live?

He answers:

I will.

The minister shall ask the bride:

N, will you give yourself to N to be his wife,
to live together in the covenant of marriage?
Will you love him, comfort him,
honour and protect him,
and, forsaking all others, be faithful to him,
as long as you both shall live?

She answers:

I will.

9 AFFIRMATION BY THE FAMILIES

If one of the following questions is used, those answering are asked to stand and may be addressed by name.

Do you, the parents of N and N, give your blessing to their marriage?

The parents of the bride and bridegroom say:

We do.

or

Do you, on behalf of your family, give your blessing to this marriage?

A member of each family says:

I do.

or

Do you, on behalf of both families, give your blessing to this marriage?

A member of one family says:

I do.

10 AFFIRMATION BY THE PEOPLE

(See People's Book, p. 82.)

The minister may ask the people:

Will you, the families and friends of N and N, who have come to share this wedding day, uphold them in their marriage?

The people say:

We will.

Alternatively, the minister may say:

I call upon you, the families and friends of N and N,
who have come to share this wedding day,
to uphold them in their marriage.

11   THE VOWS

A

The bride and bridegroom face each other and join hands.

The bridegroom says:

**I, N, in the presence of God,
take you, N, to be my wife;
to have and to hold
from this day forward,
for better, for worse,
for richer, for poorer,
in sickness and in health,
to love and to cherish,
as long as we both shall live.
This is my solemn vow.**

The bride says:

**I, N, in the presence of God,
take you, N, to be my husband;
to have and to hold
from this day forward,
for better, for worse,
for richer, for poorer,
in sickness and in health,
to love and to cherish,
as long as we both shall live.
This is my solemn vow.**

They loose hands.

The bride and bridegroom face each other and join hands.

The bridegroom says:

**I, N, take you, N,
to be my wife,
according to God's holy will.
I will love you,
and share my life with you,
in sickness and in health,
in poverty and in prosperity,
in conflict and in harmony,
as long as we both shall live.
This is my solemn vow.**

The bride says:

**I, N, take you, N,
to be my husband,
according to God's holy will.
I will love you,
and share my life with you,
in sickness and in health,
in poverty and in prosperity,
in conflict and in harmony,
as long as we both shall live.
This is my solemn vow.**

They loose hands.

The bride and bridegroom face each other and join hands.

The bridegroom says:

I, N, in the presence of God,
take you, N, to be my wife.
All that I am I give to you,
and all that I have I share with you.
Whatever the future holds,
I will love you and stand by you,
as long as we both shall live.
This is my solemn vow.

The bride says:

I, N, in the presence of God,
take you, N, to be my husband.
All that I am I give to you,
and all that I have I share with you.
Whatever the future holds,
I will love you and stand by you,
as long as we both shall live.
This is my solemn vow.

They loose hands.

or **D**

The bridegroom turns and faces the people, and says:

I ask everyone here to witness
that I, N, take N to be my wife,
according to God's holy will.

He then faces the bride, takes her hands, and says:

N,
all that I am I give to you,
and all that I have I share with you.
Whatever the future holds,
I will love you and stand by you,
as long as we both shall live.
This is my solemn vow.

They loose hands.

The bride turns and faces the people, and says:

I ask everyone here to witness
that I, N, take N to be my husband,
according to God's holy will.

She then faces the bridegroom, takes his hands, and says:

N,
all that I am I give to you,
and all that I have I share with you.
Whatever the future holds,
I will love you and stand by you,
as long as we both shall live.
This is my solemn vow.

They loose hands.

12 GIVING OF THE RINGS

The minister receives the ring(s) and may say:

Let us pray:

God of steadfast love,
by your blessing,
let these rings (this ring) be to N and N
a symbol of the vows
which they have made this day;
through Jesus Christ our Lord.
Amen.

As the giver places the ring on the ring-finger of the other's left
hand, the following words may be said:

**N, I give you this ring
as a sign of our marriage
and of the vows which we have made today.**

If only one ring is given, the following words may be said by the
receiver:

**N, I receive this ring
as a sign of our marriage
and of the vows which we have made today.**

13 PROCLAMATION OF THE MARRIAGE

The couple join hands.

The minister asks the people to stand, and addresses them:

Hear the words of our Lord Jesus Christ:
From the beginning of creation,
God made them male and female.

For this reason a man shall leave his father and mother
and be joined to his wife,
and the two shall become one.
So they are no longer two but one.
Let no one separate those whom God has joined together.

Mark 10:6-9

Before God and in the presence of us all,
N and N have made their solemn vows.
They have confirmed their marriage
by the joining of hands
and by the giving and receiving of rings (a ring).
In the name of the Father,
and of the Son, and of the Holy Spirit,
I therefore proclaim
that they are now husband and wife.

The Blessing of the Marriage

14   ACCLAMATIONS

(See People's Book, p. 83.)

The following may be said by the minister only, or used
responsively with the people.

Blessed are you, heavenly Father:
You give joy to bridegroom and bride.

Blessed are you, Lord Jesus Christ:
You have brought new life to the world.

Blessed are you, Holy Spirit of God:
You bring us together in love.

Blessed be Father, Son and Holy Spirit:
One God to be praised for ever. Amen.

15 BLESSING

The couple may kneel or stand as the minister says one of the following blessings:

God the Father make you holy in his love;
God the Son enrich you with his grace;
God the Holy Spirit strengthen you with joy.
The Lord bless you and keep you in eternal life.
Amen.

or

The riches of God's grace be upon you,
that you may live together in faith and love
and receive the blessings of eternal life.
May almighty God,
who creates you, redeems you and guides you,
bless you now and always.
Amen.

The couple stand.

16 THE PEACE

The minister gives the greeting of peace to the couple and to all the people:

The peace of the Lord be always with you.
And also with you.

The minister may give a sign of peace to the husband and the wife.

The minister may say to the couple:

In peace, greet each other with a kiss.

The couple may move to where their parents are standing and greet them.

The people sit.

17 PRAYERS

The couple may kneel.

The minister or lay person(s) may offer free prayer or may use resources from sections A, B, or C.

A

Some or all of the following petitions may be used.

Each petition or a grouping of petitions may conclude with:

Lord, hear us.
Lord, hear our prayer.

In peace, let us pray to the Lord:

All grace comes from you, O God,
and you alone are the source of eternal life.
Bless your servants N and N,
that they may faithfully live together
to the end of their lives.

May they be patient and gentle,
ready to trust each other,
and to face together the challenge of the future.

May they pray together in joy and in sorrow,
and always give thanks for the gift of each other.

Be with them in all their happiness;
that your joy may be in them,
and their joy may be full.

Strengthen them in every time of trouble,
that they may bear each other's burdens,
and so fulfil the law of Christ.

Give N and N grace, when they hurt each other,
to recognise and acknowledge their fault,
to ask each other's forgiveness,
and to know your mercy and love.

May your peace dwell in their home,
and be a sign of hope for peace in the world.

Let their home be a place of welcome,
that its happiness may be freely shared.

Through loving one another in Christ,
may they be strengthened to love Christ in their neighbour.

May they be creative in their daily work,
and find fulfilment in the life of their community.

The following petition may be included:

May N and N enjoy the gift and heritage of children.
Grant that they may be loving and wise parents,
with grace to bring up their children
to know you, to love you and to serve you.

The following petition may be included if there are
children/grandchildren of a previous marriage:

May N and N enjoy the gift and heritage of their children.
Grant them the grace to share their love (and faith)
with N and N (*names of children*)
that they may grow together as a loving family.

Bless the parents and families of N and N,
that they may be united in love and friendship.

Grant that all married people
who have witnessed these vows today
may find their lives strengthened
and their loyalties confirmed.

We ask these prayers in the name of Christ our Lord.
Amen.

or B

A selection of the following prayers may be used.

Let us pray for N and N in their life together:

Most gracious God,
we bless you for your tender love
in sending Jesus Christ to come among us,
born of a human mother.
We give you thanks that he grew up
in a home in Nazareth,
and joined in the celebration of a marriage
in Cana of Galilee.
By the power of the Holy Spirit,
give your blessing to N and N.
Let their love for each other
be a seal upon their hearts,
a mantle about their shoulders,
and a crown upon their heads.
Bless them in their work and in their companionship,
in their joys and in their sorrows.
And finally in your mercy
bring them to your heavenly home;
through Jesus Christ our Lord.
Amen.

or

Faithful Lord, source of all love,
pour down your grace upon N and N,
that they may fulfil the vows they have made today,
and reflect your steadfast love
in their life-long faithfulness to each other.
Help us to support them in their life together.
Give them courage and patience,
affection and understanding,
and love toward you,
toward each other,
and toward the world;
that they may continue to grow
in Jesus Christ our Lord.
Amen.

or

Creator God, giver of life,
bless N and N whom you have now joined in marriage.
Grant them wisdom and devotion in their life together,
that each may be for the other a strength in need,
a comfort in sorrow, and a companion in joy.
So unite their wills in your will,
and their spirits in your Spirit,
that they may live and grow together in love and peace
all the days of their life;
through Jesus Christ our Lord.
Amen.

Let us pray for N and N's families:

Gracious God,
you have called us to live in loving families,
and by your generous love
all the families on earth are blessed.
We pray today for the parents and families of N and N.
We recall the gracious influences and loving deeds
that have surrounded N and N in their homes.
And for their parents we ask continuing health,
fulfilment of life,
and the joy of knowing their children's children;
through Jesus Christ our Lord.
Amen.

Let us pray for all families:

Gracious Father,
you bless family life and renew your people.
Enrich husbands and wives, parents and children
more and more with your grace,
that, strengthening and supporting each other,
they may serve those in need
and be a sign of the fulfilment of your kingdom,
where, with your Son Jesus Christ and the Holy Spirit,
you live and reign,
one God through all ages.
Amen.

or C

Eternal God,
without your grace no promise is sure.
Strengthen N and N with patience, kindness, gentleness,
and all other gifts of the Holy Spirit,
so that they may fulfil the vows they have made.
Keep them faithful to each other and to you.
Fill them with such love and joy
that they may build a home of peace and welcome.
Guide them by your word to serve you all their days.
Enable us all, O God,
to do your will in each of our homes and lives.
Enrich us with your grace,
so that, encouraging and supporting one another,
we may serve those in need
and hasten the coming
of peace, love, and justice on earth;
through Jesus Christ our Lord.
Amen.

18   THE LORD'S PRAYER

(See People's Book, p. 84.)

The minister or lay person concludes the prayers by saying:

And now let us pray together
in the words our Saviour gave us:

either

**Our Father in heaven,
  hallowed be your name,
  your kingdom come,
  your will be done,
    on earth as in heaven.**

Give us today our daily bread.
Forgive us our sins,
  as we forgive those who sin against us.
Save us from the time of trial
  and deliver us from evil.

For the kingdom, the power, and the glory are yours
  now and for ever. Amen.

or

Our Father, who art in heaven,
  hallowed be thy name,
  thy kingdom come,
  thy will be done
    on earth as it is in heaven.
Give us this day our daily bread.
And forgive us our trespasses,
  as we forgive those who trespass against us.
And lead us not into temptation,
  but deliver us from evil.

For thine is the kingdom, the power and the glory,
  for ever and ever. Amen.

19   HOLY COMMUNION

If holy communion is to be celebrated, see section 19 at the
conclusion of this order; also v in the Notes.

20 HYMN

A hymn or song may be sung.

At the conclusion, the people remain standing for the Blessing.

21 BLESSING

**The blessing of God almighty,
the Father, the Son and the Holy Spirit,
be upon you and remain with you always.
Amen.**

22 SIGNING OF THE MARRIAGE CERTIFICATES

---

19 HOLY COMMUNION

A communion hymn may be sung.

The service of holy communion begins at The Setting of the Table. The newly-married couple may bring the gifts of bread and wine to the Lord's table.

The following form of the Great Prayer of Thanksgiving may be used at a marriage:

**The Lord be with you.
And also with you.**

**Lift up your hearts.
We lift them to the Lord.**

**Let us give thanks to the Lord our God.
It is right to give our thanks and praise.**

Loving God,
on this joyous occasion
we delight to give you thanks.
You made us in your image,
creating us male and female.
With Abraham and Sarah you made a covenant
that through them all people might be blessed.
To Mary and Joseph you gave a Son
who has wedded all people to yourself.
You have given us the gift of marriage
that we may fulfil one another in love.

And so we praise you
with the faithful of every time and place,
joining with choirs of angels and the whole creation
in the eternal hymn:

**Holy, holy, holy Lord, God of power and might,
heaven and earth are full of your glory.
Hosanna in the highest.**

**Blessed is he who comes in the name of the Lord.
Hosanna in the highest.**

We bless you that you loved the world so much
that you gave your only Son Jesus Christ to be our Saviour.
He suffered and died for the sin of the world.
You raised him from the dead
that we too might have new life.
He ascended to be with you in glory,
and by the Holy Spirit he is with us always.
He loved the church and gave himself for it,
giving us an example for the love of husband and wife.

On the night before he died,
Jesus took bread,
and when he had given you thanks
he broke it, and gave it to his disciples saying:
Take, eat. This is my body which is given for you.
Do this in remembrance of me.

After supper, he took the cup,
and again giving you thanks
he gave it to his disciples, saying:
Drink from this, all of you.
This is my blood of the new covenant
which is shed for you and for many
for the forgiveness of sins.
Do this, as often as you drink it, in remembrance of me.

Therefore,
in remembrance of all your mighty acts in Jesus Christ
we ask you to accept
this sacrifice of praise and thanksgiving,
which we offer in union with Christ's sacrifice.

Send the Holy Spirit upon us and what we do here;
that we and these gifts, touched by your Spirit,
may be signs of life and love to each other
and to all the world.

Through Christ, with Christ, in Christ,
in the unity of the Holy Spirit,
all glory is yours, eternal Father,
now and for ever.

Amen.

A Reaffirmation of Marriage

NOTES

i   This order is to be regarded as a model, and provides resources for reaffirmation of marriage which should be adapted to suit the needs of those involved.

ii   This order may be used on occasions such as:

(a) when a couple choose to reaffirm and give thanks for their marriage on a significant occasion such as an anniversary. The service may be held in a church, a home, or other venue, forming part of the celebration with family and friends;

(b) when a couple has experienced difficulties in their marriage, or after a time of separation;

(c) when a group of couples request, or are invited to make, a public reaffirmation of marriage.

iii   This order may form part of a public service of worship. It may be appropriate for the order to be included in the service of holy communion. There may be occasions, as in (b) above, when it would be more helpful for the reaffirmation of marriage to take place privately. If this order forms part of the worship of the Lord's day, it comes at an appropriate place between the Preaching of the Word and the Prayers of the People.

iv   This order is prepared for the use of one couple only. If more than one couple make a reaffirmation of marriage on the same occasion, the rubrics and text will need to be varied.

v   The following resources in The Marriage Service may be helpful for a reaffirmation of marriage:

Hymns: Note x
Scripture readings: Note xvi
Prayers: Section 17 in the service

A Reaffirmation of Marriage

1 INTRODUCTION

The minister may introduce this order by explaining the circumstances which led to its use.

The minister says:

Marriage is appointed by God.
The church believes that marriage
is a gift of God in creation
and a means of grace in which man and woman
become one in heart, mind and body.

Marriage is the sacred and life-long union
of a man and a woman
who give themselves to each other in love and trust.
It signifies the mystery of the union
between Christ and the church.

Marriage is a way of life which all people should honour;
it is not to be entered into lightly or selfishly,
but responsibly and in the love of God.

N and N are here today
to reaffirm their commitment to this way of life
which God has created and Christ has blessed.
We pray with them
that they may fulfil God's purpose in their lives.

The minister or a lay person calls the people to prayer.

Gracious God,
your generous love surrounds us,
and everything we enjoy comes from you.
We thank you for those who gave us life,
and have loved and guided us.
We are grateful for friends and relatives
whose care and love have helped us,
and whose patience and concern
are a source of strength and hope.
We thank you for the love of this couple (*or,* N and N).
Grant them sincerity
as they recommit themselves to each other.
May they put their trust in you,
the source of all life and love;
through Jesus Christ our Lord.
Amen.

2   REAFFIRMATION OF VOWS

A   THANKSGIVING

When the predominant note is thanksgiving, the following form
is used.

The husband and wife face each other, and join hands.

The husband says:

I, N, in the presence of God,
reaffirm my commitment to you, N, as your husband.
I give thanks that you have shared my life.
All that I am and all that I have
I continue to share with you.
Whatever the future holds,
I will love you and stand by you,
as long as we both shall live.

The wife says:

I, N, in the presence God,
reaffirm my commitment to you, N, as your wife.
I give thanks that you have shared my life.
All that I am and all that I have
I continue to share with you.
Whatever the future holds,
I will love you and stand by you,
as long as we both shall live.

B RECOMMITMENT

When the predominant note is recommitment, the following form is used.

The husband and wife face each other, and join hands.

The husband says:

I, N, in the presence of God,
renew my commitment to you, N, as your husband.
All that I am I give to you,
and all that I have I share with you.
Whatever the future holds,
I will love you and stand by you,
as long as we both shall live.

The wife says:

I, N, in the presence of God,
renew my commitment to you, N, as your wife.
All that I am I give to you,
and all that I have I share with you.
Whatever the future holds,
I will love you and stand by you,
as long as we both shall live.

3 BLESSING

The riches of God's grace be upon you,
that you may continue together in faith and love
and receive the blessings of eternal life.
May almighty God,
who creates you, redeems you and guides you,
bless you now and always.
Amen.

or

God the Father make you holy in his love;
God the Son enrich you with his grace;
God the Holy Spirit strengthen you with joy.
The Lord bless you and keep you in eternal life.
Amen.

The couple may kiss.

4 AFFIRMATION BY THE PEOPLE

The minister may say to the people:

Will you, the relatives and friends of N and N,
who have gathered here today,
continue to uphold them in their marriage?

We will.

5 PRAYERS

Free prayer may be offered by the minister, or a member of the family or other person. Alternatively, the following prayer(s) may be used:

Eternal God,
we pray that marriage may be held in honour everywhere:
that husbands and wives may live faithfully together;
and that members of every family
may grow in mutual understanding,
in courtesy and kindness;
that they may learn to forgive one another
as you forgive them;
that they may bear one another's burdens
and so fulfil the law of Christ.
Amen.

For an anniversary.

Gracious God,
we thank you for all the rich blessings of life;
and we rejoice today that N and N
are sharing this anniversary with each other,
(with their children and their grandchildren),
and with us.
May your love for them be their enduring treasure;
and may they continue to share each other's life
and to grow through each other's love.
In the name of Christ, we pray.
Amen.

After the restoration of a broken marriage.

Faithful God,
we thank you that you have safely brought N and N
through a time of trouble and testing,
and called them to reaffirm their commitment to each other.
May your mercy and grace be to them healing and strength;
may they continue to be honest, patient and understanding;
and as they grow together in love for each other,
may they proclaim your saving love
in Jesus Christ our Lord.
Amen.

NOTES

i   This order may form part of a regular Sunday service of the congregation and is used when parents desire to acknowledge that their child is a gift from God.

ii   The service comes at an appropriate place between the Preaching of the Word and the Prayers of the People.

iii   Those participating in the service should be visible to the congregation but should, if possible, not stand near the font.

iv   One of the parents holds the child throughout the service.

v   If parents request to give thanks publicly for their child, this order should be used soon after the child's birth or adoption, regardless of whether or not the parents intend to present their child for baptism at a later date. The Thanksgiving should be held on the first occasion on which the child is present in the worshipping community.

vi   Part or all of this order may be used in the hospital or in the home, at the discretion of the minister.

Thanksgiving
for the Gift of a Child

1 HYMN

A hymn of praise or thanksgiving may be sung.

2 PRESENTATION

(See People's Book, p. 87.)

The elder responsible for the care of the family brings the
parent(s), the child and any brothers and sisters forward and
introduces them to the congregation.

Friends,
I present to you N and N
who have come to give thanks for their child N.
(I also present N and N
who are so glad to be welcoming
a new brother/sister into their family.)
With them, we give our thanks to God.

3 INTRODUCTION

The minister says:

All life is from God,
and children are a gift from the Lord.
Within a family,
the birth/adoption of a child
is a joyous and solemn occasion.
In this event we see the wonder
of God's loving creativity among us.

We are now to share the joy of this family
whose life has been enriched
by the gift of a son/daughter.

4 PSALM

Bless the Lord, O my soul,
and all that is within me, bless his holy name.

Bless the Lord, O my soul,
and forget not all his benefits.

He satisfies you with good things,
and your youth is renewed like an eagle's.

As a father cares for his children,
so does the Lord care for those who fear him.

The merciful goodness of the Lord endures for ever
on those who fear him,
and his righteousness on children's children.

On those who keep his covenant
and remember his commandments and do them.

Bless the Lord, all you works of his,
in all places of his dominion;
bless the Lord, O my soul.

Psalm 103: 1, 2, 5, 13, 17, 18, 22

Alternatively, Psalm 23 or Psalm 100 may be used.

5   PRAYER OF THANKSGIVING

The minister or elder offers one of the following prayers and/or free prayer:

Let us pray:

O God,
like a mother who comforts her children,
you sustain, nurture and strengthen us;
like a father who cares for his children,
you look upon us with compassion and goodness.
We give you thanks for the birth (adoption) of N,
and for the joy which has come to this family.
Confirm their joy by a lively sense
of your presence with them,
and give them calm strength and patient wisdom
as they seek to bring this child to love
all that is true and noble, just and pure,
lovable and gracious, excellent and admirable,
following the example
of our Lord and Saviour, Jesus Christ.
Amen.
or
O Lord our God,
creator of heaven and earth, and our creator:
we give you thanks and praise
for the gift of this child.
We thank you for creating him/her in your image,
and breathing into him/her the breath of life.
We thank you for the love
which these parents have for each other,
and for the welcome they are giving to N.
By the power of the Holy Spirit,
fill their home with love, trust and understanding;
through Jesus Christ our Lord.
Amen.

6   STATEMENT BY PARENTS

One or both parents may say one of the following:

**We thankfully receive N
as a gift from God.
With humility and hope
we promise to love and care for him/her.**

or

**We thankfully receive N
as a gift from God.
With humility and hope
we promise to love and care for him/her,
and to set before him/her the christian faith
by teaching and example.
In this we ask for the power of the Holy Spirit
and the prayers of the church.**

7   PRAYER

The following prayer and/or free prayer is offered:

Gracious God,
from whom every family
in heaven and on earth is named:
strengthen us by the Holy Spirit
that we may witness faithfully
in our homes and in our daily lives.
May the love of Christ be made plain to N,
and may he/she be brought by grace
to the sacrament of baptism.
May he/she come, with all your people,
to the fullness of your kingdom of love and peace;
through Jesus Christ our Lord.
Amen.

8   BLESSING

The minister says:

The Lord bless you and keep you;
the Lord make his face to shine upon you,
and be gracious unto you;
the Lord lift up his countenance upon you,
and give you peace.
Amen.

Numbers 6:24-26

9   HYMN

If a hymn of praise or thanksgiving was not sung at the beginning
of this order, one may be sung here.

A Service of Healing

NOTES

i   Services of healing are of various kinds. The rite of healing may be included in The Service of the Lord's Day in response to a particular need within the congregation. Or the rite of healing may be given emphasis on a particular Sunday and a general invitation made for anyone in need of healing to come forward. In either of these cases, The Sacrament of the Lord's Supper may be included in the order of worship. The Service of Healing may be before or after communion.

Special services of healing may be held at times other than the regular Sunday service of the congregation. Again, holy communion may be celebrated. The order should always include The Gathering of the People of God (including an act of confession) and The Service of the Word (including the Prayers of the People).

A Service of Healing may also be conducted in the home or hospital for one who is unable to attend a service with the congregation. Some representatives of the congregation may be present with the minister. In these circumstances, with sensitive regard to a person's condition, the service may be considerably shortened.

ii   The council of elders, with the minister, is responsible for the oversight of the services of worship of the church. The elders, with the minister, will decide the times and the leadership of any public services of healing.

iii   This services provides:
        A — For the Healing of the Sick or Disabled;
        B — For the Healing of a Personal Relationship;
        C — For Healing Within Society.
In any one service it is not necessary for all sections to be used. The prayers in For Healing Within Society may be used in any service.

iv   The prayers of intercession in this order may include the names of all those who have requested prayer for healing, whether they are present or not. It is important that people have the opportunity before or during the service to present the names of those who are seeking prayers for healing or for whom prayer is requested. General prayers for the sick and disabled, or for the healing of broken relationships, should be offered.

v   The laying on of hands has always been a sign of blessing. It has from early times been closely associated with prayers for healing.

During the laying on of hands, it should not be expected that public free prayer will always be offered. It is appropriate for the prayer to be in silence or for those present to wait on God in silence until it seems right that one should pray audibly. It is the inclination of the heart, the longing that is often too deep for words, to which the Lord listens.

vi Anointing with oil has been a practice of the church from the beginning. (James 5:14) It is a sign of God's presence through the Holy Spirit and of the joy of those who welcome God. Therefore it should not be treated lightly. If possible, those who are to receive the anointing and others who participate in the service should be prepared beforehand by some instruction about the purpose of this symbolic act. Anointing need not always be included with the prayers for healing, but when requested it should not be denied. The anointing for healing is a solemn moment in anyone's life. Normally it is not used more than once for a particular illness, whereas the laying on of hands may be requested frequently for growth towards wholeness.

A Service of Healing

The Laying On of Hands with Prayer and Anointing

INTRODUCTION

(See People's Book, p. 91.)

The minister or leader says:

Our Lord Jesus Christ sent his disciples
to preach the good news and to heal the sick.
Through his death and resurrection he has made us whole.
We who are his disciples
bear witness to his saving love.

The following may also be read:

The apostle James wrote:
Are any among you sick?
Let them call for the elders of the church,
and let them pray over them,
anointing them with oil in the name of the Lord;
and the prayer of faith will save the sick,
and the Lord will raise them up;
and if they have committed sins,
they will be forgiven.

James 5:13-15

INVITATION

An invitation such as the following is given:

We invite you to receive the laying on of hands
with prayer in the name of Christ.

You may be ill or suffering pain;
you may be anxious or depressed;
you may be in a difficult life situation.

Whatever reasons you have for coming,
they are already known to our Lord Jesus Christ;
it is he who welcomes and receives you.

SAVIOUR OF THE WORLD

Jesus, Saviour of the world,
come to us in your mercy;
   we look to you to save and help us.

By your cross and your life laid down
you set your people free;
   we look to you to save and help us.

When they were about to perish
you saved your disciples;
   we look to you to come to our help.

In the greatness of your mercy,
loose us from our chains;
   forgive the sins of all your people.

Make yourself known as our Saviour
and mighty Deliverer;
   save and help us that we may praise you.

Come now and dwell with us,
Lord Christ Jesus;
   hear our prayer and be with us always.

And when you come in your glory,
   **make us to be one with you
   and to share the life of your kingdom.**

A: For the Healing of the Sick or Disabled

PRAYER OF INTERCESSION

Those who wish to receive the laying on of hands come forward.

General prayers are offered for the sick and disabled, and prayers for the healing of particular people.

THE LAYING ON OF HANDS

The minister lays hands on the sick person.

Others may also lay their hands on the person.

The minister says:

We lay our hands upon you, N,
in the name of our Lord Jesus Christ.

There may be a time of silence or free prayer.

The minister continues:

May almighty God,
the Father, the Son and the Holy Spirit,
bring you to wholeness in body, mind and spirit,
give you a secure hope and a confident peace,
and keep you in eternal life.
Amen.

THE ANOINTING

If anointing is to take place, the minister makes the sign of the cross with oil on the person.

The minister says:

N, we anoint you with oil
for cleansing and healing
in the name of our Lord Jesus Christ.

The minister may add:

May the Holy Spirit poured out upon you
yield the fruit of pardon, trust and joy.
Amen.

B: For the Healing of a Personal Relationship

PRAYERS OF INTERCESSION

Those who wish to receive the laying on of hands come forward.

General prayers are offered for the healing of broken relationships,
and prayers for particular situations.

THE LAYING ON OF HANDS

The minister lays hands on those concerned.

Others may also join in the laying on of hands.

The minister says:

We lay our hands upon you, N (and N),
in the name of our Lord Jesus Christ.

There may be a time of silence or free prayer.

The minister continues:

May almighty God,
the Father, the Son and the Holy Spirit,
who has broken down the barriers of hostility
and who calls us to live reconciled lives,
enable you to live in unity and peace.
Amen.

THE ANOINTING

If anointing is to take place, the minister makes the sign of the
cross with oil on the person(s).

The minister says:

N (and N), we anoint you with oil
for cleansing and healing
in the name of our Lord Jesus Christ.

The minister may add:

May the Holy Spirit poured out upon you
yield the fruit of pardon, trust and joy.
Amen.

C: For Healing Within Society

PRAYERS OF INTERCESSION

Free prayer may be offered and/or one of the following prayers said:

Almighty God,
through Jesus your Son
you created all things in heaven and earth;
all nations, authorities and powers
were created through him and for him.
In him all things are held together in unity.
Break down the barriers which separate us from each other,
and bring peace to the troubled affairs of our world.

May divisions (between N and N) be healed.
Instil within our hearts
the desire for true peace, justice and mercy,
that all people everywhere may live with dignity,
free from the fear of violence;
through Jesus Christ our Lord.
Amen.

or

O God of love,
our peace lies in conversion to your will,
our strength in confident trust;
but we would have none of it.
By the gently power of the Holy Spirit
quieten the turmoil of our minds
and open our hearts to your presence within us,
that we may be still and know that you are God;
through Jesus Christ our lord,
who lives and reigns with you and the Holy Spirit,
one God, for ever and ever.
Amen.

Conclusion

A prayer such as the following concludes A Service of Healing:

May almighty God,
the source of new life,
be your strong defence against discouragement and fear,
and kindle in your heart a sense of continuing healing;
through the One who brings salvation
and keeps you in eternal life,
Jesus Christ our Lord.
Amen.

The Service of the Lord's Day may continue at The Sacrament of
the Lord's Supper or The Sending Forth of the People of God.
A shorter form of service may conclude simply with a blessing.

Other Prayers for Use in a Service of Healing

Eternal Father,
creator of all that is,
you fashioned us in your image;
you breathed your breath into us
and we became living beings.

Lord Jesus,
you bring reconciliation and healing
to a world torn apart by violence and suffering.

Holy Spirit,
you bring new life and hope
to those who are open to your presence.

We worship and adore you, O blessed Trinity,
one God, for ever and ever.
Amen.

Heavenly Father,
you anointed your Son Jesus Christ
with the Holy Spirit and with power,
to bring to every person the blessings of your kingdom.
Anoint your church with the same Holy Spirit,
that we who share in Christ's sufferings and victory
may be witnesses to the gospel of salvation;
through Jesus Christ our Lord.
Amen.

God our Father,
giver of life and health,
send your blessing on all who are sick,
and upon those who minister to them;
that all weakness may be transformed by the risen Christ,
who lives and reigns with you and the Holy Spirit,
one God, for ever.
Amen.

If the service needs to be shortened to such an extent that a prayer of confession such as those in The Service of the Lord's Day or Resources for Leading Worship is inappropriate, at least words such as the following shall be said:

Before God, we confess that we have sinned.

Silence

May almighty God have mercy on us,
forgive us our sins,
and bring us to everlasting life.
Amen.

Almighty God,
we thank you that through these signs
you have confirmed your promise of life
in all its fullness.
Your faithfulness is beyond our understanding;
again and again we experience your love reaching out to us.
Into your hands we entrust ourselves
and all those whom you have given us.
Keep us always in the spirit of the Beatitudes:
joy, simplicity and compassion;
through Jesus Christ our Lord.
Amen.

A Service of Reconciliation

NOTES

i This short order is recommended for those occasions when it seems appropriate for a person to be reconciled to God in the presence of a representative of the whole church, normally a minister. It may be used at the close of a counselling session when something has surfaced which needs to be dealt with in the context of a prayer for forgiveness.

ii While it is envisaged that such an order would be used in a quiet place where there is little chance of intrusion, there are ways in which an order similar to this could be used in the context of a corporate act of confession at a retreat or camp. In these situations, any personal confession should be made in a place where it cannot be overheard.

iii Public confession of particular sins may be made on very rare occasions and then only if it has arisen out of some action that has hurt the whole congregation in a tangible way. We are dealing here with some of the deep stirrings of the human spirit. It is not in any circumstances to be regarded lightly.

iv The substance of a personal confession is never to be communicated outside the place and time where the confession is made. Those who are given the privilege and responsibility of hearing another person open himself or herself in confession should understand that the one who confesses comes with a trusting confidence and longing for reconciliation with God and with fellow human beings.

v The one confessing may kneel. This simple gesture may help the person to express humility and trust in God. The one in whose presence the confession is made may adopt the same position alongside the other. Care should be taken to ensure that the minister does not take up a position that makes it appear as if the confession is being made *to* another person. It is being made *in the presence of* another who is also in need of reconciliation. The one who declares forgiveness does so as a servant of God. God alone forgives and makes whole.

vi   At the words, 'I declare the forgiveness of your sins . . .', some sign such as the touch of a hand on the head, or the tracing of the cross on the forehead, may add depth to the meaning of the words. The person saying these words speaks as a representative of the church which has received the Spirit of reconciliation from the Lord himself.

(John 20:19-23)

vii   Those in whose presence confession is made need to be alert to and to deal sensitively with a person who may have a compulsive need to confess. In such a case, at the least, there should be some clear affirmation that God does forgive, and that repeated confession is neither helpful or necessary. The person may need to be directed to further counselling.

A Service of Reconciliation

A Form of Personal Confession

ACT OF CONFESSION

(See People's Book, p. 97.)

The one making confession says:

**Lord,
purify me with the fire of the Holy Spirit,
so that I may serve you
with a pure and trusting heart.**

Silence may be kept for a time.

**I confess to almighty God,
in the communion of saints in heaven and on earth,
and before you, my brother/sister,
that I have sinned.**

Here, specific things for which forgiveness is sought may be confessed.

The minister may ask questions and speak words of encouragement.

The one making confession then says:

**My sins weigh me down;
but my confidence is in the Lord Jesus Christ
who has taken upon himself the burden of our sin.**

**I ask you, my brother/sister,
to pray for me to the Lord our God.**

Free prayer is offered.

DECLARATION OF FORGIVENESS

One or more of the following is said:

God sent the Son into the world, not to condemn the world,
but that the world might be saved through him.
Those who believe in him are not condemned.

John 3:17, 18

or

The Lord breathed on his disciples and said to them:
Receive the Holy Spirit.
If you forgive the sins of any, they are forgiven;
if you retain the sins of any, they are retained.

John 20:23

or

Those who are in Christ are a new creation;
the old has passed away,
behold, the new has come.
All this is from God,
who through Christ reconciled us to himself.

2 Corinthians 5:17, 18

or

The saying is sure and worthy of full acceptance,
that Christ Jesus came into the world to save sinners.

1 Timothy 1:15

or

If we confess our sins,
God is faithful and just, and will forgive our sins
and cleanse us from all unrighteousness.

1 John 1:9

The minister says:

Our Lord Jesus Christ forgives your offences
and releases you from your burden of guilt.

By his authority,
I declare the forgiveness of your sins.

You are free:
in the name of the Father,
and of the Son,
and of the Holy Spirit.
Amen.

THE PEACE

Both stand.

The minister says:

God was in Christ, reconciling the world to himself,
not counting our trespasses against us,
and entrusting to us the message of reconciliation.
Let us therefore be ambassadors for Christ.

2 Corinthians 5:19, 20

The peace of the Lord be always with you.
And also with you.

A sign of peace may be exchanged.

NOTES

i   This service witnesses to the fact that the Holy Spirit is constantly working in the lives of God's people, awakening faith and calling them to make a new beginning in their christian pilgrimage. It may be used to meet particular situations such as the following:

* When a person has recently come to faith in Christ and desires to celebrate the experience and witness to it before his/her congregation.

* When a person has recently made a recommitment of his/her life to Christ.

* When a person intends to return to active involvement in the worship and life of the congregation and/or to seek baptism or confirmation.

ii   This order forms part of the congregation's Sunday worship. It could appropriately be placed after the Preaching of the Word and the Affirmation of Faith. It may be appropriate for the order to be followed by holy communion.

iii   The service may be adapted for different circumstances including the occasion when a number of people wish to celebrate new beginnings in faith.

A Celebration of New Beginnings in Faith

1 INTRODUCTION AND WELCOME

(See People's Book, p. 100.)

The minister and an elder stand together with the person at the front of the church.

The minister introduces the service and welcomes the person, beginning with words such as:

Brothers and sisters,
from time to time we experience a new beginning
in our faith journey,
when the Holy Spirit breaks into our lives
to inspire us, to lead us,
and to deepen our commitment to Christ.

Today we praise the Lord
for what has been happening in N's life,
recalling the many ways
in which God has blessed us . . .

We welcome you, N . . .

2 SCRIPTURE SENTENCES

The elder reads one or more Scripture sentences such as:

What does the Lord require of you
but to do justice, and to love kindness,
and to walk humbly with your God?

Micah 6:8

Ask, and it will be given to you;
seek and you will find;
knock, and it will be opened to you.

Matthew 7:7

God shows his love for us
in that while we were yet sinners
Christ died for us.

Romans 5:8

It is the Spirit himself bearing witness with our spirit
that we are children of God,
and if children, then heirs,
heirs of God and fellow heirs with Christ.

Romans 8:16, 17a

I have been crucified with Christ;
it is no longer I who live,
but Christ who lives in me.

Galatians 2:20

Be renewed in the spirit of your minds,
and put on the new nature,
created after the likeness of God
in true righteousness and holiness.

Ephesians 4:23, 24

3   WITNESS

The person may give a brief testimony to his/her experience of
Christ, or of making a new beginning in faith.

If the person is unwilling or unable to do this, the minister or
another person may outline briefly the experiences which have
brought the person to make a witness to Christ before the
congregation.

4   CONGREGATIONAL RESPONSE

(See People's Book, p. 100.)

The elder or other appropriate person may make a brief response
to the witness, concluding with:

**N, we rejoice in your experience
of the grace of the Lord Jesus Christ,
the love of God,
and the fellowship of the Holy Spirit.**

The people say:

**In the love of Christ we encourage you,
and pray that he will continue to bless you.
To his name be glory and praise.
Hallelujah!**

The elder may initiate applause.

5   HYMN

A hymn or song which is significant to the person may be sung.
(See also suggestions under 9.)

6   PRAYER WITH THE LAYING ON OF HANDS

Some of the congregation, family and friends may be invited to
come forward and gather around the person.

The person kneels.

The minister invites the elder and those who have come forward
to lay hands on the person's head.

The minister then says to the congregation:

Let us pray for N in silence.

After a time, free prayer and/or one of the following prayers may be offered by the minister and/or elder and/or other persons.

O Lord our God,
your love is rich beyond our deserving.
You never forsake us,
no matter how far we move from you.
We thank you for all you have done for N.
Strengthen him/her by the Holy Spirit,
that he/she may grow in faith
and increase in love for you.
May his/her service and witness
bring you honour and glory;
in the name of Jesus Christ our Lord.
Amen.

or

Loving God,
continue to bless your servant N.
We pray that the Holy Spirit may be present in him/her
and that he/she may know your renewing power.
Help us to see the fruit of the Spirit in him/her,
and to follow with him/her in the way of Christ;
to whom be glory with you and the Holy Spirit.
Amen.

7 BLESSING

The minister says one of the following blessings:

N, you are a child of God,
a servant of Christ,
and a temple of the Holy Spirit.
May almighty God bless you
and keep you in eternal life.
Amen.

or

N, may the Father of our Lord Jesus Christ
strengthen you through the Spirit in your inner being;
that Christ may dwell in your heart through faith,
and that you may be filled with all the fullness of God.
Amen.

Based on Ephesians 3:14-19

The people may then say or sing the Aaronic Blessing,
(*Australian Hymn Book*, 572)

**The Lord bless you and keep you;
the Lord make his face to shine upon you,
and be gracious unto you;
the Lord lift up his countenance upon you,
and give you peace.**

Numbers 6:24-26

The person stands and all return to their seats.

8 INVITATION TO DISCIPLESHIP

The minister may invite others to make a first commitment of
their life to Christ or a reaffirmation of their faith in him.

They may come forward during the singing that follows.

If people respond to the invitation, brief free prayer is offered.

9 HYMN

An appropriate hymn or song may be sung.

One of the following may be suitable, either here or at 5.

AUSTRALIAN HYMN BOOK

81	The king of love my shepherd is
85	To God be the glory, great things he has done
115	Let us sing to the God of salvation
138	And can it be that I should gain
451	Lord Jesus Christ, you have come to us
465	All my hope on God is founded
497	Just as I am, without one plea
520	Take my life, and let it be
527	Just as I am, thine own to be
537	May the mind of Christ my Saviour
573	Praise God from whom all blessings flow

OTHER SONGS

Father welcomes all his children
In the house of God
Freely, freely
Seek ye first the kingdom of God
Holy holy, holy holy
Father, we adore you
Praise the name of Jesus
Prayer of St Francis
St Patrick's Prayer

Reception
of a Member by Transfer

NOTES

i   A confirmed or baptised member may join a congregation either by transfer from another congregation of the Uniting Church in Australia or by transfer from another denomination. In each case application shall be made as required in the Regulations.

ii   The reception may be recognised during a regular Sunday service of the congregation with which the new member will be associated.

iii   No formal act is required for the reception of an adherent, but if a family is being received and includes adherents as well as baptised and/or confirmed members, it may be appropriate to include the adherents in the presentation to the congregation and the welcome.

iv   Normally this order follows the Preaching of the Word in a service which includes the celebration of holy communion.

Reception
of a Member by Transfer

(See People's Book, p. 103.)

An elder brings forward the person to be received and says:

The Uniting Church in Australia
affirms that every member of the church
is engaged to confess the faith of Christ crucified
and to be his faithful servant.
In each congregation the members are to meet regularly
to hear God's Word,
to celebrate the sacraments,
to build one another up in love,
to share in the wider responsibilities of the church,
and to serve the world.

I present to you NN
to be received as a confirmed member of this congregation,
by transfer from the . . . congregation.
or

I present to you NN
to be received as a baptised member of this congregation,
by transfer from the . . . congregation.

If the person is a confirmed member, the minister asks:

N,
do you reaffirm your allegiance to Jesus Christ
as Saviour and Lord?

I do.

Do you accept membership in this congregation,
promising to share in the life and worship of the church?

I do.

If the person is a baptised member, an adult or a child able to
speak for himself/herself, the minister asks:

**N,
do you accept membership in this congregation,
promising to share in the life and worship of the church?**

I do.

If the person to be received is an infant or young child, the
minister asks the parents or guardian:

**N (and N),
do you accept membership for N in this congregation,
promising to enable and encourage him/her
to share in the life and worship of the church?**

I(we) do.

The minister asks the congregation:

**Will you welcome N
into the fellowship of this congregation,
and will you offer him/her
your friendship and support?**

We will.

The following prayer may be used, or free prayer may be offered for the new member and the congregation.

Alternatively, this prayer may be included with other intercessions in Prayers of the People.

Let us pray:

O God our Father,
we praise you for calling us to faith
and for gathering us into the church,
the body of Christ.
We thank you for this congregation of your people
and rejoice that you have added to our number
N, our brother/sister in the faith.

Together may we live in the Spirit,
 building one another up in love,
sharing in the life of the church,
and serving the world;
for the sake of Jesus Christ our Lord.
Amen.

The minister takes the hand of the new member and says:

N, as a sign of our welcome,
we give you the right hand of fellowship.

Representatives of the council of elders and the congregation come forward and greet the new member.

One may speak words of welcome on behalf of the congregation.

Reception
of a Member-in-Association

NOTES

i   A member of another denomination who, for the time-being,
participates in the life of a congregation of the Uniting Church in
Australia may become a member-in-association. Application shall be
made as required in the Regulations.

ii   The reception may be recognised during a regular Sunday service of the
congregation with which the new member will be associated.

iii   Normally this order follows the Preaching of the Word in a service
which includes the celebration of holy communion.

Reception
of a Member-in-Association

(See People's Book, p. 106.)

An elder brings forward the person to be received and says:

The Uniting Church in Australia
provides for a member of another christian denomination
who, for the time-being,
participates in the life of a congregation of this church
to become a member-in-association.
Such a member joins in the corporate life
of the Uniting Church
while retaining membership
in his or her own denomination.

I present to you NN
to be received as a member-in-association
of this congregation.

The minister asks the person:

N,
do you reaffirm your allegiance to Jesus Christ
as Saviour and Lord?

I do.

Do you accept membership-in-association in this congregation,
promising to share in the life and worship of the church;
and accepting the way in which the Uniting Church in Australia
orders its own life,
without forsaking your own denomination?

I do.

The minister asks the congregation:

Will you welcome N
into the fellowship of this congregation;
and will you offer him/her
your friendship and support?

We will.

The following prayer may be used, or free prayer may be offered for the new member-in -association and the congregation.

Alternatively, this prayer may be included with other intercessions in Prayers of the People.

Let us pray:

O God our Father,
we praise you for calling us to faith
and for gathering us into the church,
the body of Christ.
We thank you for this congregation of your people
and rejoice that you have added to our number
N, our brother/sister in the faith.

Together may we live in the Spirit,
building one another up in love,
sharing in the life of the church,
and serving the world;
for the sake of Jesus Christ our Lord.
Amen.

The minister takes the hand of the new member and says:

N, as a sign of our welcome,
we give you the right hand of fellowship.

Representatives of the council of elders and the congregation come forward and greet the new member.

One may speak words of welcome on behalf of the congregation.

Ministry at the Time of Death

The following resources are intended for use in a short devotional service which would normally include appropriate Bible readings and free prayer.

Prayers with the Dying

SCRIPTURE SENTENCES

The steadfast love of the Lord never ceases,
his mercies never come to an end;
they are new every morning, so great is his faithfulness.

Lamentations 3:22, 23

What no eye has seen, nor ear heard,
nor the human heart conceived,
God has prepared for those who love him.

1 Corinthians 2:9

Those who are in Christ are a new creation;
the old has passed away,
behold, the new has come.
All this is from God,
who through Christ reconciled us to himself.

2 Corinthians 5:17, 18

Jesus said:
Lo, I am with you always,
to the close of the age.

Matthew 28:20b

From the cross,
Jesus cried with a loud voice and said:
Father, into your hands I commit my spirit.
And having said this, he breathed his last.

Luke 23:46

PRAYERS

Heavenly Father,
your Son Jesus Christ commended his spirit
into your hands at his last hour:
into those same hands
we now commend your servant N,
that death may be for him/her the gate to life
and to eternal fellowship with you;
through Jesus Christ our Lord.
Amen.

Go forward, N, on your pilgrim journey,
in the name of the Father
who created you;
in the name of Jesus Christ
who died and rose for you;
in the name of the Holy Spirit
who strengthens you.
May you have communion with all the saints in light;
may you rejoice with the whole company of heaven;
may your portion this day be peace,
and your dwelling place the heavenly Jerusalem.
Amen.

Heavenly Father,
bless N in this time of weakness,
and comfort him/her with the promise of eternal life,
given in the resurrection of your Son,
Jesus Christ our Lord.
Amen.

God of love, God of peace,
into your hands we commend N.
May he/she know the strength,
the courage and the comfort
that are the gifts of the Holy Spirit.
May he/she trust your sure love,
and rest secure in your everlasting arms,
now and for ever.
Amen.

Mighty God,
we commend your son/daughter N
to your everlasting love and mercy.
Give him/her joy and gladness in your presence;
give him/her the assurance of your forgiveness and love;
give him/her your peace, now and for ever.
Amen.

May God the Father, who created you,
have mercy on you.
May God the Son, Jesus Christ,
who conquered death for you,
have mercy on you.
May God the Holy Spirit, who sanctifies you,
have mercy on you.
May God almighty,
the Father, the Son and the Holy Spirit,
grant you eternal rest and peace.
Amen.

Prayers with the Family after a Death

SCRIPTURE SENTENCES

Thus says the Lord God, the Holy One of Israel:
in quietness and in trust shall be your strength.

Isaiah 30:15

I am sure that neither death, nor life,
nor angels, nor principalities,
nor things present, nor things to come,
nor powers, nor height, nor depth,
nor anything else in all creation,
will be able to separate us from the love of God
in Christ Jesus our Lord.

Romans 8:38, 39

Blessed be the God and Father of our Lord Jesus Christ,
the Father of mercies and God of all comfort,
who comforts us in all our affliction.

2 Corinthians 1:3

Jesus said:
Blessed are those who mourn,
for they shall be comforted.

Matthew 5:4

Jesus said:
Come to me, all who labour and are heavy-laden,
and I will give you rest;
for I am gentle and lowly in heart,
and you will find rest for your souls.

Matthew 11:28, 29

PRAYERS

O God our Father,
we know that you are afflicted in our afflictions.
We come to you today in sorrow,
that we may receive from you
the comfort you alone can give.
Enable us to see that in perfect wisdom,
perfect love and perfect power
you are always working for our good.
You are our dwelling-place, O God,
and underneath us are your everlasting arms.
Make us so sure of your love
that we will be able to accept
what we cannot understand.
Help us today to be thinking
not only of the darkness of death,
but of the splendour of eternal life.

Enable us even now to face life with courage and hope;
give us the grace and the strength to go on,
knowing that the best tribute we can pay our loved one
is to let his/her life be a continuing inspiration to us,
and knowing that we are constantly surrounded
by the unseen cloud of witnesses.

Comfort and uphold us,
until we share with them the light of your glory
and the peace of your eternal presence;
through Jesus Christ our Lord.
Amen.

Lord Jesus,
we wait for you to grant us your comfort and peace.
We confess that we are slow to accept death
as an inevitable part of life.
We confess our reluctance to surrender
this friend and loved one into your eternal care.
You, Lord Jesus, know the depth of our sorrow;
you also wept at the grave of your friend Lazarus.
Let the Holy Spirit come upon us now,
the Comforter you promise.
Grant us your love and peace
as we reach out to comfort one another.
Be our companion as we live through the days ahead;
and even as we mourn,
may all that we feel, think, say and do
bear witness to our faith.
Amen.

Lord Jesus,
we remember the pain you endured for us:
your agony in the garden,
your scourging, your crowning with thorns,
your death on the cross.
You had to suffer to enter your glory.
In the midst of our grief and loss,
remind us that the sufferings of this present time
are not to be compared to the glory that is to come.
In the strength of the Holy Spirit,
enable us to join our suffering with yours,
to trust in your redeeming love,
and to serve you all our days.
Amen.

The Funeral Service

NOTES

The christian recognition of death is a part of the church's offering of the whole of life to God. The Funeral Service should be seen as a time:

(a) to worship God, celebrating the death and resurrection of Jesus Christ which witness to the faithfulness of God in life and death;

(b) to give thanks for a specific person's life and mourn that person's death;

(c) to dispose reverently of a body.

The Funeral Service witnesses to the fact that death is a reality and a basic part of our common humanity that all people must face. However, as each human life is of individual worth to God, the minister should make each funeral a unique occasion.

i   The following is a suggested order of worship and a collection of appropriate resources and is not a prescribed form to be used in its entirety.

ii   In parts of the order, options are provided; some are appropriate for general use, others for tragic death, and others for the funeral of a child. The minister should exercise discernment in planning the style of the service and in selecting readings, prayers, phrases and words which are most suitable for the person whose life and death are being acknowledged.

iii   This order is arranged in two parts: the first part, The Service in the Church, may be used in church, home or funeral parlour; this part is also used where the whole of the service is conducted in the crematorium chapel or cemetery, except that 10, Prayer, is omitted.

iv   Members of the family or close friends may share in the service, particularly in the Bible readings, a tribute, and Prayers of the People.

v   A minister, priest or pastor of another parish or denomination who is pastorally involved with the family may be invited to participate.

vi   In this order of service, NNN denotes the full name of the deceased person and N the christian name only. In Prayers of the People, N may also denote the parents, the partner and family members of the deceased.

vii Provision is made in this order for the Preaching of the Word, following the reading of Bible passages. The purpose of the Funeral Service is not only to assist people to honour the life and death of a specific person but also to acknowledge God's gift of life and to witness to the faithfulness of God in both life and death. The preference, therefore, is for a brief sermon. Alternatively, the minister or a family member or friend may give a brief tribute, which may be placed prior to the Bible readings; a brief witness to the resurrection of Christ and the christian hope of all who believe in him shall then follow after the readings. Where there is inadequate time to give a brief sermon or a tribute/sermon, or where it seems inappropriate to do so, the minister shall, at the very least, give a brief personal witness to the faith of the church in the risen Lord and his promises.

viii While there is no provision made in this order for the celebration of holy communion, this central act of worship may be included if requested by the family. Because this is the celebration of the community of faith, it should be open to all people who would normally communicate. The appropriate section to use is The Sacrament of the Lord's Supper in The Service of the Lord's Day, which should follow 6, Prayers of the People in the Funeral Service, and precede 7, Commendation.

ix Where the service at the cemetery or crematorium chapel follows a service in a church or funeral parlour and where many people were not present at the earlier service, it may be appropriate for the minister to make a brief introduction before beginning 11, Scripture Sentences.

x During the Committal, the coffin should be lowered to the bottom of the grave or catafalque, or else be removed from sight. This demonstrates the reality of the physical separation that death brings.

xi Physical movement or gesture and the use of symbols, music and silence may speak more powerfully than words. Ministers are encouraged to avoid an over-dependence on words. For example, it may be helpful for the minister to face or touch the coffin during the Commendation or the Committal.

xii   In addition to the Bible readings printed in full in the order, the
       following readings may also be suitable:

OLD TESTAMENT

Job 19:1, 23-27b	I know that my Redeemer lives
Ecclesiastes 3:1-11	For everything there is a season
Isaiah 25:6-9	The Lord God will swallow up death for ever
Wisdom of Solomon 3:1-5, 9	The souls of the righteous are in the hand of God
Ecclesiasticus 44:1-15	Let us now sing the praises of the famous

PSALM

Psalm 27	The Lord is my light and my salvation
Psalm 42	My souls is athirst for the living God
Psalm 118:14-21, 28, 29	The Lord has become my salvation
Psalm 130	Out of the depths have I called you, O Lord

NEW TESTAMENT

Acts 10:34-43	God raised Jesus from death
Romans 5:5-11	God shows his love for us
Romans 6:3-11	We believe that we shall also live with him
Romans 14:7-9	Whether we live or die, we are the Lord's
2 Corinthians 1:3-7	We are comforted by God
2 Corinthians 4:7-15	He who raised the Lord Jesus will raise us
2 Corinthians 4:16 to 5:10	We have a building from God
Philippians 3:8-11, 20, 21	That I may know him and the power of his resurrection
1 Thessalonians 4:13-18	The coming of the Lord
Revelation 7:9-17	God will wipe away every tear from their eyes
Revelation 21:1-7	Behold, I make all things new
Revelation 22:1-7	The Lord God will be their light

GOSPEL

Matthew 5:1-12 — Blessed are those who mourn
Matthew 11:25-30 — Come to me and rest
Luke 23:33, 39-43 — Today you will be with me in paradise
Luke 24:1-9 — The resurrection of Jesus
John 5:19-24 — The Son gives life to whom he will
John 11:17-27 — I am the resurrection and the life

FOR THE FUNERAL OF A CHILD

Isaiah 11:6-9 — A little child shall lead them
Psalm 103:8-18 — As a father cares for his children
1 John 3:1, 2 — Beloved, we are God's children now

The Funeral Service

The Service in the Church

This part is also used where the whole of the service is conducted at the cemetery or crematorium chapel, except that 10, Prayer, is omitted.

1   INTRODUCTION

The minister says:

We are here today
to give thanks to God for the life of NNN,
(*or,* to acknowledge the passing of NNN,)
and to affirm the christian conviction
that while death is the end of human life,
it marks a new beginning in our relationship with God.
We are also here
to share the sorrow of those who mourn,
and to offer them our love and support.

Let us hear the word of Scripture,
that we may all face the future with hope.

Jesus said:
I am the resurrection and the life;
those who believe in me, though they die,
yet shall they live;
and whoever lives and believes in me
shall never die.

John 11:25, 26

and/or

The apostle Peter said:
Blessed be the God and Father of our Lord Jesus Christ!
By his great mercy
we have been born anew to a living hope
through the resurrection of Jesus Christ from the dead.

1 Peter 1:3

2 PRAYERS

The minister says:

Let us pray:

Eternal God, our heavenly Father,
your love for us is everlasting.
You alone can turn the shadow of death
into the brightness of the morning light.
By the power of the Holy Spirit,
come to us in our darkness and distress
with the light and peace of your presence.
Speak to us now through your holy word,
that our faith may be strengthened
and our hope sustained;
through Jesus Christ our Lord.
Amen.

Merciful Father, our Maker and Redeemer,
we confess that we have not always lived
as your grateful children;
we have not loved as Christ loved us.
Father, forgive us
if there have been times when we failed N.
Enable us by your grace
to forgive anything that was hurtful to us.
Lord, have mercy on us;
set us free from our sins,
and grant us healing and wholeness;
through Jesus Christ our Lord.
Amen.

The minister may also use one of the following prayers, or offer free prayer.

Almighty God, source of all wisdom,
you know all our needs.
Have compassion on us,
and in your love grant us
those things for which we are unworthy to ask,
and those things we are too blind to know we need;
for the sake of your Son, Jesus Christ our Lord.
Amen.

Help us, O God,
as we face the mystery of death,
to believe in the communion of saints,
the forgiveness of sins,
and the resurrection to life everlasting;
through Christ our Lord.
Amen

3   HYMN

A hymn of praise or of faith in God may be sung.

4   THE PROMISES OF GOD

A selection may be made from the following Bible readings; a gospel reading shall be included.

The following may be used after the final reading:

This is the word of the Lord.
Thanks be to God.

THE STEADFAST LOVE OF THE LORD NEVER CEASES

17 My soul is bereft of peace,
      I have forgotten what happiness is:

18 so I say, 'Gone is my glory,
      and my expectation from the Lord'.

19 Remember my affliction and my bitterness,
      the wormwood and the gall!

20 My soul continually thinks of it
      and is bowed down within me.

21 But this I call to mind,
      and therefore I have hope:

22 The steadfast love of the Lord never ceases,
      his mercies never come to an end;

23 they are new every morning;
      great is your faithfulness.

24 'The Lord is my portion', says my soul,
      'therefore I will hope in him'.

25 The Lord is good to those who wait for him,
      to the soul that seeks him.

26 It is good that one should wait quietly
      for the salvation of the Lord.

31 For the Lord will not cast off for ever,

32 but, though he cause grief, he will have compassion
      according to the abundance of his steadfast love;

33 for he does not willingly afflict his people
      or grieve his children.

Lamentations 3:17-26, 31-33

THE LORD IS MY SHEPHERD

1 The Lord is my shepherd;
    I shall not be in want.

2 He makes me lie down in green pastures
    and leads me beside still waters.

3 He revives my soul
    and guides me along right pathways for his name's sake.

4 Though I walk through the valley of the shadow of death,
    I shall fear no evil;
      for you are with me;
      your rod and your staff, they comfort me.

5 You spread a table before me
    in the presence of those who trouble me;
      you have anointed my head with oil,
      and my cup is running over.

6 Surely your goodness and mercy shall follow me
    all the days of my life,
      and I will dwell in the house of the Lord for ever.

Psalm 23

LORD, YOU HAVE BEEN OUR REFUGE

1 Lord, you have been our refuge
    from one generation to another.

2 Before the mountains were brought forth,
    or the land and the earth were born,
      from age to age you are God.

⁴ For a thousand years in your sight
are like yesterday when it is past
and like a watch in the night.

⁵ You sweep us away like a dream;
we fade away suddenly like the grass.

⁶ In the morning it is green and flourishes;
in the evening it is dried up and withered.

¹⁰ The span of our life is seventy years,
perhaps in strength even eighty;
yet the sum of them is but labour and sorrow,
for they pass away quickly and we are gone.

¹² So teach us to number our days
that we may apply our hearts to wisdom.

¹⁴ Satisfy us by your loving-kindness in the morning;
so shall we rejoice and be glad all the days of our life.

¹⁵ Make us glad by the measure of the days
that you afflicted us
and the years in which we suffered adversity.

¹⁶ Show your servants your works
and your splendour to their children.

¹⁷ May the graciousness of the Lord our God be upon us;
prosper the work of our hands;
prosper our handiwork.

Psalm 90:1, 2, 4-6, 10, 12, 14-17

I LIFT UP MY EYES TO THE HILLS

1 I lift up my eyes to the hills;
    from where is my help to come?

2 My help comes from the Lord,
    the maker of heaven and earth.

3 He will not let your foot be moved
    and he who watches over you will not fall asleep.

4 Behold, he who keeps watch over Israel
    shall neither slumber nor sleep;

5 The Lord himself watches over you;
    the Lord is your shade at your right hand,

6 So that the sun shall not strike you by day,
    nor the moon by night.

7 The Lord shall preserve you from all evil;
    it is he who shall keep you safe.

8 The Lord shall watch over your going out
  and your coming in,
    from this time forth for evermore.

Psalm 121

LORD, YOU HAVE SEARCHED ME OUT

1 Lord, you have searched me out and known me;
2   you know my sitting down and my rising up;
    you discern my thoughts from afar.

3 You trace my journeys and my resting-places
    and are acquainted with all my ways.

4 Indeed, there is not a word on my lips,
    but you, O Lord, know it altogether.

5   You press upon me behind and before
    and lay your hand upon me.

6   Such knowledge is too wonderful for me;
    it is so high that I cannot attain to it.

7   Where can I go then from your Spirit?
    where can I flee from your presence?

8   If I climb up to heaven, you are there;
    if I make the grave my bed, you are there also.

9   If I take the wings of the morning
    and dwell in the uttermost parts of the sea,

10   Even there your hand will lead me
    and your right hand hold me fast.

11   If I say, 'Surely the darkness will cover me,
    and the light around me turn to night',

12   Darkness is not dark to you;
    the night is as bright as the day;
      darkness and light to you are both alike.

17   How deep I find your thoughts, O God!
    how great is the sum of them!

18   If I were to count them,
    they would be more in number than the sand;
    to count them all,
      my life span would need to be like yours.

Psalm 139:1-12, 17-18

NOTHING WILL BE ABLE TO SEPARATE US FROM THE LOVE OF GOD

[18] I consider that the sufferings of this present time are not worth comparing with the glory that is to be revealed to us.

[28] We know that in everything God works for good with those who love him, who are called according to his purpose.

[31b] If God is for us, who is against us? [32] He who did not spare his own Son but gave him up for us all, will he not also give us all things with him? [33] Who shall bring any charge against God's elect? It is God who justifies; [34] who is to condemn? Is it Christ Jesus, who died, yes, who was raised from the dead, who is at the right hand of God, who indeed intercedes for us?

[35] Who shall separate us from the love of Christ? Shall tribulation, or distress, or persecution, or famine, or nakedness, or peril, or sword?

[37] No, in all these things we are more than conquerors through him who loved us. [38] For I am sure that neither death, nor life, nor angels, nor principalities, nor things present, nor things to come, nor powers, [39] nor height, nor depth, nor anything else in all creation, will be able to separate us from the love of God in Christ Jesus our Lord.

Romans 8:18, 28, 31b-35, 37-39

THANKS BE TO GOD WHO GIVE US THE VICTORY

[19] If in this life we who are in Christ only have hope, we are of all people most to be pitied.

[20] But in fact Christ has been raised from the dead, the first fruits of those who have fallen asleep. [21] For as by a man came death, by a man has come also the resurrection of the dead.

²² For as in Adam all die, so also in Christ shall all be made alive.

²³ But all in their own order: Christ the first fruits, then at his coming those who belong to Christ. ²⁴ Then comes the end, when he delivers the kingdom to God the Father after destroying every rule and every authority and power. ²⁵ For he must reign until he has put all his enemies under his feet. ²⁶ The last enemy to be destroyed is death.

³⁵ But some one will ask, 'How are the dead raised? With what kind of body do they come?' ³⁶ You foolish one! What you sow does not come to life unless it dies. ³⁷ And what you sow is not the body which is to be, but a bare kernel, perhaps of wheat or of some other grain. ³⁸ But God gives it a body as he has chosen, and to each kind of seed its own body.

⁴² So it is with the resurrection of the dead. What is sown is perishable, what is raised is imperishable. ⁴³ It is sown in dishonour, it is raised in glory. It is sown in weakness, it is raised in power. ⁴⁴ It is sown a physical body, it is raised a spiritual body. If there is a physical body, there is also a spiritual body.

⁵⁰ I tell you this, my friends: flesh and blood cannot inherit the kingdom of God, nor does the perishable inherit the imperishable.

⁵³ For this perishable nature must put on the imperishable, and this mortal nature must put on immortality. ⁵⁴ When the perishable puts on the imperishable, and the mortal puts on immortality, then shall come to pass the saying that is written:
    'Death is swallowed up in victory'.
⁵⁵ 'O death, where is thy victory?
    O death, where is thy sting?'
⁵⁶ The sting of death is sin, and the power of sin is the law.
⁵⁷ But thanks be to God, who gives us the victory through our Lord Jesus Christ.

⁵⁸ Therefore, my beloved friends, be steadfast, immovable, always abounding in the work of the Lord, knowing that in the Lord your labour is not in vain.

1 Corinthians 15:19-26, 35-38, 42-44 50, 53-58

THE FATHER FROM WHOM EVERY FAMILY IS NAMED

This may be suitable for the funeral of a child.

¹⁴ I bow my knees before the Father, ¹⁵ from whom every family in heaven and on earth is named, ¹⁶ that according to the riches of his glory he may grant you to be strengthened with might through his Spirit in your inner being, ¹⁷ and that Christ may dwell in your hearts through faith; that you, being rooted and grounded in love, ¹⁸ may have power to comprehend with all the saints what is the breadth and length and height and depth, ¹⁹ and to know the love of Christ which surpasses knowledge, that you may be filled with all the fullness of God.

Ephesians 3:14-19

A LIVING HOPE THROUGH THE RESURRECTION OF CHRIST

³ Blessed be the God and Father of our Lord Jesus Christ! By his great mercy we have been born anew to a living hope through the resurrection of Jesus Christ from the dead, ⁴ and to an inheritance which is imperishable, undefiled, and unfading, kept in heaven for you, ⁵ who by God's power are guarded through faith for a salvation ready to be revealed in the last time.

6 In this you rejoice, though now for a little while you may have to suffer various trials, 7 so that the genuineness of your faith, more precious than gold which though perishable is tested by fire, may redound to praise and glory and honour at the revelation of Jesus Christ.

8 Without having seen him you love him; though you do not now see him you believe in him and rejoice with unutterable and exalted joy. 9 As the outcome of your faith you obtain the salvation of your souls.

1 Peter 1:3-9

JESUS IS THE BREAD OF LIFE

35 Jesus said to them, 'I am the bread of life; no one who comes to me will ever hunger, and no one who believes in me will ever thirst.

36 'But I said to you that you have seen me and yet do not believe. 37 Everyone whom the Father gives me will come to me; and anyone who comes to me I will not cast out.

38 'For I have come down from heaven, not to do my own will, but the will of him who sent me; 39 and this is the will of him who sent me, that I should lose nothing of all that he has given me, but raise it up on the last day.

40 'For this is the will of my Father, that everyone who sees the Son and believes in him should have eternal life; and I will raise up that one at the last day.'

John 6:35-40

I AM THE GOOD SHEPHERD

This may be suitable for the funeral of a child.

[14] 'I am the good shepherd; I know my own and my own know me, [15] as the Father knows me and I know the Father; and I lay down my life for the sheep.

[27] 'My sheep hear my voice, and I know them, and they follow me; [28] and I give them eternal life, and they shall never perish, and no one shall snatch them out of my hand. [29] My Father, who has given them to me, is greater than all, and no one is able to snatch them out of the Father's hand. [30] I and the Father are one.'

John 10:14-15, 27-30

IN MY FATHER'S HOUSE ARE MANY ROOMS

[1] 'Let not your hearts be troubled; believe in God, believe also in me. [2] In my Father's house are many rooms; if it were not so, would I have told you that I go to prepare a place for you? [3] And when I go and prepare a place for you, I will come again and will take you to myself, that where I am you may be also.

[4] 'And you know the way where I am going.' Thomas said to him, 'Lord, we do not know where you are going; how can we know the way?' Jesus said to him, 'I am the way, and the truth, and the life; no one comes to the Father, but by me.

[18] 'I will not leave you desolate; I will come to you. [19] Yet a little while, and the world will see me no more, but you will see me; because I live, you will live also.

[27] 'Peace I leave with you; my peace I give to you; not as the world gives do I give to you. Let not your hearts be troubled, neither let them be afraid.'

John 14:1-6, 18, 19, 27

Other readings are listed in Note xii.

5   PREACHING OF THE WORD

See Note vii

6   PRAYERS OF THE PEOPLE

The minister and/or a lay person may lead the prayers in this section.

The prayers are arranged in the following seven sub-sections:

Praise for the Work of Christ
Thanksgiving for Life in the Church
A: For General Use — Thanksgiving and Intercession
B: In the Case of a Tragic Death — Thanksgiving and Intercession
C: For the Funeral of a Child — Thanksgiving and Intercession
General Intercessions
Alternative Prayers

Praise for the Work of Christ

This or a similar prayer is used on all occasions.

Let us pray:

All glory and honour, thanks and praise,
be to you, eternal God, our Father.
In your great love for the world
you gave your Son to be our Saviour;
to live our life, to know our joy and pain,
and to die our death.
We praise you for raising him from the dead,
and for receiving him at your right hand in glory.
With your church in every generation
we rejoice that he has conquered sin and death for us,
and opened the kingdom of heaven to all believers.

For this assurance of our new life in Christ,
and for the great company of the faithful
whom you have received into your eternal joy,
all praise and thanks be given to you,
our God, for ever and ever.
Amen.

Thanksgiving for Life in the Church

This prayer is used when appropriate.

Gracious God,
we thank you that you received N by baptism
into the family of your church on earth,
and granted him/her the gift of eternal life.
He/she ate the bread of life
and drank from the cup of salvation,
and gave himself/herself in love and service to Christ.

We thank you for . . .
  growth in faith . . .
  spiritual gifts . . .
  offices held and work done in the church . . .

A: For General Use –
Thanksgiving and Intercession

Let us now give thanks for N's life:

Heavenly Father,
we give thanks for the many ways
in which N shared his/her life with us and others.
In strength and in weakness, in achievement and failure,
in the brightness of joy and the darkness of despair,
we remember him/her as one of us.

We thank you for . . .

or

We remember with gratitude . . .

or

We are deeply grateful for . . .

> *early life . . .*
> *home and family . . .*
> *close relationships with family members and friends . . .*
> *commitment to daily work . . .*
> *service to the community . . .*
> *leisure activities . . .*
> *personal qualities . . .*
> *courage in facing sickness and death . . .*
> *those who have cared for N . . .*

Let us pray for those who mourn:

Merciful God,
we pray for all the members of N's family,
(remembering especially N and N and N,)
whose sense of loss is so keen
because their love is so deep.
Even when we are weighed down by grief and loneliness,
may we know that you are upholding us.
Give us the assurance of your constant care,
that we may have courage to meet the days ahead.

B: In the Case of a Tragic Death – Thanksgiving and Intercession

Let us now give thanks for N's life:

Heavenly Father,
we give thanks for the many ways
in which N shared his/her life with us and others.
In strength and in weakness, in achievement and failure,
in the brightness of joy and the darkness of despair,
we remember him/her as one of us.

We thank you for . . .

or

We remember with gratitude . . .

or

We are deeply grateful for . . .

> *early life . . .*
> *home and family . . .*
> *close relationships with family members and friends . . .*
> *commitment to daily work . . .*
> *service to the community . . .*
> *leisure activities . . .*
> *personal qualities . . .*
> *courage in facing sickness and death . . .*
> *those who have cared for N . . .*

Let us pray for those who mourn:

Merciful God,
we pray for all the members of N's family,
(remembering especially N and N and N,)
whose sense of loss is so keen
because their love is so deep.
When we are unable to understand the things that happen,
when we are weighed down by grief and loneliness,
may we know that you are upholding us.
Give us the assurance of your constant care,
that we may have courage to meet the days ahead.

C: For the Funeral of a Child –
Thanksgiving and Intercession

Let us now give thanks for N's life:

Heavenly Father,
your love for all your children is strong and enduring.
You gave N as a blessing to his/her family.

We thank you for . . .

or

We remember with gratitude . . .

or

We are deeply grateful for . . .

> *the way he/she grew and developed . . .*
> *the way in which he/she reached out to others . . .*
> *the way he/she discovered the world around him/her . . .*
> *his/her love of school and friends . . .*
> *his/her courage in suffering . . .*
> *those who have cared for N . . .*

Let us pray for those who mourn:

Merciful God,
we pray for all the members of N's family,
(remembering especially his/her parents N and N,
and his/her brother(s) and sister(s) N and N).
Your Son Jesus Christ took children
into his arms and blessed them.
When we are unable to understand the things that happen,
when we are weighed down by grief and loneliness,
may we know that you are upholding us.
Give us the assurance of your constant care,
that we may have courage to meet the days ahead.

General Intercessions

> One or more of the following prayers may conclude prayers taken
> from sections A or B or C.

Let us pray for N's friends:

We pray for those who were close to N.
May their present sorrow be so transformed by hope,
that they come in time to cherish with true thankfulness
those shared experiences which nothing can ever take away.
Give us grace to face the future with a calm mind,
a strong faith and a loving heart.

Let us pray for those in need:

We pray for our loved ones and friends
who are frail or sick or weary.
May they be conscious of your sustaining presence,
and find joy and peace in believing.
Show your mercy to all who are dying.
May they rest with confidence
in the knowledge that nothing in life or death
can separate them from your love in Christ Jesus our Lord.

Let us pray for one another:

We pray for each other here today.
Increase our trust in you,
and strengthen our love for other people.
May the Holy Spirit lead us all our days,
that we may live in joyful obedience to Jesus Christ.

*The minister and/or lay person may conclude Prayers of the
People with words such as:*

Father,
we offer all these prayers to you
in the name of Jesus Christ our Lord.
Amen.

*The Lord's Prayer may be said here if it is not to be used at the
conclusion of 7, Commendation.*

Alternative Prayers

*If prayers in section A, B or C are not appropriate, a selection from
the following may be made:*

Lord God,
today we lift our hearts in gratitude
for the life of N our friend, now gone from among us;
for all your goodness to him/her during his/her life;
for all that he/she was to those who loved him/her;
and for everything in his/her life
that reflected your goodness and love.
And now we bless you that for him/her
the suffering and difficulties of this life are past,
and he/she is in your loving hands.
Help us to be content to release him/her to you,
his/her Father and our Father.

Assure us that in your keeping he/she will be safe,
your work in him/her complete.

Surround us and all who mourn today
with your continuing compassion.
Do not let grief be without end,
or overwhelm your children,
or turn them against you.
Rather may we travel on more confidently after today,
strengthened by the reality of new life in Christ.
Then, Lord, in your good time,
reunite us with those whom we have loved
in your everlasting kingdom,
where there shall be no more tears and no more partings;
through Jesus Christ our Lord.
Amen.

Eternal God
we praise you for the joy you have given us
through the lives of your departed servants.
We thank you for them and for our memories of them.
We praise you for your goodness and mercy
which followed them all the days of their lives,
and for their faithfulness to the tasks
to which you called them.
We thank you that for them
the tribulations of this world are over and death is past;
and we pray that you will bring us with them
to the joy of your perfect kingdom;
through Jesus Christ our Lord.
Amen.

Eternal God,
before your face the generations rise and pass away.
But your kingdom stands secure and its bounds increase.
We bless you for all your servants departed in the faith;
and especially our dear ones,
who at such a time as this come very near to us.
We love them, and miss them,
and long for the day when we shall meet them again.

O Lord,
help us to follow in the steps of those
who in every age have responded to your call,
ventured their life on your faithfulness,
and lived in loving obedience to your will.
In your mercy, gather us together with them
in the kingdom of your love and joy and peace;
through Jesus Christ our Lord.
Amen.

Lord of our lives,
as we come together with a sense of common loss,
draw us closer to each other in faith and love,
that our fears may be dispelled,
our loneliness eased and our hurt healed.
Help us, O God, to emerge from these days,
looking ahead with courage and hope
and walking by faith in the light of your love;
through Christ our risen Lord.
Amen.

Father of all,
we remember with thanksgiving
your faithful people in every generation,
and those whom we love but see no longer.
Grant them your peace;
may your light shine on them for ever;
and in your loving wisdom and grace
fulfil in them your perfect will;
through Jesus Christ our Lord.
Amen.

Almighty God,
grant that, with all who have believed in you,
we may be united in the full knowledge of your love
and the unclouded vision of your glory;
through Jesus Christ our Lord.
Amen.

> The Lord's Prayer may be said here if it is not to be used at the
> conclusion of 7, Commendation.

7 COMMENDATION

The people stand.

The minister may move to stand by the coffin

The minister says:

Let us now commend N
to the love and mercy of God:

A: For General Use

either

Heavenly Father,
by your creative power you gave us the gift of life,
and in your redeeming love
you have given us new life in Christ.
Rejoicing in your gift of eternal life
and confident in the love you have for all,
we commend N into your merciful keeping.
Amen.

or

O God of eternal light,
we commend N to you.
Now that he/she has passed from this life,
may he/she know the light of your presence.
Give us such faith
that, by day and by night,
in all times and in all places,
we may without fear
entrust those who are dear to us
to your never-failing love,
in this life and in the life to come;
through Jesus Christ our Lord.
Amen.

B: For the Funeral of a Child

Holy God, loving Father,
your Son Jesus Christ loved and welcomed children,
and taught us that your kingdom
belongs to those with child-like trust in you:
we commend N to your care
in the faith of Christ our Lord,
who died and rose again to save us,
and who now lives and reigns with you and the Holy Spirit
in glory for ever.
Amen.

8   THE LORD'S PRAYER

Let us pray to God with confidence
in the words our Saviour gave us:

either

Our Father in heaven,
   hallowed be your name,
   your kingdom come,
   your will be done,
      on earth as in heaven.
Give us today our daily bread.
Forgive us our sins
   as we forgive those who sin against us.
Save us from the time of trial
   and deliver us from evil.

For the kingdom, the power and the glory are yours
   now and for ever. Amen.

or

Our Father, who art in heaven,
    hallowed be thy name,
    thy kingdom come,
    thy will be done
        on earth as it is in heaven.
Give us this day our daily bread.
And forgive us our trespasses,
    as we forgive those who trespass against us.
And lead us not into temptation,
    but deliver us from evil.

For thine is the kingdom, the power and the glory,
    for ever and ever. Amen.

9 HYMN

A hymn may be sung, celebrating God's love for us, our love for God, the victory of Christ or the presence of the Holy Spirit with us.

10 PRAYER

The following prayer shall be omitted if the whole service is being conducted at the cemetery or crematorium chapel.

either

May God in his infinite mercy bring the whole church,
living and departed in Christ,
to a joyful resurrection
in the fulfilment of his eternal kingdom.
Amen.

or

May the God of peace
who brought again from the dead our Lord Jesus,
the great Shepherd of the sheep,
by the blood of the eternal covenant,
equip you with everything good;
that you may do his will,
working in you that which is pleasing in his sight,
through Jesus Christ, to whom be glory for ever and ever.
Amen.

Hebrews 13:20-21

An appropriate Blessing may be added.

The Service at the Cemetery or in the Crematorium Chapel

If the first part of the service has been conducted in another place, it may be appropriate to welcome the people and to identify whose funeral it is.

It may also be helpful to commence this service by reading a psalm or other portion of Scripture.

11 SCRIPTURE SENTENCES

One or more of these Scripture sentences may be read while the coffin is lowered to the bottom of the grave at a burial, or while the coffin is removed from sight at a cremation.

Alternatively, one or more Scripture sentences may be read first; then, a psalm or other reading while the coffin is being removed from sight.

A: For General Use or Tragic Death

Let us hear the promises of God:

The steadfast love of the Lord never ceases,
his mercies never come to an end;
they are new every morning, so great is his faithfulness.

Lamentations 3:22, 23

Thus says the Lord God, the Holy One of Israel:
in quietness and in trust shall be your strength.

Isaiah 30:15

God is our refuge and strength,
a very present help in trouble.

Psalm 46:1

I am sure that neither death, nor life,
nor angels, nor principalities,
nor things present, nor things to come,
nor powers, nor height, nor depth,
nor anything else in all creation,
will be able to separate us from the love of God
in Christ Jesus our Lord.

Romans 8:38, 39

What no eye has seen, nor ear heard,
nor the human heart conceived,
God has prepared for those who love him.

1 Corinthians 2:9

Blessed be the God and Father of our Lord Jesus Christ,
the Father of mercies and God of all comfort,
who comforts us in all our affliction.

2 Corinthians 1:3

Those who are in Christ are a new creation;
the old has passed away,
behold, the new has come.
All this is from God,
who through Christ reconciled us to himself.

2 Corinthians 5:17, 18

Blessed are those who mourn,
for they shall be comforted.

Matthew 5:4

Jesus said:
Come to me, all who labour and are heavy-laden,
and I will give you rest;
for I am gentle and lowly in heart,
and you will find rest for your souls.

Matthew 11:28, 29

God so loved the world that he gave his only Son,
that whoever believes in him should not perish
but have eternal life.

John 3:16

Jesus said:
I am the resurrection and the life;
those who believe in me, though they die,
yet shall they live;
and whoever lives and believes in me shall never die.

John 11:25, 26

B: For the Funeral of a Child

Let us hear the promises of God:

The Lord God will feed his flock like a shepherd;
he will gather the lambs in his arms,
he will carry them close to his heart.

Isaiah 40:11

As a father pities his children,
so the Lord pities those who fear him.
For he knows our frame;
he remembers that we are dust.

Psalm 103:13, 14

Blessed are those who mourn,
for they shall be comforted.

Matthew 5:4

12 COMMITTAL

At a cremation, the minister invites the people to stand.

At a burial, while earth is cast on the coffin, or at a cremation, while the coffin is being removed from sight, the minister says:

We have entrusted N to the hands of God.
We now commit his/her body
to the ground (*or*, to the elements),
(earth to earth) ashes to ashes, dust to dust;
in sure and certain hope of the resurrection to eternal life
through our Lord Jesus Christ,
who died, was buried, and rose again for us.
To God be glory for ever.
Amen.

or

Now that the earthly life of N has come to an end,
we commit his/her body
to be buried (*or*, to be cremated),
confident of the resurrection to eternal life
through our Lord Jesus Christ.
To God be glory for ever.
Amen.

or

We have entrusted N to the hands of God.
We now commit his/her body
to the ground (*or*, to the elements),
(earth to earth), ashes to ashes, dust to dust;
trusting in the infinite mercy of God
and the victory over death of Christ our Lord.
To God be glory for ever.
Amen.

13 AFFIRMATION OF FAITH

One or more of these affirmations may be read.

'Blessed are the dead who die in the Lord henceforth.'
'Blessed indeed', says the Spirit,
'that they may rest from their labours'.

Revelation 14:13

They shall hunger no more,
neither thirst any more;
for the Lamb in the midst of the throne will be their shepherd,
and he will guide them to springs of living water;
and God will wipe away every tear from their eyes.

Revelation 7:16, 17

You, O Christ, are the king of glory,
the eternal Son of the Father.
When you became incarnate to set us free
you humbly accepted the Virgin's womb.
You overcame the sting of death,
and opened the kingdom of heaven to all believers.
You are seated at God's right hand in glory.
We believe that you will come to be our judge.
Come then, Lord, and help your people,
bought with the price of your own blood,
and bring us with your saints
to glory everlasting.

Te Deum Laudamus, Part 2

Save your people, Lord, and bless your inheritance.
Govern and uphold them now and always.
Day by day we bless you.
We praise your name for ever.
Keep us today, Lord, from all sin.
Have mercy on us, Lord, have mercy.
Lord, show us your love and mercy;
for we put our trust in you.
In you, Lord, is our hope:
and we shall never hope in vain.

Versicles and Responses after the Te Deum Laudamus

14 PRAYERS

One or more of these prayers may be used, or the minister may
offer free prayer.

Eternal Father, God of all consolation,
be our refuge and strength in sorrow.
As your Son, our Lord Jesus Christ,
by dying for us conquered death,
and by rising again restored us to life,
enable us to go forward in faith to meet him,
that, when our life on earth has ended,
we may be united with all who love him
in your heavenly kingdom,
where every tear will be wiped away;
through Jesus Christ our Lord.
Amen.

Almighty God,
Father of all mercies and giver of all comfort;
look graciously, we pray, on those who mourn,
that, casting all their care on you,
they may know the consolation of your love;
through Jesus Christ our Lord.
Amen.

O God,
whose mercies cannot be numbered;
let the Holy Spirit lead us
with the company of the whole church
in holiness and righteousness;
in the confidence of a loving faith;
and in the strength of a sure hope.
May we live in favour with you, most gracious Lord,
and in perfect love for all;
through Jesus Christ our Lord.
Amen.

O Lord,
support us by your grace
through all the hours of life's day;
until the shadows lengthen,
the busy world is hushed,
the fever of life is over,
and the evening comes.
Then, Lord, in your mercy,
grant us a safe lodging,
a holy rest,
and peace at the last;
through Christ our Lord.
Amen.

15 BLESSING

If not previously used, one of the prayers in 10 may be used here.

either

The grace of the Lord Jesus Christ
and the love of God
and the fellowship of the Holy Spirit
be with you all.
Amen.

2 Corinthians 13:14

or

The peace of God which passes all understanding
keep your hearts and minds in the knowledge and love of God,
and of his Son, Jesus Christ our Lord.

And the blessing of God almighty,
the Father, the Son and the Holy Spirit,
be upon you and remain with you always.
Amen.

Based on Philippians 4:7

Prayers for Other Pastoral Occasions

The following resources are intended for use in a short devotional
service which would normally include appropriate Bible readings
and free prayer.

Prayers after the Birth of a Still-born Child or the Death of a Newly-born Child

PRAYERS WITH THE PARENTS

Merciful God,
you strengthen us by your power and wisdom.
Be gracious to N and N in their grief,
and surround them with your unfailing love;
that they may not be overwhelmed by their loss,
but have confidence in your goodness,
and courage to meet the days to come;
through Jesus Christ our Lord.
Amen.

Gracious Father,
in darkness and in light,
in trouble and in joy,
help us to trust your love,
to serve your purpose,
and to look forward in hope
to your heavenly kingdom;
through Jesus Christ our Lord.
Amen.

A PRAYER OF COMMENDATION

Let us commend this child
to the love of God our Father:

Heavenly Father,
your Son Jesus Christ took children
into his arms and blessed them.
We entrust this child (*or*, N) to your care
in the faith of Christ our Lord,
who died and rose again to save us,
and who now lives and reigns with you
and the Holy Spirit in glory for ever.
Amen.

Prayers for the Burial or Scattering of Ashes

FOR THE BURIAL OF ASHES
OR SCATTERING ON LAND

God our Father,
in loving care your hand has created us,
and as the potter fashions the clay
you have made us in the image of your Son.
Through the Holy Spirit
you have breathed into us the gift of life,
and in the sharing of love
you have enriched our knowledge of you
and of each other.
We claim your love today
as we commit these remains of N,
earth to earth, ashes to ashes, dust to dust,
in sure and certain hope of the resurrection to eternal life
through Jesus Christ our Lord.
Amen.

Glory to the Father,
and to the Son,
and to the Holy Spirit:
as it was in the beginning,
is now,
and will be for ever.
Amen.

or

Dear God,
the earthly life of N is ended.
With gratitude for the life we shared with him/her,
and with confidence in your enduring love,
we commit these remains to this resting place;
earth to earth, ashes to ashes, dust to dust,
knowing that all things work together for good
for those who love you;
through Jesus Christ our Lord.
Amen.

Glory to the Father,
and to the Son,
and to the Holy Spirit:
as it was in the beginning,
is now,
and will be for ever.
Amen.

FOR THE SCATTERING OF ASHES ON WATER

Almighty Father,
at the beginning of time
your Spirit moved over the face of the waters,
bringing order out of chaos.
In the fullness of time
you sent your Son as Saviour,
giving your people a spring of water
welling up to eternal life.
Therefore, in confidence and faith in you,
we commit to the water
these remains of our loved one N,
trusting in the wideness of your mercy
revealed in Jesus Christ our Lord.
Amen.

Glory to the Father,
and to the Son,
and to the Holy Spirit:
as it was in the beginning,
is now,
and will be for ever.
Amen.

On the Anniversary of a Death

PRAYERS

O God,
today brings us sad memories.
Sometimes we can forget,
yet deep down the pain remains,
for you have given us tender hearts.
Even a glimpse of a place or a photograph,
the sound of a tune or a word,
and especially a day like this can make us feel again
that emptiness which nothing on earth can fill.
May we not be overcome by our sorrow
as those who have no hope.
Help us to face life with steadfast faith,
remembering that the one we loved
has been added to that unseen cloud of witnesses
who constantly surround us.
Hasten the time when the memories which distress us
will be the very things
that enrich our life and deepen our love;
through Jesus Christ our Lord.
Amen.

Loving God,
today our minds are filled with memories of N.
So much of the life we shared together
has come flooding back,
and the pain of separation is reawakened.
At a time when the feeling of loss is so acute,
may our sense of your loving care be very strong.

We thank you for all the friends
that we enjoyed together with N,
and for their continuing love and care.
We thank you that the shared experiences
that grew out of our life with N
are still enriching our relationships with others.

God our Father,
as we remember today
how much our life was made radiant
by the love between human beings,
a love that was nourished by our love for you,
help us to offer that same love to other people.
Graciously meet our many needs,
according to your glorious riches in Christ Jesus;
and to you, our God, be glory for ever.
Amen.

The Ordering of the Church

Ordination
of a Minister of the Word

NOTES

i   Ordination of a minister of the Word is an act of the presbytery which has pastoral responsibility for the ordinand, or, if the ordinand is to minister within another presbytery, the presbytery having pastoral responsibility may arrange for that other presbytery to ordain. (Regulation 2.3.1(c))

ii   The service is conducted at a time and place determined by the presbytery and in the presence of a congregation, normally one which has had, or will have a significant association with the ordinand. (Regulation 2.3.3)

iii   Before the service commences the ordinand, with members of his/her family, if appropriate, may be escorted into the church by the secretary of presbytery and sit in a front pew or other convenient place.

iv   The chairperson of the presbytery, or another of its members appointed by the presbytery, presides at The Service of Ordination and shall ask the questions of the ordinand, offer the ordination prayer and make the Declaration of Ordination. (Regulation 2.3.4)

v   Other people may be invited by the presbytery to lead parts of The Gathering of the People of God and The Service of the Word. The presbytery determines who presides at The Sacrament of the Lord's Supper. Normally the chairperson, if a minister of the Word, presides. The presbytery also determines whether the newly-ordained minister shall take part in the service following the ordination.

vi   The Preaching of the Word should be an exposition of one or more of the Bible readings and should affirm the dignity and importance of the office of the ministry of the Word. The sermon may also include an exhortation to the people to share in the one ministry of Christ.

vii   Normally The Charge is delivered by the chairperson. However, so that ordination may be seen as the action of Christ through his whole church, as well as through the presbytery in particular, it may be appropriate for another person such as the moderator of the synod, a past chairperson of presbytery or a member of the theological faculty to give The Charge (see the appendix to this order)

viii The 'narration of steps' presented by the secretary of presbytery is a brief account of the steps that have led to the ordination, i.e. the ordinand's reception as a candidate and completion of educational and other requirements of the Ministerial Education Council, the presbytery's belief in the suitability of the character and abilities of the ordinand for the ministry of the Word, and the presbytery's decision to ordain. The minute of presbytery recording this decision should be quoted.

ix The ordinand's statement to the presbytery and congregation is a brief statement of faith and affirmation of his/her sense of calling to the ministry. Other matters such as thanks to family and church members are more appropriately expressed at a social gathering after the service.

x The questions to the ordinand (14) and the ordination prayer (15) are those revised by the Uniting Church in Australia Fourth Assembly (May 1985).

xi The presbytery appoints those of its members who are to take part in the laying on of hands. There shall be at least two ministers of the Word and two lay persons. (Regulation 2.3.4) In special circumstances, members of other presbyteries may also be invited to participate in this act.

xii If liturgical colours are used, the colour for a Service of Ordination is red. If a minister's stole is presented to the ordinand, it should be red. However, if the ordinand does not intend to use a set of liturgical stoles, it may be appropriate to make the presentation of a Uniting Church blue scarf. It is appropriate for the chairperson of presbytery to wear a scarf of office if he/she is wearing liturgical dress.

xiii If the ordination takes place in the parish in which the ordinand is to minister, an act of induction may follow the ordination.

xiv The presbytery determines the use of the offering money. It is recommended that this be for ministerial training or for the work of the presbytery.

xv   The following Bible readings may be appropriate for both a Service of Ordination and a Service of Induction:

OLD TESTAMENT

Exodus 33:12-17	My presence will go with you
Numbers 11:16, 17, 24, 25	Bearing the burden of the people
Isaiah 6:1-8	Here am I! Send me
Isaiah 43:8-13	You are my witnesses
Isaiah 52:7-10	Your God reigns
Isaiah 55:6-11	My word shall not return to me empty
Isaiah 61:1-3	The Spirit of the Lord God is upon me
Jeremiah 1:4-10	Before you were born I consecrated you
Jeremiah 31:31-34	A new covenant
Ezekiel 33:1-9	The watchman's duty

PSALM

Psalm 23	The Lord is my shepherd
Psalm 84:1-7	How dear to me is your dwelling
Psalm 96	Worship the Lord in the beauty of holiness
Psalm 100	We are his people and the sheep of his pasture

NEW TESTAMENT

Acts 20:28-35	Guardian of the flock
Romans 10:9-17	Those who preach good news
Romans 12:1-13	Use the gifts God has given
1 Corinthians 1:18-31	We preach Christ crucified
1 Corinthians 3:10-17	No other foundation but Christ
1 Corinthians 12:4-13	Varieties of gifts
2 Corinthians 4:1, 2, 5-7	We preach Jesus Christ as Lord
2 Corinthians 5:14-20	Ambassadors for Christ
Ephesians 4:1-6, 11-13	The calling to which you have been called
Ephesians 4:7-16	The gifts of the ascended Christ to his church
Hebrews 12:1-6, 12-14	Jesus, the pioneer and perfecter of our faith
1 Peter 4:7-11	Good stewards of God's varied grace
1 Peter 5:1-4	Tend the flock of God

GOSPEL

Matthew 9:35-38	The Lord of the harvest
Matthew 10:1-7	The call of the Twelve
Matthew 10:24-33	Everyone who acknowledges me
Matthew 18:15-20	Where two or three are gathered in my name
Matthew 28:16-20	Make disciples of all nations
Mark 10:35-45	Whoever would be great among you
Luke 10:1-12	The Lord of the harvest
Luke 12:32-40	Vigilant servants
Luke 22:14-30	I am among you as one who serves
John 10:11-18	The good shepherd
John 12:20-26	Sir, we wish to see Jesus
John 13:12-20	I have given you an example
John 14:25-31	The Holy Spirit will teach you all things
John 15:9-17	I have called you friends
John 20:19-23	The commission to declare God's forgiveness
John 21:15-19	Feed my sheep

Ordination
of a Minister of the Word

The Gathering of the People of God

The people stand as those who are leading the worship enter the church.

1 HYMN

2 WELCOME AND GREETING

The chairperson of presbytery says:

The Presbytery of . . .
has resolved to ordain NNN
to the ministry of the Word and sacraments
in the church of our Lord Jesus Christ.

I welcome you all to this joyful occasion,
and greet you in the name of God:

The grace of the Lord Jesus Christ
and the love of God
and the fellowship of the Holy Spirit
be with you all.
And also with you.

2 Corinthians 13:14

3 SCRIPTURE SENTENCES

The chairperson may say appropriate words of Scripture.
This may be in responsive form with the people.

4 PRAYERS

These or other appropriate prayers are offered:

Let us adore God:

God our Father,
we worship you in wonder and in love.
Our minds cannot contain you,
nor our words express you;
yet in Christ we see your glory,
hear your word of truth
and know your forgiving love.

Father, Son and Holy Spirit, gracious Trinity,
we bless and adore you.
Accept our offering of praise and thanksgiving
which we bring in the name of Jesus Christ
our Saviour and Lord,
to whom be glory for ever and ever.
Amen.

Let us confess our sin:

**Loving God, Lord of the church,
we confess that we have sinned against you
in thought, word and deed.
We have not loved you with all our heart
or served you with all our strength.
We have been blind to the vision of a renewed world
and deaf to your call to discipleship.
We have been indifferent to the suffering of others
and unwilling to forgive one another.
In your mercy, Lord,
pardon and restore us,
that together in the one ministry of Christ
we may serve you with joy
all the days of our life. Amen.**

The saying is sure and worthy of full acceptance,
that Christ Jesus came into the world to save sinners.

1 Timothy 1:15

Hear then Christ's word of grace to us:
Your sins are forgiven.
Thanks be to God.

Almighty God, Lord of the world,
we bless you for calling us
into the community of your universal church.
We praise you that in every generation
you have given ordained ministers to your church
that your people may be nourished in faith
and equipped for service.
We pray that through the Word and sacraments
your church may be renewed
and strengthened to do your will.
We ask this through Christ our Lord.
Amen.

The Service of the Word

If only two Bible readings are used, an Old Testament or epistle reading and a gospel reading shall be read.

If a psalm is used, it may be printed in the order of service, to be said or sung by the people.

5   FIRST READING

6   PSALM

7   SECOND READING

8   GOSPEL

The following may be used after this final reading:

This is the word of the Lord.
Thanks be to God.

9   HYMN OR ANTHEM

10   PREACHING OF THE WORD

11 NICENE CREED

We believe in one God,
  the Father, the Almighty,
  maker of heaven and earth,
  of all that is, seen and unseen.

We believe in one Lord, Jesus Christ,
  the only Son of God,
  eternally begotten of the Father,
  God from God, Light from Light,
  true God from true God,
  begotten, not made,
  of one Being with the Father;
  through him all things were made.
  For us and for our salvation
    he came down from heaven,
    was incarnate by the Holy Spirit of the Virgin Mary
    and became truly human.
    For our sake he was crucified under Pontius Pilate;
    he suffered death and was buried.
    On the third day he rose again
    in accordance with the Scriptures;
    he ascended into heaven
    and is seated at the right hand of the Father.
    He will come again in glory
      to judge the living and the dead,
    and his kingdom will have no end.

We believe in the Holy Spirit, the Lord, the giver of life,
  who proceeds from the Father,
who with the Father and the Son
     is worshipped and glorified,
who has spoken through the prophets.
We believe in one holy catholic and apostolic Church.
We acknowledge one baptism for the forgiveness of sins.
We look for the resurrection of the dead,
     and the life of the world to come. Amen.

> The people sit.

The Service of Ordination

12 PRESENTATION OF THE ORDINAND

> The secretary of presbytery brings the ordinand forward to stand
> before the chairperson, and says:

N, I present NNN
for ordination as a minister of the Word.

> The secretary gives a brief 'narration of steps'.

> The chairperson then asks the ordinand:

N, are you willing to be ordained
as a minister of the Word?

I am.

> The ordinand may make a brief statement concerning his/her faith
> and call to ministry.

13 THE CHARGE

See Note vii and the Appendix to this order.

Another appropriate place for The Charge is before 18, The Peace.

14 THE VOWS

The ordinand stands.

The chairperson says:

NN,
in the name of Jesus Christ, the only Head of the church,
we are here to ordain you as a minister of the Word
by prayer and the laying on of hands.

In this ordination,
the Uniting Church in Australia acts and speaks
within the one holy catholic and apostolic Church.
We believe that God in Christ acts and speaks
through all that the church does in obedience to his will.
We declare that God gives you grace and authority
for this ministry.

Therefore, that we may know
that you desire to receive this ministry of Christ
through the gift of the Holy Spirit,
we ask you these questions:

Do you confess anew Jesus Christ as Lord?

I do so confess.

Do you believe that you are truly called
by God and the church
to the office and work of a minister of the Word?

I do so believe.

Do you receive the witness to Christ
in the holy Scriptures of the Old and New Testaments;
and do you undertake to preach from these,
proclaiming Christ as Saviour of the world?

I do.

Do you receive baptism and the eucharist,
instituted by our Lord as signs and seals of the gospel;
and do you resolve to celebrate these sacraments
with the people of God?

I do.

Do you accept the Apostles' and Nicene Creeds
as safeguarding and witnessing to the faith
of the holy catholic Church;
and do you intend to use them in worship and instruction?

I do.

Do you adhere to the Basis of Union
of the Uniting Church in Australia;
and do you submit yourself to the church's discipline?

I do.

Do you commit yourself to the study
of the confessional documents of the church
as enjoined in the Basis of Union?

I do.

Relying on the power of the Holy Spirit,
will you be diligent in the study of the Bible;
will you seek to live a holy and disciplined life;
will you be faithful in prayer?

With God's help, I will.

Will you endeavour to be a faithful pastor of God's people;
will you equip them for their ministry,
and work with them in building up the body of Christ?

With God's help, I will.

Will you strive for peace and unity
among all christian people,
and especially among those whom you serve?

With God's help, I will.

May the One
who has given you the will to do these things,
give you the grace to perform them;
that the work which God has begun in you
may be brought to fulfilment.

The people say:

Faithful is God,
who has called you and who will not fail you.

15 THE ORDINATION

The chairperson addresses the people:

Beloved in Christ,
let us pray in silence for N,
before we ordain and send him/her forth to the work
for which we believe he/she has been called
by the Holy Spirit.

Let us pray.

Holy God,
you have promised to hear the prayers
of those who pray in the name of Christ.
Grant that what we have asked in faith
may be granted according to your will;
through Jesus Christ our Lord.
Amen.

We praise you, eternal God,
because in your infinite love and goodness
you have given us your only Son Jesus Christ
to be the Saviour of the world,
the Shepherd of our souls and the Head of your church.

We praise you because our risen and ascended Lord
has poured forth his gifts abundantly;
and has formed throughout the world
a holy people for your possession,
to participate in his ministry
and to fulfil your gracious purposes.

Now we give you thanks that you have called N,
whom we ordain in your name,
to be a minister of the Word in your church.
And we pray that the HolySpirit will endow him/her
with grace and power to fulfil this calling,
so that your people may be strengthened
and your holy name be glorified for ever;
through Jesus Christ our Lord.
Amen.

Hands are laid on the ordinand's head and the following words are
said by the chairperson.

If there is more than one ordinand, these words are said for each
one, hands having been laid on that ordinand's head.

N, servant of Christ, receive the Holy Spirit
for the office and work of a minister of the Word,
now committed to you by the laying on of our hands;
that you may faithfully preach the gospel,
administer the sacraments,
and exercise pastoral care;
in the name of the Father, and of the Son,
and of the Holy Spirit.

The people respond:

Amen.

The Aaronic Blessing may be said or sung by the people
(*Australian Hymn Book, 572*), or said by the chairperson.

The Lord bless you and keep you;
the Lord make his face to shine upon you,
and be gracious unto you;
the Lord lift up his countenance upon you,
and give you peace.

Numbers 6:24-26

Alternatively, the chairperson may offer this ascription of glory:

Now to him who is able to keep you from falling
and to present you without blemish
before the presence of his glory with rejoicing,
to the only God,
our Saviour through Jesus Christ our Lord,
be glory, majesty, dominion, and authority,
before all time and now and for ever. Amen.

Jude 24, 25

16 DECLARATION OF ORDINATION

The newly-ordained minister stands and faces the people.

The chairperson declares:

In the name of our Lord Jesus Christ,
the only King and Head of the church,
and by the authority of the Presbytery of . . . ,
we declare that NNN
is now a minister of the Word
in the church of God

The people may applaud.

This may be followed by the singing of a Doxology, e.g. *Australian Hymn Book, 573-577.*

The people sit.

17 PRESENTATION OF THE BIBLE

N, receive this Bible
as a sign of the authority given you
to preach the Word of God
and to administer the holy sacraments.
Keep the trust committed to you
as a minister of Christ.

A ministerial stole may be presented.

THE CHARGE

If not included at 13.

18 THE PEACE

The chairperson shall invite the members of the presbytery to come forward and give the newly-ordained minister the right hand of fellowship.

The people stand.

The newly-ordained minister gives the greeting of peace:

The peace of the Lord be always with you.
And also with you.

A sign of peace is given by the minister and exchanged among the people.

The people sit.

19 OFFERING

20 PRAYERS OF THE PEOPLE

Intercessions may include:

The minister and his/her family
The parish is which the minister will serve
The life and mission of the Uniting Church in Australia
    and of the church universal

The Sacrament of the Lord's Supper

21 HYMN

22 GREAT PRAYER OF THANKSGIVING

See Note v.

The following seasonal addition shall be included in the Great
Prayer of Thanksgiving:

We praise you, O God,
for the gift of the Holy Spirit,
for the church he brought to birth,
for the power of Word and sacrament,
and for those whom you have called
to minister within your church.

23 BREAKING OF THE BREAD

24 HOLY COMMUNION

25 PRAYER AFTER COMMUNION

The Sending Forth of the People of God

26 HYMN

27 DISMISSAL AND BLESSING

The chairperson says:

Go forth into the world in peace;
be of good courage;
hold fast that which is good;
render to no one evil for evil;
strengthen the faint-hearted;
support the weak;
help the afflicted;
honour all people;
love and serve the Lord,
rejoicing in the power of the Holy Spirit.

And the blessing of God almighty,
the Father, the Son and the Holy Spirit,
be upon you and remain with you always.
Amen.

APPENDIX

THE CHARGE

The purpose of The Charge is to remind the ordinand of the dignity and importance of the office to which he/she is called, and to exhort him/her to holiness of life and faithful discipleship.

The following is modelled on the pattern that has come down to us in the churches of the Reformed tradition. It contains those things which appropriately may be included in a charge, but it is not intended that The Charge should always be given in this form.

My brother/sister in the Lord,
in the Bible readings and the preaching of the Word we have
been reminded of the dignity and importance of the office to
which you are called. In the name of our Lord Jesus Christ, we
exhort you to remember that the church sets you apart to be a
messenger of good tidings, a steward of sacred mysteries and a
guardian of the Lord's family. Take up this office with humility
of spirit and gratitude of heart, and always have printed in your
mind how great a treasure is committed to your care.

We exhort you to be a faithful ambassador of Christ, and to
remember that you have a duty to save souls by proclaiming
that Jesus is Saviour and Lord. In all your associations with
people who have not as yet come to faith, you will respect their
opinions, honour all that is worthy in their lives, and love them
as God's children. But you will remember that they are Christ's
sheep who are scattered abroad, the sheep for whom he shed his
blood, and by your faithful discipleship and christian grace you
will seek to bring them safely home to the fold of God's love.

We exhort you to take good care of the people committed to
your charge in the congregations which you will serve. The holy
catholic Church which you love is the body of Christ. And if it
should come about that any member of his body is hurt as a
result of your negligence, you know how much it will grieve the
Lord Jesus. Accordingly, you will recall constantly the holy
purpose of your ministry to the people of God, and you will
continue your work, your care and diligence, until you bring
them to the fullness of the knowledge of God and to maturity
of faith in Christ.

We are confident that you have considered these things already,
and that you have decided, by God's grace, to devote yourself
completely to this ministry for the rest of your life. Because your
office is of such excellence and such difficulty, you will need to
call upon all the gifts and graces that God offers you.

We exhort you to be a faithful student of the holy Scriptures; you cannot perform the difficult task of leading people to salvation without God's teaching and guidance, so you must read and study the Bible well. The Word of God not only will control your teaching and inspire your exhortation of God's people; it also will nourish your own mind and sustain your own spirit, so that you may grow in your ministry.

We exhort you to be constant in prayer to God our Father, by the mediation of our Saviour Jesus Christ, asking for the daily assistance of the Holy Spirit. Pray for God's world and its peoples; pray for the holy catholic Church, and especially for those congregations committed to your care; pray for your family and loved ones; pray for yourself, that your personal life may be a godly example for the people to follow, and that you may be saved from being preoccupied by the shallow opinions and false values of this world.

This ministry will make great demands on you; but you will not be alone, nor will you fulfil it in your strength alone. God will give you chosen people to share your life and ministry; you will be surrounded with the love and encouragement of God's faithful people; most of all, God gives you the Holy Spirit to be with you for ever.

And so we charge you: love God with all your heart and soul and mind and strength; proclaim that Jesus Christ is Saviour and Lord; rely on the Holy Spirit to stir up the gifts and graces within you. May you faithfully fulfil your ministry, and at the last may you receive the unfading crown of glory, and come, with all God's people, to the joy of our promised inheritance.

> If The Charge is placed before 18, The Peace, the one who has given the Charge may be the first person to give the newly-ordained minister the right hand of fellowship and/or a sign of peace.

Recognition of a Minister
from Another Denomination

NOTES

i   When a minister of the Word from another denomination is accepted
    by a synod of the Uniting Church in Australia, this may be recognised
    in one of two ways:

    (a) If the minister to be recognised has been associated with a presbytery
    of the Uniting Church in Australia, that presbytery may arrange a
    Service of Recognition to welcome him/her into the Uniting Church.
    Subsequently the minister will be inducted into a settlement by that or
    another presbytery.

    The presbytery determines the form of service which is to include The
    Service of Recognition.

    After the Declaration and Welcome, the chairperson of presbytery shall
    invite the members of presbytery to come forward and give the newly-
    recognised minister the right hand of fellowship. The people standing,
    the newly-recognised minister shall then give the greeting of peace.

    Other people may be invited by the presbytery to lead parts of the
    worship. Holy communion may be celebrated at a Service of
    Recognition. The presbytery determines who presides at The
    Sacrament of the Lord's Supper. Normally the chairperson, if a minister
    of the Word, presides. The presbytery also determines whether the
    newly-recognised minister shall take a part in the service following the
    recognition.

    (b) The presbytery within whose bounds the minister to be recognised
    is to take up a settlement may arrange a Service of Recognition and
    Induction. The Service of Recognition is placed immediately before
    The Service of Induction.

    In 9 of the Induction service, Questions to the Minister, the third
    paragraph becomes:
    >   In view of this solemn trust,
    >   we ask you to show that you desire, by God's grace,
    >   to continue your ministry in this parish.

    The following question is omitted from Questions to the Minister:
    >   Do you confess anew Jesus Christ as Lord?

ii Nothing should be said or done in The Service of Recognition which
    may give the impression of reordination. In particular, the laying on of
    hands must be avoided.

Recognition of a Minister from Another Denomination

The Service of Recognition

Following The Service of the Word, the chairperson of presbytery addresses the minister to be recognised:

NN,
the Synod of . . .
has resolved to accept you as a minister of the Word
in the Uniting Church in Australia.

We are here to affirm and celebrate
your admission to the Uniting Church,
and to recognise you as a minister of the Word
in this church.

You have already been ordained to the office and work
of a minister of the Word and sacraments
in the church of Jesus Christ.

Therefore, that we may know
that you desire, by God's grace, to continue your ministry
within the Uniting Church in Australia,
we ask you these questions:

Do you confess anew Jesus Christ as Lord?

I do so confess.

Do you believe that you are truly called
by God and the church
to the office and work of a minister of the Word?

I do so believe.

Do you adhere to the Basis of Union
of the Uniting Church in Australia;
and do you submit yourself to the church's discipline?

I do.

Do you commit yourself to the study
of the confessional documents of the church
as enjoined in the Basis of Union?

I do.

PRAYER

The people stand.

The minister kneels.

The chairperson of presbytery offers this prayer:

We praise you, eternal God,
because in your infinite goodness
you have given us your only Son Jesus Christ
to be the Saviour of the world,
the Shepherd of our souls and the Head of your church.

We praise you because our risen and ascended Lord
has poured forth his gifts abundantly;
and has formed throughout the world
a holy people for your possession,
to participate in his ministry
and to fulfil your gracious purposes.

We give you thanks that you have called N
to be a minister of the Word in your church.
And we pray that the Holy Spirit will endow him/her
with grace and power to fulfil this calling,
so that your people may be strengthened
and your holy name be glorified for ever;
through Jesus Christ our Lord.
Amen.

DECLARATION AND WELCOME

The minister stands and faces the people.

The chairperson declares:

In the name of our Lord Jesus Christ,
the only King and Head of the church,
and by the authority of the Synod of . . .
and the Presbytery of . . .,
we now declare that NNN
is a minister of the Word
within the Uniting Church in Australia.

We welcome you as a colleague and friend
and offer you our love and our prayers
as you begin your ministry among us.

The people may applaud.

This may be followed by the singing of a Doxology, e.g. *Australian Hymn Book, 573-577.*

The people sit.

Induction of a Minister of the Word

NOTES

i   The induction of a minister of the Word into a parish settlement is an act of the presbytery which has oversight of the parish. (Regulation 2.4.24(a))

ii   The service is conducted at a time and place determined by the presbytery, normally in one of the churches of the parish, and in the presence of members of the presbytery and of the congregations of the parish.

iii   The induction of a minister of the Word into a settlement or appointment other than a parish settlement is performed by a presbytery, a synod or the Assembly, as appropriate, and this order of service should be adapted to suit the circumstances. (Regulation 2.4.24(b) and (c))

iv   For the induction of a minister of the Word of the Uniting Church in Australia into an ecumenical appointment or a united/joint parish, representatives of other denominations may be associated with the presbytery. However, the act of induction should be performed by the chairperson of presbytery or other appropriate officer of the Uniting Church.

v   The chairperson of presbytery, or another of its members appointed by the presbytery, presides at the induction service and shall put the questions to the minister to be inducted, offer the Induction Prayer and make the Declaration of Induction.

vi   Members of the presbytery or parish may be invited by the presbytery to lead other parts of the service.

vii   The chairperson should consult with the minister to be inducted in the planning of the service.

viii   Before the service commences the minister to be inducted, with members of his/her family, if appropriate, may be escorted into the church by the secretary of the parish council and sit in a front pew or other convenient place.

ix   If clergy or representatives of other churches are to be present, they should be asked prior to the service if they are willing to participate in the way suggested in 15.

x   If liturgical colours are used, the colour for a service of induction is red. Alternatively, the minister being inducted and others may wear the Uniting Church blue scarf. It is appropriate for the chairperson of presbytery to wear a scarf of office if he/she is wearing liturgical dress.

xi   A local or parish choir or other musical group may contribute to the service both by leading in the singing of the hymns and by an anthem. Depending on the content of the anthem, it may be sung after 4 or before 19.

xii   The presbytery determines the use of the offering money. It is recommended that this be for ministerial training or for the work of the presbytery.

xiii   The sacrament of the Lord's supper may be included in an induction service. However, see notes on this in *A Leaders' Guide to Uniting in Worship*.

xiv   Bible readings appropriate both for an ordination service and an induction service are set out in Note xv of the Ordination of a Minister of the Word.

Induction of a Minister of the Word

The Gathering of the People of God

The people stand as those who are leading the worship enter the church.

1 WELCOME AND GREETING

The chairperson of presbytery says:

The Presbytery of . . .
has resolved to induct NNN
to the ministry of the Word and sacraments
in the *Parish of* . . .

N, we rejoice that God has called you
by the voice of the church
to serve Jesus Christ in this *parish* and presbytery.

I welcome you all to this joyful occasion,
and greet you in the name of God:

The grace of the Lord Jesus Christ
and the love of God
and the fellowship of the Holy Spirit
be with you all.
And also with you.

2 Corinthians 13:14

2 HYMN OF PRAISE

3 PRAYERS

These or other appropriate prayers are offered.

Let us adore God:

God our Father,
we worship you in wonder and in love.
Our minds cannot contain you,
nor our words express you;
yet in Christ we see your glory,
hear your word of truth
and know your forgiving love.

Father, Son and Holy Spirit, gracious Trinity,
we bless and adore you.
Accept our offering of praise and thanksgiving
which we bring in the name of Jesus Christ
our Saviour and Lord,
to whom be glory for ever and ever.
Amen.

Let us confess our sin:

**Loving God, Lord of the church,
we confess that we have sinned against you
in thought, word and deed.
We have not loved you with all our heart
or served you with all our strength.
We have been blind to the vision of a renewed world
and deaf to your call to discipleship.
We have been indifferent to the suffering of others
and unwilling to forgive one another.**

In your mercy, Lord,
pardon and restore us,
that together in the one ministry of Christ
we may serve you with joy
all the days of our life. Amen.

The saying is sure and worthy of full acceptance,
that Christ Jesus came into the world to save sinners.

1 Timothy 1:15

Hear then Christ's word of grace to us:
Your sins are forgiven.
Thanks be to God.

Father,
we thank you that by the Holy Spirit
you have guided *this parish* to seek a minister,
and your servant N to respond.
Inspire and sustain your people
in the worship and service of *this parish*,
that their prayer and work may begin in you,
and by you be completed;
through Jesus Christ our Lord.
Amen.

The Service of the Word

4   FIRST READING

ANTHEM

If not sung before 19.

5 GOSPEL

The following may be used after this final reading:

This is the word of the Lord.
Thanks be to God.

APOSTLES' CREED

The people stand.

**I believe in God, the Father almighty,
creator of heaven and earth.**

**I believe in Jesus Christ, God's only Son, our Lord,
who was conceived by the Holy Spirit,
born of the Virgin Mary,
suffered under Pontius Pilate,
was crucified, died, and was buried;
he descended to the dead.
On the third day he rose again;
he ascended into heaven,
he is seated at the right hand of the Father,
and he will come to judge the living and the dead.**

**I believe in the Holy Spirit,
the holy catholic Church,
the communion of saints,
the forgiveness of sins,
the resurrection of the body,
and the life everlasting. Amen.**

The people sit.

7 PREACHING OF THE WORD

8 HYMN

The Service of Induction

9 QUESTIONS TO THE MINISTER

The chairperson addresses the minister:

N, my brother/sister in Christ,
you are called to be a servant and a shepherd in this *parish*.
It is your work to preach Christ's gospel,
to call people to repentance,
to assure them of God's mercy, and to baptise.
You will teach, inspire and encourage,
both by word and example,
the people entrusted to your care.
You will lead them in worship,
and celebrate the Lord's supper with them.

You will take Christ the Good Shepherd as your example,
caring for his people and serving with them
in their witness to the world.

In view of this solemn trust,
we ask you to reaffirm
the declaration of faith and obedience
that you made at your ordination,
and to show that you desire, by God's grace,
to continue your ministry in this *parish*.

Do you confess anew Jesus Christ as Lord?

I do so confess.

Do you receive the witness to Christ
in the holy Scriptures of the Old and New Testaments?

I do.

Do you accept the discipline of the Uniting Church
and the oversight of this presbytery?

I do.

Will you take part in the work of this presbytery
and other councils of the Uniting Church,
and will you share in the life and witness
of the wider church?

I will.

> Representative people of the parish (elders, members of the parish
> council, or people from other areas of parish life) come forward.
>
> The first person brings a copy of the Bible.
>
> The second person brings a baptismal ewer or jug of water.
>
> The third person brings a communion plate and chalice, with
> bread and wine.
>
> Each person speaks before giving the symbol to the minister being
> inducted. The minister holds it until he/she has made response to
> the chairperson's question, and then places it as indicated below.
>
> Then a group of people comes, representing the congregation(s)
> for which the minister will have pastoral responsibility. These may
> be from various age groups such as a senior member, a younger
> adult, a youth and a child.

Any other minister or ministers in settlement in the parish and any lay person(s) working as part of the ministry team shall then come forward.

The first person says:

Receive this holy Bible.
It is your duty to proclaim God's Word to God's people.

The chairperson continues:

Jesus said:
Go into all the world
and preach the gospel to the whole creation.

Mark 16:15

Will you study and proclaim these Scriptures,
being a faithful teacher in this *parish*
and a prophet of God to the world?

I will, by the grace of God.

The minister opens the Bible and places it on the lectern or pulpit.

The second person says:

Receive this water.
It is your duty to baptise with water
in the name of the holy Trinity.

The chairperson continues:

Jesus said:
Go therefore and make disciples of all nations,
baptising them in the name of the Father
and of the Son and of the Holy Spirit.

Matthew 28:19

Will you administer the sacrament of baptism
in this *parish?*

I will, by the grace of God.

> The minister pours the water into the font.

> The third person says:

Receive this bread and wine.
It is your duty to break the bread and offer the cup
at the table of the Lord.

> The chairperson continues:

Jesus said:
I am the bread of life;
whoever comes to me shall not hunger,
and whoever believes in me shall never thirst.

John 6:35

Will you celebrate the Lord's supper
with God's family in this *parish?*

I will, by the grace of God.

> The minister places the bread and wine on the communion table.

> One of the representative group of people says:

We come, representing the congregations
of the *Parish of* . . .
It is your duty to care for the people
entrusted to you.

The chairperson continues:

The apostle Peter said:
Tend the flock of God that is your charge,
not by constraint but willingly,
not as domineering over those in your charge,
but being an example to the flock.

1 Peter 5:2, 3

Will you exercise pastoral care of the family of God
in the congregations of this *parish?*

I will, by the grace of God.

The representatives return to their places.

If there is one other minister or one lay worker, he/she comes
forward and says:

N, I welcome you to this *parish.*
I offer you my friendship and support
as we join together in this work
to which God has called us,
and as we share with the people of this *parish*
in the wider ministry of Christ.

If there are two or more other ministers and/or lay workers, they
come forward.

The chairperson may introduce them by name and office.

One of them says:

N, we welcome you to this *parish.*
As members of the ministry team,
we offer you our friendship and support
as we join together in this work
to which God has called us,
and as we share with the people of this *parish*
in the wider ministry of Christ.

The chairperson continues:

The apostle Peter said:
As each has received a gift, employ it for one another,
as good stewards of God's varied grace.

1 Peter 4:10

Addressing the minister to be inducted and other member(s) of the ministry team, the chairperson says:

N and N, you have been called by God
to work together in this *parish*.
Will you promise, in faith and obedience to Christ,
to share this ministry;
supporting one another in love,
and through your harmony of spirit
inspiring all God's people here
in their common ministry for Christ?

We will, by the grace of God.

10 HYMN

The people remain standing after the hymn.

11 INDUCTION PRAYER

The minister to be inducted kneels and the chairperson says:

Let us pray:

Almighty God,
in every age you have chosen servants
to speak your word and lead your people.
We thank you for N
whom you have called to serve you.

Fill him/her with the Holy Spirit
and give him/her gifts for ministry in this place.
May he/she have the same mind that was in Christ Jesus,
and be a faithful disciple,
being an example to the people of God
and witnessing before the world;
through Jesus Christ our Lord.
Amen.

The Aaronic Blessing may be said or sung by the people
(*Australian Hymn Book, 572*), or said by the chairperson.

The Lord bless you and keep you;
the Lord make his face to shine upon you,
and be gracious unto you;
the Lord lift up his countenance upon you,
and give you peace.

Numbers 6:24-26

Alternatively, the chairperson may say:

The God of all grace,
who has called you to his eternal glory in Christ,
establish and strengthen you in all things,
to the glory of his name
and the good of his church on earth.

Based on 1 Peter 5:10

12 DECLARATION OF INDUCTION

The minister stands and faces the people.

The chairperson says:

In the name of our Lord Jesus Christ,
the only King and Head of the church,
and by the authority of the Presbytery of . . . ,
we now declare NNN to be inducted
into the ministry of *the Parish of* . . .

The people may applaud.

This may be followed by the singing of a Doxology, e.g. *Australian Hymn Book, 573-577.*

The people sit.

The Response

13 WELCOME BY THE PRESBYTERY

The chairperson invites members of the presbytery to come forward and give the newly-inducted minister the right hand of fellowship.

14 QUESTIONS TO THE PEOPLE

The chairperson or secretary of the parish council comes forward, invites the members and adherents of the congregations within the parish to stand, and addresses the newly-inducted minister:

N, I greet you as our new minister.
I present to you the people of God in this *parish,*
ministers with you in the gospel,
and I commend them to your prayers.

On their behalf, I give you the right hand of fellowship.

The chairperson says:

My brothers and sisters in Christ,
the church declares that her members
shall acknowledge Jesus Christ as Saviour and Lord,
confess the christian faith,
accept the discipline of the church
and share in her ministry.

Will you therefore take part
in the public worship of God,
and contribute to the work of God as you are able;
will you endeavour to make a christian witness
in the community by word and action?

We will, the Lord being our helper.

Will you honour N as your pastor and leader;
will you listen for God's Word in his/her preaching;
will you welcome him/her into your homes;
will you provide for him/her that which is necessary
for his/her physical welfare;
and will you at all times support him/her
with your love and prayers?

We will, the Lord being our helper.

The people sit.

15 WELCOME BY OTHER CHURCHES

The chairperson of presbytery may welcome and introduce clergy
or representatives of other churches who are present.

The chairperson invites them to come forward and give the newly-
inducted minister the right hand of fellowship.

16 THE PEACE

The people stand.

The newly-inducted minister gives the greeting of peace:

The peace of the Lord be always with you.
And also with you.

A sign of peace is given by the minister and exchanged among the people.

The people sit.

17 RESPONSE BY THE MINISTER

The newly-inducted minister makes a brief response.

18 OFFERING

ANTHEM

If not sung before 5.

19 PRAYERS OF THE PEOPLE

The prayers are led by a member of presbytery or a representative group of people from presbytery and/or parish.

Intercessions may include:
   The minister and his/her family
   The congregations within the parish
   The life and mission of the presbytery
   The Uniting Church in Australia
   The church universal

The last person to lead in prayer says:

And now let us pray to the Father
in the words our Saviour gave us:

**Our Father in heaven,
  hallowed be your name,
  your kingdom come,
  your will be done,
    on earth as in heaven.
Give us today our daily bread.
Forgive us our sins
  as we forgive those who sin against us.
Save us from the time of trial
  and deliver us from evil.**

**For the kingdom, the power, and the glory are yours
  now and for ever. Amen.**

The Sending Forth of the People of God

20 HYMN

21 BLESSING

The chairperson says:

May the Spirit of truth lead you into all truth,
give you grace to confess that Jesus Christ is Lord,
and to proclaim the Word and works of God.

And the blessing of God almighty,
the Father, the Son and the Holy Spirit,
be upon you and remain with you always.
Amen.

NOTES

i   The service is held at a time and place arranged by the presbytery, normally within the congregation in which the candidate holds membership, and is led by the minister(s) and others appointed by the presbytery.

ii Normally this order follows the Preaching of the Word and the Affirmation of Faith. It is appropriate that holy communion be celebrated.

iii The Scripture readings used may be the lectionary readings for the day or a selection from the following:

Isaiah 6:1-8	1 Corinthians 1:18-31	Luke 10:1-12
Isaiah 55:6-11	2 Corinthians 5:14-20	John 12:20-26
Jeremiah 1:4-9	Matthew 10:24-33	John 15:9-17

Commissioning of a Lay Preacher

1   SENTENCES

There are diverse gifts:
  but it is the same Spirit who gives them.

There are different ways of serving God:
  but it is the same Lord who is served.

God works through people in different ways:
  but it is the same God
  whose purpose is achieved through them all.

Each one of us is given a gift by the Spirit:
  and there is no gift without its corresponding service.

There is one ministry of Christ:
  and in this ministry we all share.

Together we are the body of Christ:
  and individually members of it.

Based on 1 Corinthians 12:4 ff.
and Basis of Union, para. 13

2 PRESENTATION

The presiding minister addresses the people:

The Uniting Church provides for the excercise
by men and women
of the gifts God bestows upon them
for the building up of the church.

The office of lay preacher
is a ministry in which persons may participate
in the proclamation of the gospel.

The church seeks to recognise those
who are called by God to the work of preaching
and who have the gifts of the Spirit for this ministry.
The church provides for their training and accreditation.

In the act of commissioning,
lay preachers of the Uniting Church in Australia
are authorised to lead worship and preach
in the churches of the parishes in which they hold membership,
and in other churches to which they may be invited.

The candidate is presented to the presiding minister by a lay member of presbytery, normally from the candidate's parish.

I present NN.
He/she has successfully completed the preparation
required by the church,
and has made application through the Parish of . . .
to the Presbytery of . . .
for accreditation as a lay preacher.
The presbytery has now resolved to commission him/her.

3   THE VOWS

The minister asks the candidate:

N,
do you confess anew Jesus Christ as Lord?

I do.

Do you receive the witness to Christ
in the holy Scriptures of the Old and New Testaments;
and do you undertake to preach from these?

I do.

Will you seek to live and work within the faith and unity
of the one holy catholic and apostolic Church?

I will.

Do you adhere to the Basis of Union
of the Uniting Church in Australia?

I do.

Relying on God's grace,
do you promise to carry out the duties of your office?

I do.

The minister says:

May God give you strength to fulfil these vows;
and to him be the glory
in the church and in Christ Jesus
from generation to generation for ever.
Amen.

4 ACT OF COMMISSIONING

Those appointed by the presbytery to join with the presiding minister in the laying on of hands come forward.

The minister says:

Beloved in Christ,
let us pray in silence for N
before we commission him/her for the work
to which we believe the Holy Spirit has called him/her.

The candidate kneels.

After a time of silence the minister says:

Almighty God,
in every age you have chosen servants
to speak your word to your people.
We thank you that you have called N to serve you.
May he/she have the same mind which was in Christ Jesus
and be a faithful disciple,
proclaiming the truth of the gospel;
through Jesus Christ our Lord.
Amen.

Hands are laid on the candidate's head and the presiding minister says:

N, receive the Holy Spirit
for the ministry of lay preacher.

The people respond:

Amen.

The Aaronic Blessing may be said or sung by the people,
(Australian Hymn Book, 572), or said by the minister.

**The Lord bless you and keep you;
the Lord make his face to shine upon you,
and be gracious unto you;
the Lord lift up his countenance upon you,
and give you peace.**

Numbers 6:24-26

Alternatively, the minister says this blessing:

The God of all grace,
who has called you to his eternal glory in Christ,
establish and strengthen you in all things,
to the glory of his name
and the good of his church on earth.

Based on 1 Peter 5:10

5 DECLARATION

The candidate stands.

The presiding minister says:

**In the name of our Lord Jesus Christ,
I declare you to be a lay preacher
in the Uniting Church in Australia.**

The people may applaud.

A representative of the presbytery presents the Lay Preacher's certificate.

A lay preacher or elder from the parish presents a Bible on behalf of the parish.

The new lay preacher is given the right hand of fellowship by members of the presbytery and others as appropriate.

The new lay preacher may make a brief statement concerning his/her call to this ministry.

6 PRAYERS

Intercessions for the following may be included in Prayers of the People:
The newly-commissioned lay preacher and his/her family
The life and mission of the congregations within the parish
The work of the presbytery
The witness of lay preachers within the Uniting Church in Australia

Commissioning of Elders

NOTES

i   This service forms part of the regular Sunday service of the congregation.

ii   Normally this order follows the Preaching of the Word and the Affirmation of Faith. It is appropriate that holy communion be celebrated.

iii   The Scripture readings used may be the lectionary readings for the day or a selection from the following:

Exodus 18:13-25	Ephesians 4:1-7, 11-16	Luke 12:32-40
Numbers 11:16, 17, 24, 25	1 Peter 5:1-4	John 15:1-11
Romans 12:1-13	Luke 5:1-11	John 21:15-19

Commissioning of Elders

1 SENTENCES

(See People's Book, p. 109.)

There are diverse gifts:
  but it is the same Spirit who gives them.

There are different ways of serving God:
  but it is the same Lord who is served.

God works through people in different ways:
  **but it is the same God
  whose purpose is achieved through them all.**

Each one of us is given a gift by the Spirit:
  and there is no gift without its corresponding service.

There is one ministry of Christ:
  and in this ministry we all share.

Together we are the body of Christ:
  and individually members of it.

*Based on 1 Corinthians 12:4 ff.
and Basis of Union, para. 13*

2 PRESENTATION

The minister addresses the people:

The Uniting Church provides for the excercise
by men and women
of the gifts God bestows upon them
for the building up of the church.

Having sought the guidance of the Holy Spirit,
we are now to commission as elders
those whom we have elected to this ministry.

A representative of the congregation presents the candidates and says:

On behalf of the people of this congregation,
I present the following persons
to be *commissioned* or *recommissioned* as elders:

The representative reads the names of the candidates.

The candidates stand together facing the congregation and the minister addresses them:

Brothers and sisters,

or

N and N,

the congregation has elected you
to serve Jesus Christ as elders.

The responsibilities of the council of elders
include the following:

to share with the minister
   in building up the congregation in faith and love;

to nurture the members in their growth in grace;

to visit regularly the members and adherents;

to share with the minister
   in the conduct of worship
   and the administration of the sacraments,
   the spiritual oversight of the congregation,
   and in christian education and evangelistic outreach;

to maintain the membership rolls of the congregation
   and to exercise pastoral discipline;

to make recommendations to the parish council
   concerning applicants for training for ministry.

3   THE VOWS

The minister asks the candidates:

Do you confess anew Jesus Christ as Lord?

I do.

Do you believe that you are called by God
through the church to this ministry?

I do.

Will you seek to live and work within the faith and unity
of the one holy catholic and apostolic Church?

I will.

Do you adhere to the Basis of Union
of the Uniting Church in Australia?

I do.

Relying on God's grace,
do you promise to carry out the duties of your office?

I do.

Will you, the members of this congregation,
accept these brothers and sisters (*or*, N and N) as elders?

We will.

Will you encourage them in love
and support them in their ministry,
serving with them the one Lord Jesus Christ?

We will.

May God give you strength to fulfil these vows;
and to him be the glory
in the church and in Christ Jesus
from generation to generation for ever.
Amen.

The people sit.

4 ACT OF COMMISSIONING

Those appointed by the council of elders to join with the minister
in the laying on of hands come forward.

The minister says:

Beloved in Christ,
let us pray in silence for these people
before we commission them for the work
to which we believe the Holy Spirit has called them.

The candidates kneel.

After a time of silence the minister says:

Almighty God,
in every age you have chosen servants
to lead and care for your people.
We thank you that you have called N and N
to serve you.
May they have the same mind which was in Christ Jesus
and be faithful disciples,
giving example to Christ's flock
and witnessing to the truth of the gospel;
through Jesus Christ our Lord.
Amen.

The minister and those appointed lay hands on the head of each candidate in turn, and the minister says:

N, receive the Holy Spirit
for the ministry of elder.

The people respond:

Amen.

When all the candidates have received the laying on of hands, the Aaronic Blessing may be said or sung by the people, *(Australian Hymn Book, 572)*, or said by the minister.

The Lord bless you and keep you;
the Lord make his face to shine upon you,
and be gracious unto you;
the Lord lift up his countenance upon you,
and give you peace.

Numbers 6:24-26

Alternatively, the minister says this blessing:

The God of all grace,
who has called you to his eternal glory in Christ,
establish and strengthen you in all things,
to the glory of his name
and the good of his church on earth.

Based on 1 Peter 5:10

5   DECLARATION

The candidates stand.

The minister says:

In the name of our Lord Jesus Christ,
I declare you to be elders
of the Uniting Church in Australia
in the . . . Congregation.

The people may applaud.

The minister and other elders give the right hand of fellowship to
the new elders.

6   PRAYERS

Intercessions for the following may be included in Prayers of the
People:
   The newly-commissioned elders and their families
   The life and mission of the congregation
   The witness of elders within the Uniting Church in Australia

Resources for Leading Worship

Resources for Leading Worship

Greetings

1   The Lord be with you.   *Ruth 2:4*
    And also with you.   *2 Thessalonians 3:16*

2   Grace to you and peace
    from God our Father and the Lord Jesus Christ.
                                                                 Romans 1:7
                                                               and elsewhere.

3   The grace of the Lord Jesus Christ
    and the love of God
    and the fellowship of the Holy Spirit
    be with you all.
    And also with you.   *2 Corinthians 13:14*

4   Grace be with you all
    who love our Lord Jesus Christ with love undying.
                                                             Ephesians 2:24

5   Peace be to you all,
    and love with faith,
    from God the Father and the Lord Jesus Christ.
                                                             Ephesians 6:23

6   The peace of the Lord be always with you.
    And also with you.   *2 Thessalonians 3:16*

7   The grace of our Lord Jesus Christ
    be with you all.
    And also with you.   *2 Thessalonians 3:18*

8 Grace, mercy, and peace
from God our Father and Christ Jesus our Lord.

1 Timothy 1:2
2 Timothy 1:2

9 Grace and peace be yours in fullest measure,
through the knowledge of God and of Jesus our Lord.

2 Peter 1:2

10 Grace to you and peace,
from God who is and who was and who is to come,
and from Jesus Christ, the faithful witness,
the first-born from the dead.   *Revelation 1:4, 5*

Scripture Sentences

The sentence of the day, or words from the psalm or other reading for the day, or one of the following:

1 Surely the Lord is in this place.
   This is none other than the house of God,
   and this is the gate of heaven.   *Genesis 28:16, 17*

2 Send out your light and your truth,
   that they may lead me,
   and bring me to your holy hill and to your dwelling.
                                             Psalm 43:3

3 Worship the Lord in the beauty of holiness;
   let the whole earth tremble before him.   *Psalm 96:9*

4 This is the day which the Lord has made;
   let us rejoice and be glad in it.   *Psalm 118:24*

5 I was glad when they said to me:
   Let us go to the house of the Lord.   *Psalm 122:1*

6 Our help is in the name of the Lord,
   who has made heaven and earth.   *Psalm 124:8*

7 Let our prayer be set forth in your sight as incense,
   the lifting up of our hands as the evening sacrifice.
                                             Psalm 141:2

8 Seek the Lord while he may be found;
   call upon him while he is near.   *Isaiah 55:6*

9 From the rising of the sun to its setting,
   my name is great among the nations;
   and in every place incense is offered to my name,
   and a pure offering;

for my name is great among the nations,
says the Lord of hosts. *Malachi 1:11*

10 The Lord is in his holy temple;
let all the earth keep silence before him. *Habakkuk 2:20*

11 The hour is coming, and now is,
when the true worshippers will worship the Father
in spirit and in truth,
for such the Father seeks to worship him. *John 4:23*

12 God is spirit,
and those who worship him
must worship in spirit and in truth. *John 4:24*

13 God was in Christ, reconciling the world to himself,
not counting our trespasses against us,
and entrusting to us the message of reconciliation.
1 Corinthians 5:19

14 At the name of Jesus every knee shall bow,
and every tongue confess that Jesus Christ is Lord,
to the glory of God the Father. *Philippians 2:10, 11*

15 Rejoice in the Lord always;
again I will say, Rejoice.
Have no anxiety about anything; but in everything,
by prayer and supplication with thanksgiving,
let your requests be made known to God.
Philippians 4:4, 6

16 If then you have been raised with Christ,
seek the things that are above, where Christ is,
seated at the right hand of God. *Colossians 3:1*

17   Since we have a great high priest
who has passed through the heavens,
Jesus, the Son of God,
let us hold fast our confession.
Let us with confidence draw near to the throne of grace,
that we may receive mercy
and find grace to help in time of need.   *Hebrews 4:14, 16*

18   Through Jesus, let us continually offer up to God
the sacrifice of praise, that is,
the tribute of lips which acknowledge his name.
Hebrews 13:15

19   Blessed be the God and Father of our Lord Jesus Christ.
By his great mercy
we have been born anew to a living hope
through the resurrection of Jesus Christ from the dead.
1 Peter 1:3

20   God is light, and in him is no darkness at all.
If we walk in the light, as God is in the light,
we have fellowship with one another,
and the blood of Jesus his Son cleanses us from all sin.
1 John 1:7

21   Beloved, let us love one another;
for love is of God,
and those who love are born of God and know God.
1 John 4:7

22   Holy, holy, holy, is the Lord God Almighty,
who was, and is, and is to come.   *Revelation 4:8*

23 The kingdom of the world
has become the kingdom of our Lord and of his Christ,
and he shall reign for ever and ever.   *Revelation 11:15*

24 Behold, the dwelling of God is with us.
God will dwell with us, and we shall be his people.
                                               Revelation 21:3

25 In the name of the Father,
and of the Son,
and of the Holy Spirit.

> One of these sentences may be appropriate when holy
> communion is to be celebrated:

26 Taste and see that the Lord is good;
happy are they who trust in him.   *Psalm 34:8*

27 How shall I repay the Lord
for all the good things he has done for me?
I will lift up the cup of salvation
and call upon the name of the Lord.
I will fulfil my vows to the Lord
in the presence of all his people.   *Psalm 116:12-14*

28 Jesus said:
Come to me all who labour and are heavy laden,
and I will give you rest.
Take my yoke upon you, and learn from me;
for I am gentle and lowly of heart,
and you will find rest for your souls.
For my yoke is easy, and my burden is light.
                                           Matthew 11:28-30

29   They will come from east and west,
      and from north and south,
      and sit at table in the kingdom of God.   *Luke 13:29*

30   God so loved the world that he gave his only Son,
      that whoever believes in him
      should not perish but have eternal life.   *John 3:16*

31   Jesus said:
      I am the bread of life;
      whoever comes to me shall not hunger,
      and whoever believes in me shall never thirst.   *John 6:35*

32   Christ our Passover has been sacrificed for us;
      therefore let us keep the feast.   *1 Corinthians 5:7, 8*

33   Because there is one bread,
      we who are many are one body,
      for we all partake of the same bread.   *1 Corinthians 10:17*

34   The apostle Paul said:
      As often as you eat this bread and drink the cup,
      you proclaim the Lord's death until he comes.
      Whoever, therefore, eats the bread
      or drinks the cup in an unworthy manner
      will be guilty of profaning
      the body and blood of the Lord.
      Let us therefore examine ourselves,
      and so eat of the bread and drink of the cup.
                       1 Corinthians 11:26-28

35   Hear what the apostle Paul says:
This saying is true and worthy of full acceptance,
that Christ Jesus came into the world to save sinners.

1 Timothy 1:15

36   Hear what Saint John says:
If anyone sins, we have an advocate with the Father,
Jesus Christ the righteous;
and he is the perfect offering for our sins,
and not for ours only,
but for the sins of the whole world.   *1 John 2:1, 2*

Prayers of Invocation and Adoration

1   Let us glorify and adore the one true God,
    Father, Son and Holy Spirit:

    Almighty God the Father,
    gracious Lord of all,
    whose glory knows no bounds:
    we worship and adore you.

    Lord Jesus Christ the Son,
    eternal Word of God,
    whose mercy never ends:
    we worship and adore you.

    Most good and loving Spirit,
    source of power and life,
    whose goodness lasts for ever:
    we worship and adore you.

    Father, Son and Holy Spirit: one eternal God,
    resplendent in brightness,
    radiant in purity,
    inconceivable in majesty,
    to you we give all blessing, glory, honour and power,
    always, now and ever, and to the ages of ages.

2   Lord our God,
    great, eternal, wonderful, utterly to be trusted:
    you give life to all;
    you help those who come to you;
    you give hope to those who appeal to you.
    Set our hearts and minds at peace,
    that we may now bring our prayers to you
    confidently and without fear;
    through Jesus Christ our Lord.

3 You are holy,
   O Lord, our Creator and Father,
   giving us mercies without number.
   You are holy,
   O Saviour Jesus Christ,
   loving us and setting us free.
   You are holy,
   O Spirit of truth and peace,
   leading us in ways that are right.
   O holy, eternal Trinity,
   we praise you for ever and ever.

4 We wait for your loving-kindness, O God,
   in the midst of your temple.
   Let us rise to the limits of time
    and behold your eternity;
   let us run to the edges of space
   and gaze into your immensity;
   let us penetrate the barriers of sound
   and pass into your silence.

   In the midst of your temple,
   in the presence of your holy people,
   we wait in silence for your loving-kindness, O God.

5 Eternal God,
   you have shined in our hearts
   to give the knowledge of your glory
   in the face of Jesus Christ:
   give us now such knowledge of your grace
   that we may worship and adore you.

6 Let us acknowledge the greatness and majesty of God
as we offer our humble adoration:

Blessed are you, almighty Father,
sovereign ruler of all creation:
we glorify and adore you.

Blessed are you, Lord Jesus Christ,
loving Saviour of the world:
we glorify and adore you.

Blessed are you, eternal Spirit,
gracious source of light and life:
we glorify and adore you.

Father, Son and Holy Spirit,
Lord God of endless power and might,
we praise your name for ever and ever.

7 Mighty God,
we meet to celebrate your greatness.
We join with the hosts of heaven
to sing your praises and to offer you worship.
For you are worthy of adoration from every mouth,
and every tongue should praise you.
You created the earth by your power;
you save the human race by your mercy;
and make it new by your grace.
Father, Son and Holy Spirit,
we offer you our grateful praise.

8 God of eternity,
before you lips are silenced in awe and wonder.
Mere words fail to praise the fullness of your Word for us
spoken in Jesus Christ.
Let our lives reflect his love by all we say and do,
and so return to you all praise and glory.

9 Eternal Lord God,
   you are worshipped and adored by all the hosts of heaven:
   we join our thanks and praise with the triumph song
   of prophets and apostles, saints and martyrs,
   praying that your grace may enable us,
   unworthy as we are,
   to worship you adoringly on earth;
   through Jesus Christ our Lord.

10 O God, our God, how great you are.
   On the first day of the week
   we commemorate your creation of the world
   and all that is in it.
   Thank you for the light which wakes us
   morning by morning,
   and for the greater light which shines in Jesus Christ.

   O God, our God, how great you are.
   On the first day of the week
   you raised Jesus from the dead.
   Raise us with him to new life.

   O God, our God, how great you are.
   Again on the first day of the week
   you sent the Holy Spirit on your disciples.
   Do not deprive us of your presence,
   but renew the Spirit in us day by day.

11 Come, Holy Spirit of God,
   restore the lives which, without you, are lifeless and dead;
   kindle the hearts which, without you, are cold and dull;
   enlighten the minds which, without you,
   are dark and blind;
   fill the church which, without you, is an empty shrine;
   and teach us how to praise and pray.

12 Most wonderful God,
   it is you who inspires every noble thought
   and every loving deed.
   When we draw near to you in worship,
   save us from wanderings of mind and coldness of heart,
   that with a deep longing for more truth
   and a warm desire for more love,
   we may know you, embrace you, and worship you
   in the incarnate life of our Saviour, Jesus Christ.

13 O God of truth,
   you are worthy of nobler praises than we can offer
   and of purer worship than we can imagine.
   Assist us in our prayers and draw us to yourself,
   that what is lacking in our words and thoughts
   may be supplied by your overflowing love;
   through Jesus Christ our Lord.

14 Let us glorify and adore the one true God:

   Glory to you,
   Father, Son and Holy Spirit,
   loving God in three persons.
   We gladly proclaim your majesty and power,
   your greatness and sovereignty,
   always, now and ever,
   and to the ages of ages.

15 Almighty God,
   you have been the dwelling place of your people
   in all generations;
   your mercies are more than we can number,
   and your compassion is without end.

Grant us now the help of the Holy Spirit,
that we may praise you for your goodness and mercy,
receive your word with joy and thanksgiving,
and give ourselves again to you in love and service;
through Jesus Christ our Lord.

16 God of Abraham and Ruth,
you call us to embark on a journey of faith.
We stand before you,
ready to hear your call and to follow where you lead;
for you have claimed us by your mercy,
and set before us eternal promises in Jesus Christ,
in whom alone we give you all glory
in the power of the Holy Spirit.

17 O God all-powerful, true and incomparable,
we adore you.
You are present in all things, yet limited by none,
untouched by place, unaged by time,
unhurried by the years, undeceived by words,
not subject to birth nor in need of protection;
you are above all corruption,
you are beyond all change,
living in light that none can approach,
invisible, yet you make yourself known to us;
and you are found by all who seek you
with their whole heart.
You are the God of Israel
and of all who hope in Christ.
You are God; we adore you.

18   O Lord God,
      you have called us to prayer.
      Stir our hearts with the thought of your goodness,
      and grant us the spirit of true devotion;
      that we may worthily praise the One who died for our sins
      and opened to us the gates of eternal life,
      our Saviour, Jesus Christ.

19   God our Father,
      we worship you in wonder and in love.
      Our minds cannot contain you,
      nor our words express you;
      yet in Christ we see your glory,
      hear your word of truth
      and know your forgiving love.

      Father, Son and Holy Spirit, gracious Trinity,
      we bless and adore you.
      Accept our offering of praise and thanksgiving
      which we bring in the name of Jesus Christ
      our Saviour and Lord,
      to whom be glory for ever and ever.

20   O living God,
      awaken us to your presence,
      that we may know the power of that endless life
      which you have given to us your children;
      through Jesus Christ our Lord.

21   God the Father, God beyond us, we adore you.
      You are the depth of all that is.
      You are the ground of our being.
      We can never grasp you, yet you grasp us.
      The universe speaks of you,
      and your love comes to us through Jesus.

God the Son, God beside us, we adore you.
You are the perfection of humanity.
You have shown us what human life should be like.
In you we see divine love and human greatness combined.

God the Spirit, God around us, we adore you.
You draw us to Jesus and the Father.
You are the power within us.
You give us abundant life
and can make us the people we are meant to be.

Father, Son, and Holy Spirit:
God, beyond, beside, and around us;
we adore you.

22 Eternal God and Father,
in you is the source of all life,
the fount of all wisdom,
the well-spring of all grace.
Your days are without end,
your loving mercies without number.

We depend on you;
and we remember your goodness to us
and to those who have gone before us.
We tell your story in every generation:
you are our familiar God,
God of Abraham, Isaac and Jacob,
God of Sarah, Rebekah and Rachel,
God and Father of our Lord Jesus Christ,
God of a pilgrim people, your church.

But you are not our captive God,
not a god of our own making,
not bound by us, not controlled by us.
You are ahead of us, leading us,
guiding us and calling us;
you are the Lord God,
the all-wise, all-compassionate.
To you we lift up our hearts and we worship you,
one God, for ever and ever.

23   Blessed are you, Lord God almighty, for ever and ever.
Yours, O Lord, is the greatness and the might
and the glory and the victory and the majesty;
for all that is in the heavens and on the earth is yours;
yours is the kingdom,
and you are exalted as head over all.
Therefore we adore you now and always.

24   Lord Jesus,
preaching good tidings to the people,
proclaiming release to captives,
setting at liberty those who are bound:
we adore you.

Lord Jesus,
friend of the outcast and the poor,
feeder of the hungry,
healer of the sick:
we adore you.

Lord Jesus,
denouncing the oppressor,
exposing the hypocrite,
overcoming evil with good:
we adore you.

Lord Jesus,
pattern of gentleness,
teacher of holiness,
prophet of the kingdom of heaven:
we adore you.

Lord Jesus,
dying to save us from our sin,
rising to give us eternal life,
ascending to prepare our heavenly home:
we adore you.

25   Most wonderful God,
you are beyond our sight, above our thought,
infinite, eternal, and unsearchable:
your wisdom shines in all your works;
your glory is shown in your goodness to all people;
your grace and truth are revealed in Christ.
Therefore we adore you, our God,
for ever and ever.

26   God of all glory,
on this first day you began creation,
bringing light out of darkness.
On this day you began your new creation,
raising Jesus Christ out of the darkness of death.
On this Lord's day, grant that we,
the people you create by water and the Spirit,
may be joined with all your works
in praising you for your great glory.
Through Jesus Christ,
in union with the Holy Spirit,
we praise you now and for ever.

27 Great and marvellous are your works, Lord God almighty;
just and true are your ways, O King of saints.
Who shall not stand in awe before you, O Lord,
and glorify your holy name?
Therefore with your whole church in heaven and on earth
we worship and adore you,
Father, Son, and Holy Spirit;
to whom be glory for ever and ever.

28 Lord God our heavenly Father,
we praise and adore you;
we celebrate your mighty power and your love.
You have guided and preserved us in all our ways;
you are worthy of all praise and honour and love.
Your glory is beyond all thought;
you are alpha and omega, the first and the last;
you are beyond all letters and all words,
beyond all that we can say or think.
Accept our praise and adoration, we pray,
through the merits of your Son,
our Saviour Jesus Christ.

29 Most blessed, most holy God,
before the brightness of your presence
the angels and archangels veil their faces.
Most blessed, most holy God,
in silent reverence and with adoring love
we behold your infinite glory.
We worship you, eternal Trinity,
Father, Son, and Holy Spirit.
Blessing, and glory, and honour, and power
are yours for ever and ever.

30 Let us offer our adoration to God,
the Maker and Redeemer of all:

Almighty and everlasting God,
Father, Son, and Holy Spirit,
sovereign Ruler of all creation:
as we call upon your glorious name
we give you praise,
we offer you worship,
we bow in adoration.

You alone are our hope,
you alone are our salvation,
you alone are our life.

To you belong all majesty and glory,
dominion and power,
always, now and ever,
and to the ages of ages.

31 Almighty God our heavenly Father,
you have made us for yourself
and called us into this fellowship of your people.
While we worship you here today,
may we receive your blessing;
and may we be equipped by the Holy Spirit
to witness for you throughout this coming week;
through Jesus Christ our Lord.

32 Let us bow in adoration before the Lord of all:

Glory to you,
Father, Son, and Holy Spirit,
sovereign Ruler of all creation,
Lord of inconceivable majesty,
God of love, mercy and power.
We magnify your glorious name,
always, now and ever,
and to the ages of ages.

33 People ought to praise you, God of earth and heaven.
All of us ought to praise you.
You are always there, never growing old,
fresh as each new day.
You were in Jesus, showing us your love by his death,
and by his resurrection
giving us hope of living with you for ever.
You bring life and light to the world by the Holy Spirit,
making every moment your moment,
and every day your day of coming to the rescue.

To God the Father, God the Son, and God the Holy Spirit
let all the world give praise,
today, and every day, and for ever and ever.

Calls to Confession of Sin

1   Purge me from sin, and I shall be pure;
    wash me, and I shall be clean indeed.   *Psalm 51:7*

2   The sacrifice of God is a troubled spirit;
    a broken and contrite heart, O God, you will not despise.
                                                    Psalm 51:17

3   He was wounded for our transgressions,
    he was bruised for our iniquities;
    upon him was the chastisement that made us whole,
    and with his stripes we are healed.
    All we like sheep have gone astray;
    we have turned every one to our own way;
    and the Lord has laid on him the iniquity of us all.
                                                    Isaiah 53:5, 6

4   Thus says the high and lofty One,
    who inhabits eternity, whose name is Holy:
    I dwell in the high and holy place,
    and also with those
    who are of a contrite and humble spirit,
    to revive the spirit of the humble,
    and to revive the heart of the contrite.   *Isaiah 57:15*

5   To the Lord our God belong mercy and forgiveness,
    though we have rebelled against him,
    and have not obeyed the voice of the Lord our God
    by following his laws which he set before us. *Daniel 9:9, 10*

6   Rend your hearts and not your garments.
    Return to the Lord, your God;
    for God is gracious and merciful,
    slow to anger, and abounding in steadfast love.   *Joel 2:13*

7   Jesus said:
Come to me, all who labour and are heavy laden,
and I will give you rest.

Matthew 11:28

8   I will arise and go to my father, and I will say to him:
Father, I have sinned against heaven and before you;
I am no longer worthy to be called your son.

Luke 15:18, 19

9   If we say we have no sin,
we deceive ourselves, and the truth is not in us.
If we confess our sins,
God is faithful and just,
and will forgive our sins
and cleanse us from all unrighteousness.

1 John 1:8, 9

10   Behold, I stand at the door and knock.
If those who hear my voice open the door,
I will come in to them and eat with them,
and they with me.

Revelation 3:20

11   In silence let us confess our sins;
for the Lord is merciful and compassionate to all.

12   Dearly beloved,
we have come together
in the presence of almighty God, our heavenly Father,
to set forth God's praise,
to hear God's holy Word,
and to ask, for ourselves and on behalf of others,
those things that are necessary
for our life and our salvation.
And so that we may prepare ourselves
in heart and mind to worship God,
let us bow in silence,

and with penitent and obedient hearts confess our sins,
that we may obtain forgiveness
by God's infinite goodness and mercy.

13 Let us in silence confess our sin
and seek God's mercy and forgiveness.

14 Dear friends in Christ,
God is steadfast in love and infinite in mercy;
God welcomes sinners and invites them to the table.
Let us confess our sin,
confident in God's forgiveness.

15 We have come, as God's family, into our Father's presence.
Let us now, in silence,
tell God that we are sorry for the wrong we have done,
and ask for forgiveness.
For the Lord is a God of tenderness and compassion,
slow to anger, and rich in graciousness.

16 Christ our Lord calls all who love him
earnestly to repent of their sin
and live in peace with one another.
Therefore, let us confess our sin
before God and one another.

17 Let us confess our sins against God and our neighbour.

18 Dear friends in Christ,
here in the presence of almighty God
let us bow in silence,
and with penitent and obedient hearts confess our sins,
so that we may obtain forgiveness
by God's infinite goodness and mercy.

Prayers of Confession

1   Most merciful God,
     we confess that we have sinned against you
     in thought, word, and deed,
     by what we have done,
     and by what we have left undone.
     We have not loved you with our whole heart;
     we have not loved our neighbours as ourselves.
     We are truly sorry and we humbly repent.
     For the sake of your Son Jesus Christ,
     have mercy on us and forgive us;
     that we may delight in your will
     and walk in your ways,
     to the glory of your name.

2   O God,
     we confess the blindness that is not even aware of sinning;
     the pride that dares not admit that it is wrong;
     the selfishness that can see nothing but its own will;
     the righteousness that knows no fault;
     the callousness that has ceased to care;
     the defiance that does not regret its own sins;
     the evasion that always tries to make excuses;
     the coldness of heart that is too hardened to repent.
     God, we are sinners; be merciful to us.

3   Almighty God,
     you love us, but we have not loved you;
     you call, but we have not listened.
     We walk away from neighbours in need,
     wrapped up in our own concerns.
     We have gone along with evil,
     with prejudice, warfare, and greed.

God our Father,
help us to face up to ourselves,
so that, as you move toward us in mercy,
we may repent, turn to you, and receive forgiveness;
through Jesus Christ our Lord.

4   Heavenly Father,
we confess that we have sinned against you
and our neighbour.
We have walked in darkness rather than in light;
we have named the name of Christ,
but have not departed from iniquity.
Have mercy on us, we pray;
for the sake of Jesus Christ forgive us all our sins;
cleanse us by your Holy Spirit;
quicken our consciences;
and enable us to forgive others;
that we may henceforth serve you in newness of life,
to the glory of your holy name.

5   God our Father,
you love us with an everlasting love.
But we confess, with sorrow,
that we have loved neither you nor our neighbour
as we should.
You have called us to be your people,
but we confess, with shame,
that our response has been half-hearted and indecisive.
Loving God,
enable us to face up to what we really are,
that, turning to you in penitence and faith,
we may receive forgiveness and healing;
through Jesus Christ our Lord.

6   Merciful God,
     we have sinned in what we have thought and said,
     in the wrong we have done,
     and in the good we have not done.
     We have sinned in ignorance;
     we have sinned in weakness;
     we have sinned through our own deliberate fault.
     We repent and turn to you.
     Forgive us, for our Saviour Christ's sake,
     and renew our lives to the glory of your name.

7   Holy God,
     we confess that often we have failed
     to be an obedient church.
     We have not done your will;
     we have broken your law;
     we have rebelled against your love;
     we have not loved our neighbours;
     and we have not heard the cry of the needy.
     Forgive us, we pray.
     Free us for joyful obedience;
     through Jesus Christ our Lord.

8   Almighty and most merciful Father,
     we have strayed from your ways like lost sheep.
     We have left undone what we ought to have done,
     and we have done what we ought not to have done.
     We have followed our own ways
     and the desires of our own hearts.
     We have broken your holy laws.
     Yet, good Lord, have mercy on us;
     restore those who are penitent,
     according to your promises declared to all people
     in Jesus Christ our Lord.

And grant, merciful Father, for his sake,
that we may live a godly and obedient life,
to the glory of your holy name.

9   O God,
we confess the things we try to hide from you;
the things we try to hide from others;
the things we try to hide from ourselves.
We confess the worry and heartbreak
that we have caused others,
and the things we have said and done
which make it hard for them to forgive us.
We confess the times we have made it easy
for others to go wrong;
we confess the harm we have done, and cannot undo,
making it hard for us to forgive ourselves.
Lord, have mercy, forgive us and renew us.

10 Most merciful God,
we confess that we have sinned against you
in thought, word, and deed.
We have not loved you with our whole heart.
We have not loved our neighbours as ourselves.
We pray you, of your mercy,
to forgive what we have been,
to help us to amend what we are,
and to direct what we shall be;
that we may delight in your will
and walk in your ways;
through Jesus Christ our Lord.

11   Almighty God our Father,
we have sinned against you and one another;
we have sinned in thought, word, and deed,
by what we have done,
and by what we have left undone.
In your mercy forgive what we have been,
help us to correct what we are,
and direct what we shall be;
through Jesus Christ our Lord.

12   Almighty God, our heavenly Father,
we have sinned against you and against one another,
in thought and word and deed,
in the evil we have done
and in the good we have not done,
through ignorance, through weakness,
through our own deliberate fault.
We are truly sorry and repent of all our sins.
For the sake of your Son Jesus Christ, who died for us,
forgive us all that is past;
and grant that we may serve you in newness of life
to the glory of your name.

13 Almighty God, most merciful Father,
who created us for life together:
we confess that we have turned from your way.
We have not loved you with all our heart;
we have not loved one another as you commanded.
We have been quick to claim our own rights,
but careless of the rights of others.
We have taken much and given little.
Holy God, whose compassion never ends,
we ask you to forgive us our sins,
and to blot out all our guilt,
that we may know again the joy of your Spirit;
through Jesus Christ our Lord.

If a prayer of confession is to include the three-fold response 'Lord, have mercy' (*Kyrie, eleison*), the prayer should be structured in the form of three short sentences.

After the call to confession, silence should be kept for a time to enable people to make their personal confession of sin. A short period of silence should also be observed after each of the three parts of the prayer, to enable people to relate the words of the sentences to their own lives.

Worship leaders are encouraged to prepare their own sentences, basing them on the theme of the day or on one or more of the Scripture readings.

The three-fold prayer is usually a confession of our human frailty and sin or an affirmation of the grace and goodness of God. A prayer may include both elements, beginning with confession of sin and concluding with the affirmation of God.

The people's response may be said or sung. Some settings provide for the response to be sung after each of the three sections of the prayer. Other settings are written for use at the conclusion of the prayer; in which case the people may say the responses during the prayer and then join with the choir in singing the whole of 'Lord, have mercy'.

The following are given as examples:

CONFESSION

14 Because we nurture too many grudges against others:
Lord, have mercy.
Lord, have mercy.

Because we are sometimes unwilling to forgive:
Christ, have mercy.
Christ, have mercy.

Because we are slow to seek peace and reconciliation:
Lord, have mercy.
Lord, have mercy.

15 For our foolish or careless use
of the gifts of your creation:
Lord, have mercy. .
Lord, have mercy.

For our indifference to the needs of others,
our brothers and sisters for whom you died:
Christ, have mercy.
Christ, have mercy.

For our neglect of the means of grace,
for superficial worship, for selfish prayer:
Lord, have mercy.
Lord, have mercy.

16 We have failed to love you with all our heart
and to be good stewards of your creation:
Lord, have mercy.
Lord, have mercy.

We have failed to take up the cross of discipleship
and to be good stewards of your gospel:
Christ, have mercy.
Christ, have mercy.

We have failed to be faithful members of your church
and to be good stewards of your spiritual gifts:
Lord, have mercy.
Lord, have mercy.

17 Always ready to forgive the penitent sinner:
Lord, have mercy.
Lord, have mercy.

Never despairing of our frail human nature:
Christ, have mercy.
Christ, have mercy.

For ever willing to help us make a new beginning:
Lord, have mercy.
Lord, have mercy.

18 Lord Jesus Christ,
you came into this world to save sinners:
Lord, have mercy.
Lord, have mercy.

You suffered and died upon the cross
that our sins might be forgiven:
Christ, have mercy.
Christ, have mercy.

You live for ever, our risen and ascended Saviour,
making intercession for us:
Lord, have mercy.
Lord, have mercy.

19 Your grace is a never-ending fountain of love:
Lord, have mercy.
Lord, have mercy.

You offer life-giving water to all without cost:
Christ, have mercy.
Christ, have mercy.

You call us to drink of thirst-quenching Spirit:
Lord, have mercy.
Lord, have mercy.

20 Lord Jesus,
you came to reconcile us to the Father
and to one another:
Lord, have mercy.
Lord, have mercy.

Lord Jesus,
you heal the wounds of sin and division:
Christ, have mercy.
Christ, have mercy.

Lord Jesus,
you offer us the chance to start again:
Lord, have mercy.
Lord, have mercy.

21 Because our personal sins grieve you
and hurt other people:
Lord, have mercy.
Lord, have mercy.

Because our social sins hold others
in bondage and oppression:
Christ, have mercy.
Christ, have mercy.

Because you grant us the joy of forgiveness
whenever we return to you in genuine repentance:
Lord, have mercy.
Lord, have mercy.

22 We have journeyed into the far country
and wasted our gifts and resources:
Lord, have mercy.
Lord, have mercy.

We have turned our back on family and friends
and sought our own selfish pleasures:
Christ, have mercy.
Christ, have mercy.

But patiently waiting, you have kept on loving us,
and then welcomed us home with rejoicing:
Lord, have mercy.
Lord, have mercy.

Declarations of Forgiveness and Prayers for Forgiveness

1 God so loved the world that he gave his only Son,
that whoever believes in him should not perish
but have eternal life.   *John 3:16*

2 God sent his Son into the world,
not to condemn the world,
but that the world might be saved through him.
Those who believe in him are not condemned.
                                            John 3:17, 18

3 While we were yet helpless,
at the right time Christ died for the ungodly.   *Romans 5:6*

4 God shows his love for us
in that, while we were yet sinners,
Christ died for us.   *Romans 5:8*

5 Those who are in Christ are a new creation;
the old has passed away,
behold, the new has come.
All this is from God,
who through Christ reconciled us to himself.
                                        2 Corinthians 5:17, 18

6 God was in Christ, reconciling the world to himself,
not counting our trespasses against us,
and entrusting to us the message of reconciliation.
                                            2 Corinthians 5:19

7　God has forgiven us all our trespasses,
　　having cancelled the bond which stood against us
　　with its legal demands;
　　this God set aside, nailing it to the cross. *Colossians 2:13, 14*

8　The saying is sure and worthy of full acceptance,
　　that Christ Jesus came into the world to save sinners.
　　　　　　　　　　　　　　　　　　　　　　　　1 Timothy 1:15

9　God is light, and in him is no darkness at all.
　　If we walk in the light, as God is in the light,
　　we have fellowship with one another,
　　and the blood of Jesus his Son cleanses us from all sin.
　　　　　　　　　　　　　　　　　　　　　　　　　　1 John 1:7

10　If we confess our sins,
　　God is faithful and just, and will forgive our sins
　　and cleanse us from all unrighteousness.　　*1 John 1:9*

11　If any one sins,
　　we have an advocate with the Father,
　　Jesus Christ the righteous;
　　and he is the perfect offering for our sins,
　　and not for ours only
　　but also for the sins of the whole world.　　*1 John 2:1, 2*

DECLARATIONS OF FORGIVENESS

12　The good news is that all who trust in Christ
　　will have their sins forgiven
　　and receive the gift of eternal life.

As you hold this faith,
I declare that you are set free from all your sins
in the name of the Father,
and of the Son,
and of the Holy Spirit,
to whom be glory for ever and ever.

13   By the authority of Jesus Christ
I declare that God has mercy on you,
pardons you and sets you free.
Know that your sins are forgiven
through Jesus Christ our Saviour.
God strengthen you in all goodness
and keep you in eternal life.

14   Good people,
I now declare to you that almighty God,
who absolves all who truly repent,
grants you the forgiveness of all your sins.
I give you this glad assurance
in the name of the Father,
and of the Son,
and of the Holy Spirit,
to whom be glory for ever and ever.

15   Our heavenly Father, in tender mercy,
has given his Son Jesus to die for us,
and for his sake, forgives us all our sins.
By the authority of Christ,
I therefore declare to you the forgiveness of all your sins,
in the name of the Father,
and of the Son,
and of the Holy Spirit.

16   My brothers and sisters in Christ,
      you have confessed your sins to God.
      Therefore, in the name of God,
      Father, Son, and Holy Spirit,
      I assure you that you are forgiven.
      You are set free from your sins by the power of Christ,
      who raises you up to new life in the Spirit.
      To the only God our Saviour,
      who so graciously forgives us and sets us free,
      be glory, majesty, power and authority,
      before all ages, now and for evermore.

17   Christ Jesus came into the world to save sinners.
      Hear then the word of grace and the assurance of pardon:
      Your sins are forgiven.

18   You have opened your hearts to God in confession;
      may they remain open
      to receive God's forgiveness and peace,
      as we declare to you
      that you are released from all your sins,
      in the name of the Father,
      and of the Son,
      and of the Holy Spirit,
      to whom be glory for ever and ever.

19   God is love.
      Through Christ your sins are forgiven.
      Take hold of this forgiveness
      and live your life in the power of the Holy Spirit.

20 Dear friends,
the gospel by which we seek to live states unequivocally
that nothing can separate us from the love of God
in Christ Jesus our Lord.
On the authority of this gospel
I declare to all who truly repent:
in Jesus Christ you are forgiven;
for which we give glory
to the Father, the Son, and the Holy Spirit,
for ever and ever.

PRAYERS FOR FORGIVENESS

21 Almighty God have mercy on you,
pardon and deliver you from all your sins,
confirm and strengthen you in all goodness,
and keep you in eternal life;
through Jesus Christ our Lord.

22 Merciful Lord,
grant to your faithful people pardon and peace,
that they may be cleansed from all their sins,
and serve you with a quiet mind;
through Jesus Christ our Lord.

23 Almighty God have mercy on you,
forgive you all your sins through our Lord Jesus Christ,
strengthen you in all goodness,
and by the power of the Holy Spirit
keep you in eternal life.

24 The almighty and merciful God
grant us pardon and remission of all our sins,
time for amendment of life,
and the grace and comfort of the Holy Spirit.

25 Almighty God,
who has promised forgiveness
to all who turn to him in faith,
pardon you and set you free from all your sins,
strengthen you to do his will,
and keep you in eternal life;
through Jesus Christ our Lord.

Prayers for Illumination

1   O Lord our God,
    you have given your word
    to be a lamp to our feet and a light to our path.
    Grant us grace to receive your truth in faith and love,
    that we may be obedient to your will
    and live always for your glory;
    through Jesus Christ our Lord.

2   O God,
    you have prepared for those who love you
    such good things as pass our human understanding:
    pour into our hearts such love towards you,
    that, loving you above all things,
    we may obtain your promises
    which exceed all that we can desire;
    through Jesus Christ our Lord.

3   Come upon us now, O Holy Spirit,
    and give us holy thoughts which are translated into prayer,
    holy prayers which are translated into love,
    and holy love which is translated into life;
    for the sake of Christ Jesus our Lord.

4   O God,
    because we are not able to please you
    unless you live in us and we live in you,
    mercifully grant that the Holy Spirit
    may in all things direct and rule our hearts;
    through Jesus Christ our Lord.

5   Lord Jesus,
    open our deaf ears
    and give sight to our blind eyes,
    that we may receive your word of grace
    and rejoice to see your coming kingdom.

6 O God of light and truth,
   pour down on us the spirit of wisdom and understanding.
   Through hearing the holy Scriptures,
   may we receive by faith the words of eternal life;
   through Jesus Christ our Lord.

7 Let the words of my mouth
   and the meditation of our hearts
   be acceptable in your sight, O Lord,
   our strength and our redeemer.   *Psalm 19:14*

8 O God,
   let the gospel of your Son come to us,
   not only in word and sign, but in power and love.
   May the Holy Spirit teach us now,
   that we may receive with understanding
   what you have revealed,
   and eagerly do what you have commanded;
   through Jesus Christ our Lord.

9 Loving God,
   you have so made us that we cannot live by bread alone,
   but by every word that proceeds from your holy mouth.
   Cause us now to hunger after your word,
   and in that food to find our daily need;
   through Jesus Christ our Lord.

10 Most wonderful God,
   let the same mind be in us
   which was in Christ Jesus our Lord.
   When we speak,
   let us speak with the will to proclaim your truth.

When we listen,
let us listen with the will to understand and obey;
in Jesus' name we pray.

11   O God,
you commanded the light to shine out of darkness:
shine into our hearts,
to give the light of the knowledge of your glory
in the face of Jesus Christ;
to whom with you and the Holy Spirit
be honour and glory, now and for ever.

12   Holy God,
your word is sharper than a two-edged sword,
piercing both heart and conscience with many wounds.
Let the sword of the Spirit pierce us through,
and grant that the wounds
which are made by your justice and righteousness
may be healed by your mercy and grace;
through Jesus Christ our Lord.

13   Prepare our hearts, O Lord, to receive your word.
Silence in us any voice but your own,
that hearing, we may also obey your will;
through Jesus Christ our Lord.

14   Guide us, O God, by your word and Holy Spirit,
that in your light we may see light,
in your truth find freedom,
and in your will discover our peace;
through Christ our Lord.

Ascriptions of Glory

1   O the depth of the riches and wisdom
and knowledge of God.
How unsearchable are God's judgments
and how mysterious are God's ways.
To God be glory for ever and ever.   *Romans 11:33, 36*

2   Now to the One
who is able to do far more abundantly
than all that we ask or think,
to God be glory in the church and in Christ Jesus
to all generations, for ever and ever.   *Ephesians 3:20, 21*

3   Now to the King of ages,
immortal, invisible, the only God,
be honour and glory for ever and ever.   *1 Timothy 1:17*

4   Now to the blessed and only Sovereign,
the King of kings and Lord of lords,
who alone has immortality
and dwells in unapproachable light,
be honour and eternal dominion.   *1 Timothy 6:15, 16*

5   To the God of all grace,
who has called you to eternal glory in Christ,
be the dominion for ever and ever.   *1 Peter 5:10, 11*

6   Now to the One who is able to keep you from falling
and to present you without blemish
before the presence of his glory with rejoicing,
to the only God our Saviour,
through Jesus Christ our Lord,
be glory, majesty, dominion, and authority,
before all time and now and for ever.   *Jude: 24, 25*

7   To Jesus Christ the faithful witness,
     the first-born of the dead,
     who loves us and has freed us from our sins by his blood,
     and made us a kingdom, priests to his God and Father,
     to him be glory and dominion for ever and ever.

     Revelation 1:5, 6

8   Worthy is the Lamb who was slain,
     to receive power and wealth and wisdom
     and might and honour and glory and blessing.

     Revelation 5:12

9   To God who sits upon the throne and to the Lamb
     be blessing and honour and glory and might
     for ever and ever.   *Revelation 5:13*

10   Blessing, glory and wisdom,
     thanksgiving and honour, power and might
     be to our God for ever and ever.   *Revelation 7:12*

11   And now let us ascribe to our God
     blessing and glory and wisdom,
     thanksgiving and honour, power and might,
     for ever and ever.   *Based on Revelation 7:12*

12   Great and wonderful are your deeds,
     O Lord God the Almighty.
     Just and true are your ways,
     O King of the ages.
     Who shall not fear and glorify your name, O Lord?
     For you alone are holy.   *Revelation 15:3, 4*

13   Glory to the Father,
         and to the Son,
         and to the Holy Spirit:
         as it was in the beginning,
         is now,
         and will be for ever.

14   Christ has died,
         Christ is risen,
         Christ will come again.

15   Dying you destroyed our death,
         rising you restored our life.
         Lord Jesus, come in glory.

16   And now to the holy name of God,
         the Father, the Son, and the Holy Spirit,
         let us ascribe in the church
         all honour and glory, might and majesty,
         dominion and blessing, now and for ever.

17   Christ is Victor.
         Christ is King.
         Christ is Lord of all.

Sentences Before the Offering

Occasionally the sentence of the day may be appropriate.

1 Ascribe to the Lord the glory due to his name;
    bring an offering, and come before him. *1 Chronicles 16:29*

2 The earth is the Lord's and all that is in it,
    the world and all who dwell therein.   *Psalm 24:1*

3 Bless the Lord, O my soul,
    and all that is within me, bless his holy name.
    Bless the Lord, O my soul,
    and forget not all his benefits.   *Psalm 103:1, 2*

4 How shall I repay the Lord
    for all the good things he has done for me?
    I will fulfil my vows to the Lord
    in the presence of all his people.   *Psalm 116:12, 14*

5 Honour the Lord with your substance
    and with the first fruits of all your produce. *Proverbs 3:9*

6 Going into the house,
    they saw the child with Mary his mother,
    and they fell down and worshipped him.
    Then, opening their treasures, they offered him gifts.
                                  Matthew 2:11

7 Let your light so shine before others,
    that they may see your good works
    and give glory to your Father who is in heaven.
                                  Matthew 5:16

8 Do not lay up for yourselves treasures on earth,
where moth and rust consume
and where thieves break in and steal;
but lay up for yourselves treasures in heaven,
where neither moth nor rust consumes
and where thieves do not break in and steal.
For where your treasure is,
there will your heart be also. *Matthew 6:19-21*

9 Freely you have received,
freely give. *Matthew 10:8b*

10 Having gifts that differ according to the grace given to us,
let us use them:
whoever contributes, with generosity;
whoever gives help, with enthusiasm;
whoever does acts of mercy, with cheerfulness.
Romans 12:6, 8

11 You know the grace of our Lord Jesus Christ:
though he was rich, yet for our sake he became poor,
so that by his poverty you might become rich.
2 Corinthians 8:9

12 They who sow sparingly will also reap sparingly;
they who sow bountifully will also reap bountifully.
2 Corinthians 9:6

13 Every one must do as they have made up their mind,
not reluctantly or under compulsion,
for God loves a cheerful giver. *2 Corinthians 9:7*

14 Do not neglect to do good
and to share what you have,
for such sacrifices are pleasing to God. *Hebrews 13:16*

Prayers Over the Gifts

1   We bless you, Lord God, creator of the world;
    from you every good and perfect gift comes.
    Accept these offerings of ours
    as firstfruits of our love and gratitude,
    and enable us to give ourselves wholly
    in the life of your kingdom;
    through Jesus Christ our Lord.

2   Blessed are you, Lord God our Father;
    through your goodness we have these gifts to share.
    Accept and use our offerings for your glory
    and for the service of your kingdom.

3   Everything in heaven and earth comes from you, Lord.
    We give you only what is yours.
    May you be praised for ever and ever.

4   May the Holy Spirit be upon us now
    to cleanse our hearts,
    to hallow our gifts,
    and to perfect the offering of ourselves
    for love of Jesus Christ our Lord.

5   We bring our gifts to you, Lord God,
    in gratitude and hope.
    In dedicating them, we dedicate ourselves again
    to be your people in the world,
    in the strength and enabling power
    of Jesus Christ our Lord.

6   We offer these gifts, Lord,
    for the work of your church
    and the welfare of your people;
    acknowledging with gratitude that we could give nothing
    if you had not first given to us.
    The money we have not brought today
    is also a trust from you.
    Help us to use all we have
    in accordance with your good will
    and for the glory of your name;
    through Jesus Christ our Lord.

7   We praise you, Lord Jesus Christ, for your generosity:
    you were rich, yet for our sake you became poor,
    so that through your poverty we might become rich.
    With our praise, O Lord, accept these gifts,
    and use them for the enrichment of others
    and for the glory of your name.

8   Out of the fullness of your gifts, O Lord,
    we bring these offerings now.
    In dedicating this money to the work of Christ's church
    we dedicate also ourselves,
    and pledge that we will live this week
    in the service of Christ,
    through the power of the Holy Spirit.

9   Merciful Father,
    receive and bless the offering of our worship and our gifts,
    and so consecrate our bodies, minds and spirits
    by the operation of your Holy Spirit,
    that we may give ourselves to you, a living sacrifice,
    dedicated and fit for your acceptance;
    through Jesus Christ our Lord.

10 Bless our gifts, Lord God,
    and grant that this offering may be for us
    a sign of a greater giving:
    the offering of our time and our talents,
    our loyalty and our love,
    indeed, the offering of our whole life
    for the service of Jesus Christ our Lord.

11 Lord God of power and might,
    graciously receive the gifts we offer;
    and let all our service give you glory and praise;
    through Christ our Lord.

12 Lord God,
    you have given us more than we asked for
    and more than we deserve.
    May we show a like generosity
    in all that we do for you and for our neighbours;
    through Jesus Christ our Lord.

13 Almighty God,
    you give all good gifts,
    you inspire all good works.
    As we make these offerings now,
    we pray that you will guide those
    who plan the use of the church's resources.
    In all things, may your will be done;
    through Jesus Christ our Lord.

14   Father in heaven,
we set before you our gifts
as signs that we are yours,
that we are committed to the mercy and faithfulness,
the justice and peace,
which Christ has come to bring.
Grant that in whatever we undertake
we may be empowered by your Spirit
to do it in the name of Christ your Son,
who lives and reigns for ever and ever.

15   Creator Spirit,
without whose power no good was ever done:
we believe it to be your will
to make one great family on earth,
living together in love and joy and peace
as citizens of heaven.
Fulfil this holy purpose through us your servants.
Take the labour of our hands and minds,
our time, our talents and our possessions,
and make of this rough-hewn humanity
a perfect fellowship

Thanksgivings

The opening dialogue 'The Lord be with you . . .' may be used to introduce prayers of thanksgiving even when holy communion is not being celebrated.

1   The Lord be with you.
    And also with you.

    Lift up your hearts.
    We lift them to the Lord.

    Let us give thanks to the Lord our God.
    It is right to give our thanks and praise.

Eternal God,
we thank you for the refreshment we receive
as we celebrate, Sunday by Sunday,
the day of creation,
the day of resurrection,
the day the Spirit came upon the church.

You divide day from night,
and invite us to live as children of the light.
You raised Jesus from the dead,
and offer us life in all its fullness.
You gather disciples together,
and set us on fire to proclaim your power in every age.

We thank you that our life and ministry
are set in a time of challenge;
that our faith is tested,
our ways rough and uncharted;
and we thank you for your promise
to save us from the time of trial.
Thus you teach us to depend on your grace,
and to live close to you in humility and hope.

Draw us closer to those whom you love;
attune our ears to the cry of the poor;
open our eyes to see Christ in those around us.
Make us instruments of peace and reconciliation,
in your way and in your time.
And do not leave us alone
until we come to your eternal kingdom;
through Jesus Christ our Lord.

2 The Lord be with you.
And also with you.

Lift up your hearts.
We lift them to the Lord.

Let us give thanks to the Lord our God.
It is right to give our thanks and praise.

Holy God, we praise you.
Let the heavens be joyful,
and the earth be glad.

We bless you for creating the whole world,
for your promise to your people Israel,
and for the life we know in Jesus Christ your Son.

Born of Mary, he shares our life.
Eating with sinners, he welcomes us.
Leading his followers, he guides us.
Dying on the cross, he rescues us.
Risen from the dead, he gives new life.

Send to us the Holy Spirit,
that your people may become one.
Unite us in faith, inspire us to love,
encourage us with hope,
that, being made one with Christ,
we may be one with each other
and one in ministry to all the world,
until Christ comes in final victory.

We praise you, almighty Father,
through Christ your Son,
in the Holy Spirit.

3 The Lord be with you.
And also with you.

Lift up your hearts.
We lift them to the Lord.

Let us give thanks to the Lord our God.
It is right to give our thanks and praise.

Almighty and merciful God,
from whom comes every good and perfect gift:
we praise you for your mercies,
for your goodness that has created us,
your grace that has sustained us,
your discipline that has corrected us,
your patience that has borne with us,
and your love that has redeemed us.
Help us to love you,
and to be thankful for all your gifts
by serving you and delighting to do your will;
through Jesus Christ our Lord.

4 The Lord be with you.
And also with you.

Lift up your hearts.
We lift them to the Lord.

Let us give thanks to the Lord our God.
It is right to give our thanks and praise.

Accept, O God, our thanks and praise
for all you have done for us.
We thank you for the splendour of the whole creation,
for the beauty of this world,
for the wonder of life,
and for the mystery of love.
We thank you for the blessing of family and friends,
and for the loving care which surrounds us on every side.
We thank you for setting us tasks
which demand our best efforts,
and for leading us to accomplishments
which satisfy and delight us.
We thank you also for those disappointments and failures
that lead us to acknowledge our dependence
on you alone.
Above all, we thank you for your Son Jesus Christ:
for the truth of his word and the example of his life;
for his steadfast obedience,
by which he overcame temptation;
for his dying, through which he overcame death;
for his rising to life again,
in which we are raised to the life of your kingdom.
Grant us the gift of your Spirit,
that we may know Christ and make him known;
and through him, at all times and in all places,
may give thanks to you in all things.

5 The Lord be with you.
And also with you.

Lift up your hearts.
We lift them to the Lord.

Let us give thanks to the Lord our God.
It is right to give our thanks and praise.

Almighty God,
we your unworthy servants give you humble thanks
for all your goodness and loving-kindness
to us and to all whom you have made.
We bless you for our creation, preservation,
and all the blessings of this life;
but above all for your immeasurable love
in the redemption of the world by our Lord Jesus Christ;
for the means of grace, and for the hope of glory.
And, we pray, give us such an awareness of your mercies,
that with truly thankful hearts
we may show forth your praise,
not only with our lips, but in our lives,
by giving up ourselves to your service,
and by walking before you
in holiness and righteousness all our days;
through Jesus Christ our Lord,
to whom with you and the Holy Spirit
be honour and glory throughout all ages.

This prayer is also No. 50 in 'A Treasury of Prayers', *People's Book*.

6 The Lord be with you.
And also with you.

Lift up your hearts.
We lift them to the Lord.

Let us give thanks to the Lord our God.
It is right to give our thanks and praise.

We give you thanks, O God,
for revealing your power in the creation of the universe,
and for your providence in the life of the world;
for men and women made in your image
to rule in your name over all that you have made.
We bless your holy name, good Lord.

For the victory of light over darkness, and truth over error;
for the knowledge of your prophetic word
setting us free from fear and despair;
for the advancement of your reign of justice and peace,
of holiness and love:
we bless your holy name, good Lord.

For the revelation of your kingdom in our midst
by your Son, Jesus Christ,
who came on earth
to manifest and to accomplish your will;
for his humble birth and his holy life,
and for his words and miracles;
for his sufferings and death,
and his entry into kingship
by his resurrection and ascension:
we bless your holy name, good Lord.

For the founding of the universal church,
spread to the ends of the earth;
for the coming of your kingdom within us
by the gifts of your Holy Spirit;
for the advent of your kingdom at the end of time
when you will be all in all:
we bless your holy name, good Lord.

7   The Lord be with you.
     And also with you.

     Lift up your hearts.
     We lift them to the Lord.

     Let us give thanks to the Lord our God.
     It is right to give our thanks and praise.

     Father,
     through Jesus Christ and in the power of the Holy Spirit,
     receive our thanksgivings:
     for the creation of the universe through your Word,
     for making us in your own image and likeness,
     for the revelation of your purposes
     through the law and the prophets,
     we give you thanks and praise.

For the gift of your Son, Jesus Christ our Lord:
for his lowly birth of Mary,
for his baptism in the Jordan,
for his ministry of preaching, teaching and healing,
we give you thanks and praise.

For his steadfast love in going to Jerusalem,
for his agony in the garden of Gethsemane,
for his suffering and death on the cross,
we give you thanks and praise.

For his resurrection from the dead
and his ascension to your right hand in glory,
for his eternal intercession for us,
for the promise of his coming again to be our judge,
we give you thanks and praise.

For the outpouring of your Spirit on the church,
for the commissioning of your church to make disciples,
for the spreading of your kingdom throughout the world,
we give you thanks and praise.

Here any special thanksgivings may be offered.

So, Father, we offer ourselves to be a living sacrifice;
through Jesus Christ our Lord,
through whom you give us everything that is good,
who with you, Father, and the Holy Spirit, is God,
living and reigning for ever.

8 The Lord be with you.
And also with you.

Lift up your hearts.
We lift them to the Lord.

Let us give thanks to the Lord our God.
It is right to give our thanks and praise.

The special thanksgivings that are indented are suggestions which may be varied or omitted.

You are worthy to receive our prayers and praises,
heavenly Father, eternal Lord God;
and with all the church in heaven and on earth
we praise you for your majesty and glory,
for your goodness and grace.
We thank you for the wonders of creation,
and for the revelation of yourself to the world:
  for your gift of life to us
  for your mercy and grace throughout our lives
  for the joy of loving and being loved
  for all that is true and noble, all that is good and pure
For these gifts we give you thanks and praise.

We thank you that you so loved the world
that you sent your Son to be our Saviour,
that whoever believes in him should have eternal life:
   for his dwelling among us, full of grace and truth
   for his dying for us on the cross
   for his rising again to be our eternal priest and king
   for his promise that he will come again and be our judge
For the gift of Jesus Christ we give you thanks and praise.

We thank you for the presence and work
of the Holy Spirit:
   for creating fellowship in the truth
   for sanctifying your family, the church
   for spreading the gospel throughout the world
   for revealing the things of Christ
For the gift of your holy and life-giving Spirit
we give you thanks and praise.

And so, Father, in his power,
we offer ourselves to be a living sacrifice in your service;
strengthen us to serve you,
and gather us and all people to your kingdom;
through Jesus Christ our Lord.

9 The Lord be with you.
And also with you.

Lift up your hearts.
We lift them to the Lord.

Let us give thanks to the Lord our God.
It is right to give our thanks and praise.

Father,
you are worthy of praise from every creature,
and we give you our thanks and praise
for your goodness and love.
You formed us in your image,
and set us over the whole world to serve you, our Creator.

But we disobeyed your will,
and turned against each other.
Yet you did not leave us.
Again and again you called us to yourself;
and in the fullness of time
you sent your only Son to be our Saviour.
Great and wonderful are all your works,
Lord God almighty;
just and true are all your ways.

He came to dwell among us,
and laid down his life for us.
By his death he has destroyed death,
and by his rising again he has given us eternal life.
In him you have forgiven our sins,
and made us worthy to stand before you.
In him you have brought us out of darkness
into his marvellous light.
Through him you have made all things new.
Glory to you, our Father, for ever and ever.

And that we might no longer live for ourselves,
but for you,
through him you sent the Holy Spirit
as your gift to those who believe,
to complete his work on earth
and to lead us into all truth.

Here any special thanksgivings may be offered.

Father, through Jesus Christ your Son
we have been accepted and made your children
by water and the Spirit.
So, through him, we now offer ourselves again to you
to be a living sacrifice to your praise and glory.

10   The Lord be with you.
And also with you.

Lift up your hearts.
We lift them to the Lord.

Let us give thanks to the Lord our God.
It is right to give our thanks and praise.

We thank you, O God,
for you are gracious.
You have loved us from the beginning of time
and you have remembered us when we were in trouble.
Your mercy endures for ever.

We thank you, O God,
for you came to us in Jesus Christ,
who has redeemed the world
and saved us from our sins.
Your mercy endures for ever.

We thank you, O God,
for you send us your Holy Spirit,
to comfort us
and to lead us into all truth.
Your mercy endures for ever.

Intercessions

The range of intercessory prayer is so wide that only a few prayers are included here.

At the conclusion of this section, topics for intercessory prayer, without resources, are listed.

For the Mission of the Church

1   O Loving God,
      you have made of one blood all the peoples of the earth,
      and sent your blessed Son to preach peace
      to those who are far off and to those who are near.
      Grant that people everywhere may seek after you
      and find you;
      bring the nations into your fold;
      pour out your Spirit on all flesh;
      and hasten the coming of your kingdom;
      through Jesus Christ our Lord.

2   Gracious God,
      you have called us to be the church of Jesus Christ.
      Keep us one in faith and service,
      breaking bread together
      and telling the good news to the world;
      that all may believe you are love,
      turn to your ways, and live to your glory;
      through Jesus Christ our Lord.

3 We praise you, Lord of all,
for the gifts of Christ our ascended King:
for apostles, prophets, evangelists, pastors and teachers.
Hear our prayer for all who do not know your love
and have not heard the gospel of our Saviour Jesus Christ.
Send out your light and truth
through the messengers of your word;
help us to support them by our prayers and offerings,
and hasten the coming of your kingdom;
through Jesus Christ our Lord.

4 The whole world lives in your love, holy God,
and we are your people.
Send us out in faith to tell your story
and to demonstrate your truth to every race and nation;
so that, won by your powerful word,
people may join together to give you praise,
living to serve you in Jesus Christ our Lord.

5 O God of all the nations of the earth,
remember the multitudes
who have been created in your image but have not known
the redeeming work of our Saviour.
Grant that,
by the prayers and labours of your holy church,
they may be brought to know and worship you
as you have been revealed in your Son, Jesus Christ;
to whom be glory for ever and ever.

For the Unity of the Church

6 Almighty Father,
whose blessed Son before his passion
prayed for his disciples
that they might be one, as you and he are one:

grant that your church,
being bound together in love and obedience to you,
may be united in one body by the one Spirit;
that the world may believe in him whom you have sent,
your Son Jesus Christ our Lord;
who lives and reigns with you
in the unity of the Holy Spirit,
one God, now and for ever.

7   Lord Jesus Christ, you said to your apostles:
I leave you peace, my peace I give you.
Look not on our sins, but on the faith of your church,
and grant us the peace and unity of your kingdom
where you live for ever and ever.

8   God the Father of our Lord Jesus Christ,
our only Saviour, the Prince of Peace:
give us grace seriously to lay to heart
the great dangers we are in by our unhappy divisions.
Take away all hatred and prejudice,
and whatever else may hinder us
from godly union and peace;
that, as there is but one body, and one Spirit,
and one hope of our calling,
one Lord, one faith, one baptism,
one God and Father of us all,
so we may be all of one heart, and of one mind,
united in one holy bond of truth and peace,
of faith and love,
and may with one mind and one mouth glorify you;
through Jesus Christ our Lord.

For a Meeting of a Church Council

9   Almighty God,
    in Jesus Christ you called disciples,
    and by the Holy Spirit made them one church
    to serve you:
    be with members of our . . .
    Help them to welcome new things you are doing
    in the world,
    and to respect old things you keep and use.
    Save them from empty words and senseless controversy.
    Let the Holy Spirit guide and rule as decisions are made,
    so that our church may be united in service to the world
    and in love and obedience to Jesus Christ;
    who, having gone before us,
    is coming again to meet us in his kingdom.

10 Almighty God,
    you judge your people with wisdom
    and rule them with love:
    give a spirit of discernment and understanding
    to all the members of the . . . of our church;
    that they may make wise decisions
    which will give glory to you
    and bring blessings to your people.
    Grant this through our Lord Jesus Christ.

11 Lord Jesus Christ,
    by the presence and power of the Holy Spirit
    you presided over the first assembly of your apostles
    in Jerusalem,
    and you have promised to be with your church
    to the close of the age:
    grant your gracious presence and blessing
    to the members of . . .

Deliver them from prejudice and error;
enlighten them with wisdom from above;
and so guide all their decisions
that your kingdom may be advanced,
and congregations of your church may be built up
in faith and love;
to the glory of your holy name.

For the World

12   God our Father,
in Jesus Christ you have ordered us to live
as loving neighbours.
Though we are scattered in different lands,
speak different languages or descend from different races,
give us loving concern for all people,
so that we may become one people,
sharing the governing of the world
under your guiding purpose.
May greed, war, and lust for power be curbed,
and all people enter into the community of love
promised in Jesus Christ our Lord.

13   O merciful Creator,
your hand is open wide
to satisfy the needs of every living creature:
make us always thankful for your loving providence;
and grant that we, remembering the account
that we must one day give,
may be faithful stewards of your good gifts;
through Jesus Christ our Lord.

14 Creator God,
you made all things in your wisdom,
and in your love you save us.
We pray for the whole creation.
Order unruly powers, deal with unrighteousness,
feed and satisfy those who thirst for justice,
so that your children may freely enjoy
the earth you have made,
and cheerfully sing your praises;
through Jesus Christ our Lord.

For the Peace of the World

15 Almighty God,
from whom all thoughts of truth and peace proceed:
kindle, we pray, in the hearts of all people
the true love of peace;
and guide with your pure and peaceable wisdom
those who take counsel for the nations of the earth;
that in tranquillity your kingdom may go forward,
till the earth is filled with the knowledge of your love;
through Jesus Christ our Lord.

16 Eternal God,
our only hope, our help in time of trouble:
help the nations of the world
to work out their differences.
Do not let threats multiply,
or power be used without compassion.
May your word rule the words of world leaders,
so that they may agree and settle claims peacefully.
Restrain those who are impulsive,
that desire for vengeance
may not overwhelm our common welfare.

Give peace in our time, O Lord;
through Jesus Christ,
the Prince of Peace and Saviour of us all.

17   God of the nations,
whose kingdom rules over all:
have mercy on our broken and divided world.
Shed abroad your peace in the hearts of all people,
and banish from them the spirit that makes for war;
that all races and peoples may learn to live
as members of one family,
and in obedience to your laws;
through Jesus Christ our Lord.

18   Almighty God,
whose will is to restore all things in your beloved Son,
the king of all the world:
govern the hearts and minds of those in authority,
and bring the families of the nations,
divided and torn apart by the ravages of sin,
to be subject to Christ's just and gentle rule;
who is alive and reigns with you and the Holy Spirit,
one God, now and for ever.

For our Nation

19   Lord God almighty,
you have made all the peoples of the earth for your glory,
to serve you in freedom and in peace:
give to the people of our country
a zeal for justice and the strength of forbearance,
that we may use our liberty
in accordance with your gracious will;
through Jesus Christ our Lord.

20   O God, our help in ages past,
in your sight nations rise and fall,
and pass through times of peril:
be near to judge and save when our country is in trouble.
Grant our leaders your wisdom,
that they may search for your will and see it clearly.
Where as a nation we have turned from your path,
reverse our ways and help us to repent.
Give your light and truth to guide;
through Jesus Christ,
who is King of kings and Lord of this world.

21   Almighty God, the fountain of all goodness,
bless our sovereign lady, Queen Elizabeth,
and all who hold public office in this land;
that they may order all things
in wisdom, righteousness and peace,
to the honour of your holy name,
and the good of your church and people;
through Jesus Christ our Lord.

In Time of Drought, Flood or Bushfire

22   All things look to you, O Lord,
to give them their food in due season:
be merciful to all your people,
and hear our prayer for those whose lives and livelihood
are threatened by drought (*or* flood, *or* fire).
Guide and bless the labours of your people,
that all may enjoy the good gifts of your creation
and give you thanks with grateful hearts.
We ask this through our Lord Jesus Christ.

For Commerce and Industry

23   Almighty God,
whose Son Jesus Christ in his earthly life
shared our toil and hallowed our labour:
be present with your people where they work.
Make responsive to your will
those who carry on the industries
and commerce of this land;
and give to us all a pride in what we do,
and a just return for our labour;
through Jesus Christ our Lord.

For Industrial Peace

24   Almighty and everlasting God,
grant that we may live and work together
in unity and peace.
Give to all a spirit of respect and trust,
and an earnest desire to seek for justice
and the common good;
through Jesus Christ our Lord.

For Daily Work

25   Almighty God our heavenly Father,
you declare your glory and show forth your handiwork
in the heavens and in the earth:
deliver us in our various occupations
from the service of self alone,
that we may do the work you give us to fulfil
in truth and beauty, and for the common good;
for the sake of him who came among us
as one who serves, Jesus Christ our Lord.

26 Almighty God,
   you have so linked our lives with one another
   that all we do affects, for good or ill, the lives of others.
   So guide us in the work we do,
   that we may do it not for self alone,
   but for the common good.
   And as we seek a proper return from our own labour,
   make us mindful of the rightful aspirations
   of other workers,
   and arouse our concern for those who are out of work;
   through Jesus Christ our Lord.

For Families

27 Almighty God, our heavenly Father,
   whose Son Jesus Christ shared at Nazareth
   the life of an earthly home:
   bless our homes, we pray.
   Help parents to impart the knowledge of you
   and your love;
   and children to respond with love and obedience.
   May our homes be blessed with peace and joy;
   through Jesus Christ our Lord.

For Schools, Universities, and Other Places of Learning

28 Almighty Father,
   who commanded us to love you with all our mind:
   look with your gracious favour
   on our universities, colleges and schools.

Bless all who teach and all who learn;
grant that they may seek and love the truth,
grow in wisdom and knowledge,
and in humility of heart always look to you,
the source of all wisdom and understanding.
We ask this through Jesus Christ our Lord.

For Social Justice

29 Almighty God,
who created us in your own image:
grant us grace fearlessly to contend against evil
and to make no peace with oppression.
And may we reverently use our freedom,
employing it in the maintenance of justice
in our communities and among the nations,
to the glory of your holy name;
through Jesus Christ our Lord.

For Social Service

30 Heavenly Father,
whose blessed Son came not to be served but to serve:
bless all who follow in his steps
and give themselves to the service of others;
that with wisdom, patience and courage
they may minister in his name
to the suffering, the friendless and the needy;
for the love of him who laid down his life for us,
your Son, our Saviour Jesus Christ.

For those who are Unemployed

31 God of compassion,
we remember those who suffer want and anxiety
because they have no work.
Guide the people of this land to use our wealth
so that all may find fulfilling employment
and receive just payment for their labour;
through Jesus Christ our Lord.

For those who are Disabled

32 God of compassion,
in Jesus Christ you cared for those who were blind or deaf,
crippled or slow to learn.
Though all of us need help,
give special care to those who are disabled,
particularly those we name in silence . . .
By our concern may they know the love you have for
them,
and come to trust you;
through Jesus Christ who came to heal.

TOPICS FOR INTERCESSORY PRAYER

The Universal Church

The World Council of Churches and its agencies
Member churches of the World Council of Churches
The Roman Catholic Church
Other churches
The World Alliance of Reformed Churches

The World Methodist Council
Bible societies of the world
The Christian Conference of Asia
The Pacific Conference of Churches
International and ecumenical consultations
Missionary societies working for the spread of the gospel
Churches under persecution
People working in foreign countries in obedience to Christ

The World

The United Nations and its agencies
   (The General Secretary)
The British Commonwealth of Nations
   (Queen Elizabeth II)
The leaders of the nations
International agencies of relief and compassion
International agencies working in developing countries
Developing nations
Nations with the power and resources to work for justice
   for all people
Nations at war
Nations divided by civil strife and political unrest
Prisoners of conscience
Those countries where the gospel is not being clearly
   proclaimed and heard
People who are suffering from a natural disaster
People who have lost loved ones in international travel
Those who manage international trade and the world's
   monetary system
Those who work for the preservation of natural resources
   and the environment

The Church in Australia

The Australian Council of Churches and its agencies
Member churches of the Australian Council of Churches
The Roman Catholic, Lutheran, Baptist and other
   churches
Evangelistic witness for Christ
Ecumenical co-operation in christian education and social
   responsibility
The Assembly of the Uniting Church (The President and
   the General Secretary)
The Assembly Commission on Doctrine
The Assembly Commission on Ecumenical Affairs
The Assembly Commission on Liturgy
The Joint Board of Christian Education
The Assembly Commission for Mission (World Mission,
   Frontier Services, National Mission, Evangelism and
   Social Responsibility)
The Uniting Aboriginal and Islander Christian Congress
The Ministerial Education Commission
Other agencies of the Assembly (Finance Committee,
   Beneficiary Fund, Defence Forces Chaplaincy
   Committee, Legal Reference Committee)
The Assembly Standing Committee
The Synod in our own state (The Moderator and the
   Secretary of Synod)
The Standing Committee and other councils of the Synod
The Presbyteries within our state's Synod
Our own Presbytery (The Chairperson of Presbytery, the
   Secretary of Presbytery, the Presbytery Officer, the
   Presbytery Youth Worker)
The Pastoral Relations Committee and other councils of
   Presbytery

Theological Colleges and Lay Training Centres
Primary, Secondary and Tertiary schools and colleges
    under the care of the church
Aged Care homes and institutions
Central Missions and their agencies
Hospitals and other institutions of the Uniting Church
Industrial, hospital and prison chaplains
Ministers, deaconesses, lay preachers, lay pastors and lay
    workers
Elders, youth leaders and musicians

Australia

The Federal Parliament in Canberra (The Prime Minister
    and the Leader of the Opposition)
The members of Cabinet and all members of the Federal
    Parliament
Embassy staff working in foreign countries
The Governor General in Canberra and our state
    Governor
Our State Parliament (The Premier and the Leader of the
    Opposition)
The members of Cabinet and all members of the State
    Parliament
Our near neighbours (New Zealand, Niugini and the
    Solomon Islands, The Philippines, Indonesia, Fiji,
    Tonga, Samoa, New Caledonia, French Polynesia,
    Vanuatu, Kiribati, Tuvalu, Nauru, etc.)
Australian Aborigines
Those who have migrated recently to Australia
Members of minority ethnic and cultural groups
All those more than forty groupings for whom English is
    not their first language
Those elected to participate in local government

Our National, Social, Cultural and Economic Life

Universities, school and colleges
Hospitals and all those who work in the medical services
Those who work in science and technology
Those who grow food and all who live in rural Australia
Those who prepare and market food and all who live in
  cities
Those who work at home
Those who work in the private sector
Those who work in government departments
The trade union movement
Those who work in finance, commerce and management
Those who manufacture and sell
Those who work in skilled trades
Those who provide legal services
Those who serve in the armed forces
Those who construct and maintain essential services
Those who work in international communications
  systems
Those who provide public transport
Carpenters, mechanics, clothing manufacturers and all
  who work with their hands
Architects, planners and builders
Entertainers and those who work in the Arts
Writers, poets and publishers
Journalists, film makers and all who work in the media and
  public communications
Those who are physically disabled
The unemployed, those who are unable to work and
  those who are unable to find work
Those who are addicted to drugs
Those who suffer sexual confusion
Those in marital difficulty

Families where there is only one parent
Those who live below the poverty line
The homeless and those who are inadequately housed
Those who work in social welfare and agencies of
    compassion
Prisoners
The Police Force
Those who misuse freedom and live outside the law
Those involved in vice and organised crime

Local Community and Congregation

Kindergardens, schools and colleges
Hospitals and clinics
Service groups (Rotary, Kiwanis, Lions, Apex, etc.)
Sporting clubs
Local government agencies and services
Senior citizens complexes and nursing homes
Community organisations
The Inter-Church Council or Ministers' Fellowship
    Group
Other denominations working in our parish area
Other Uniting Church congregations in our parish
The Parish Council (The Chairperson and the Secretary)
Our Council of Elders and Meeting of the Congregation
Other committees of the congregation (Finance, Church
    Property, Worship, Evangelism, Education,
    Stewardship, etc.)
Bible study groups and house churches
Fellowship groups
The Sunday school and christian education programs
Those who are sick, physically, emotionally or spiritually
Those who are frail and housebound
Those who are aged

Those recently retired
Those in mid-life
Young families
Newly-married couples
Those who are single or who live alone
Children, youth and young adults
All who do not know and love Christ

Commemorations of the Faithful Departed

1   In you, Father, we are one family in earth and heaven.
    We remember in your presence those who have died,
    giving thanks especially for those
    who have revealed to us your grace in Christ.
    Help us to follow the example of your saints in light
    and bring us with them
    to the fullness of your eternal joy;
    through Jesus Christ our Lord.

2   Eternal God,
    we rejoice to know of all who, through the ages,
    have placed their trust in you:
    apostles, prophets, saints and martyrs
    and all the humble believers
    whose names are long forgotten.
    Give us the assurance
    that we belong to that great company
    and that we too may find the peace
    that passes understanding;
    through Jesus Christ our Lord.

3   Eternal God,
    whether we live or die we belong to you,
    for you are our everlasting refuge.
    We remember with thankfulness
    the good and faithful of all generations,
    and especially our own loved ones
    who, having finished their life on earth,
    now rejoice before you in the fullness of light.
    Grant us, in this life,
    to remain always in their company,
    and in the life to come
    to dwell with them for ever;
    through Jesus Christ our Lord,
    who lives and reigns with you and the Holy Spirit,
    ever one God, world without end.

4   Almighty God,
    we remember before you all who have lived among us:
    who have directed our steps in Christ's way,
    opened our eyes to the truth,
    inspired our hearts by their witness,
    and strengthened our wills by their devotion.
    We rejoice in their lives dedicated to your service.
    We honour them in their death,
    and pray that we may be united with them
    in the glory of Christ's resurrection.

5   We praise you, Lord God,
    for your faithful servants in every age;
    and we pray that we,
    with all who have died in the faith of Christ,
    may be brought to a joyful resurrection
    and the fulfilment of your eternal kingdom;
    through Jesus Christ our Lord.

6 Eternal Father,
God of the living and not of the dead:
we thank and praise you for the faithful of all generations
who served you in godliness and love
and are now with you in glory.
We thank you for those who have enriched the world
with truth and beauty,
for the wise and good of every land and age.
Teach us to follow them as they followed Christ;
that at the last we may receive with them
the prize of eternal life;
through Jesus the Christ, our Lord.

7 We bless you, O God,
for all your saints who have departed this life
in the faith of Christ,
especially those whom we remember today with love.
And we pray that we may lead faithful and godly lives
in this world,
and finally share with all the saints in everlasting joy;
through Jesus Christ our Lord.

8 Father,
we thank you for all the people, great and humble,
who have maintained the fabric of the world's life
in the past
and left us a great inheritance.
We pray that, building with them
on the same sure foundation,
our Saviour Jesus Christ,
we may be counted worthy also to share with them
in the life of your heavenly kingdom.

9   We thank you, Lord God,
    for the grace you gave to those
    who lived according to your will
    and are now at rest.
    We pray that their good example
    may encourage and guide us
    all the days of our life;
    through Jesus Christ our Lord.

10 God of all times and places,
    we remember with gratitude before you
    all the faithful departed,
    especially those whom we have loved.
    Make us worthy to inherit, with them,
    those good things beyond our seeing,
    beyond our hearing, beyond our imagining,
    which you have prepared for those who love you;
    through Jesus Christ our Lord.

Concluding Collects for Prayers of the People

1 Eternal God,
   ruler of all things in heaven and earth,
   accept the prayers of your people,
   and strengthen us to do your will;
   through Jesus Christ.

2 Almighty God,
   you have given us grace at this time with one accord
   to make our common supplications to you;
   and you have promised, through your well-beloved Son,
   that when two or three are gathered together in his name
   you will be in the midst of them.
   Fulfil now, O Lord, our desires and petitions
   as may be best for us;
   granting us in this world knowledge of your truth,
   and in the age to come life everlasting.

   This prayer is also No. 3 in 'A Treasury of Prayers', *People's Book*.

3 Lord our God,
   accept the fervent prayers of your people.
   In your great mercy,
   look with compassion on us
   and on all who turn to you for help;
   for you are gracious, O Lover of souls.
   To you we give glory, O blessed Trinity,
   now and for ever.

4 Heavenly Father,
you have promised through your Son Jesus Christ
that when we meet in his name
and pray according to his mind,
he will be among us and will hear our prayer.
In your love and wisdom fulfil our desires,
and give us your greatest gift,
which is to know you, the only true God,
and Jesus Christ our Lord;
who is alive and reigns with you and the Holy Spirit,
one God, now and for ever.

5 Hear our prayers, almighty God,
in the name of Jesus Christ,
who prays with us and for us.
To him be praise for ever.

6 Lord Jesus Christ,
you stretched out your arms of love
on the hard wood of the cross
that everyone might come within the reach
of your saving embrace.
So clothe us in your Spirit
that we, reaching forth our hands in love,
may bring those who do not know you
to the knowledge and love of you;
for the honour of your name.

7   O God,
     the author of peace and lover of concord,
     to know you is eternal life
     and to serve you is perfect freedom.
     Guide us by your truth,
     and order us in all our ways,
     that we may do what is right in your eyes;
     through Jesus Christ our Lord.

8   Heavenly Father,
     you sent your Son Jesus Christ
     to preach peace to those who are far off
     and to those who are near.
     Pour out your Spirit on the whole creation;
     bring the nations of the world into your fellowship;
     and hasten the coming of your kingdom;
     through Jesus Christ our Lord.

9   Mighty God,
     whose Word we trust,
     whose Spirit prays in our prayers:
     accept our requests
     and further those which will serve your purpose
     in the earth;
     through Jesus Christ, who rules over all things.

10   God of mercy,
     you have promised to hear what we ask
     in the name of Christ.
     Accept and fulfil our petitions, we pray,
     not as we ask in our ignorance,
     nor as we deserve in our sinfulness,
     but as you know and love us in Jesus Christ our Lord.

11 Into your hands, O God,
    we commend all for whom we pray,
    trusting in your mercy;
    through Jesus Christ our Lord.

12 Eternal God,
    you create us by your power and redeem us by your love.
    Guide and strengthen us by your Spirit,
    that we may give ourselves in love and service
    to one another and to you;
    through Jesus Christ our Lord.

Invitations to the Lord's Table

1   Hear the gracious words of our Saviour Jesus Christ:

Come to me, all who labour and are heavy laden,
and I will give you rest.
Take my yoke upon you, and learn from me;
for I am gentle and lowly in heart,
and you will find rest for your souls.   *Matthew 11:28, 29*

and/or

I am the bread of life.
Those who come to me shall not hunger,
and those who believe in me shall never thirst.
No one who comes to me will I cast out.   *John 6:35, 37*

and/or

Behold, I stand at the door and knock;
if those who hear my voice open the door,
I will come in to them and eat with them,
and they with me.   *Revelation 3:20*

2   This is the joyful feast of the people of God.

Taste and see that the Lord is good;
happy are they who trust in him.   *Psalm 34:8*

and/or

Blessed are those who hunger and thirst for righteousness,
for they shall be satisfied.   *Matthew 5:6*

and/or

They will come from east and west
and from north and south,
and sit at table in the kingdom of God.   *Luke 13:29*

and/or

According to Luke,
when our risen Lord was sharing an evening meal
with two friends in a home at Emmaus,
Jesus took the bread, and blessed and broke it,
and gave it to them.
Then their eyes were opened and they recognised him.

Luke 24:30, 31

and/or

This is the Lord's table.
Our Saviour invites those who trust him
to share the feast which he has prepared.

3 Come, let us take this holy sacrament
of the body and blood of Christ
in remembrance that he died for us,
and feed on him in our hearts by faith with thanksgiving.

4 I welcome you
to the worship of this congregation of God's people
and to the celebration of holy communion.
This is the Lord's table.
It is open to all members of the Uniting Church
and to all persons who in any fellowship of Christ's people
may receive holy communion in that fellowship.

Basis of Union, Appendix 1

5   This is the table of our Lord Jesus Christ.
    In great humility and love
    Jesus lived among us, he became one of us.
    He came, not to call the righteous,
    but sinners to repentance.
    He came, not to condemn us,
    but to save us from our sins.
    He understands our doubts, our lack of faith,
    our longing for more love, more holiness of life;
    and even now he accepts us as we are
    and calls us to be his disciples.

    Come then to this holy feast.
    Come to our crucified Saviour and risen Lord.
    The Master is here and is calling to you.
    Come and receive the signs of his presence,
    the body and blood of our Lord Jesus Christ.

6   Jesus is the Lamb of God
    who takes away the sin of the world.
    Happy are those who are called to his supper.

7   This is the Lord's table.
In this sacrament of his broken body
and outpoured blood,
the risen Lord feeds his baptised people
on their way to the final inheritance of the kingdom.
Through faith and the gift of the Holy Spirit,
we have communion with our Saviour;
we make our sacrifice of praise and thanksgiving;
we proclaim the Lord's death;
we grow together into Christ;
we are strengthened for our participation
in the mission of Christ in the world;
and we rejoice in the foretaste of the kingdom
which he will bring to consummation.

Basis of Union, para. 8

8   Draw near with faith.
Receive the body of our Lord Jesus Christ
which he gave for you,
and his blood which he shed for you.

Eat and drink in remembrance that he died for you,
and feed on him in your hearts by faith with thanksgiving.

Prayers of Approach

1   O God,
    by the blood of Jesus you have made us free
    to enter boldly into your holy presence
    by the new and living way he has opened for us.
    Help us to approach you in sincerity
    and in full assurance of faith.
    Accept and use both us and these gifts of bread and wine
    for the glory of your holy name.

2   Most blessed, most glorious God,
    before the brightness of your presence
    the angels and archangels veil their faces.
    Most blessed, most glorious God,
    in silent reverence and with adoring love
    we approach the mercy seat of your table,
    that here we may be nourished with heavenly food.

3   Father,
    by the blood of your dear Son
    you have consecrated for us a new and living way
    into the holiest of all.
    Help us in faith to enter with him,
    and grant that, being pure in heart by grace,
    we may share in his true, pure, and immortal sacrifice;
    through Jesus Christ our Lord.

4 Almighty Father,
we are unworthy to celebrate this sacrament,
but in your Son Jesus Christ
you have drawn near to us;
it is in his name that we draw near to you.
In obedience to his command
we present this bread and this cup.
All that we have comes from you,
and what we give you is your own.

5 Holy God,
by the blood of your dear Son
you have consecrated for us a new and living way
into the holiest of all.
Grant us, we pray, the assurance of your mercy,
and sanctify us by your heavenly grace;
that, approaching you with a pure heart
and cleansed conscience,
we may offer to you a sacrifice in righteousness;
through Jesus Christ our Lord.

See also:

Be present, risen Lord Jesus . . . page 81.

We do not presume to come to your table . . . page 81.

We give you thanks, O Father . . . No 2 in 'A Treasury of Prayers',
People's Book, page 212.

Prayers after Communion

1   Father, we thank you
    that you feed us who have received these holy mysteries
    with the spiritual food
    of the body and blood of our Saviour, Jesus Christ.
    We thank you
    for this assurance of your goodness and love,
    and that we are living members of his body
    and heirs of his eternal kingdom.
    Accept this our sacrifice of praise and thanksgiving,
    and help us to grow in love and obedience,
    that with all your saints we may worship you for ever.

2   Loving God,
    we thank you that you have fed us in this sacrament,
    united us with Christ,
    and given us a foretaste of the heavenly banquet
    in your eternal kingdom.
    We offer ourselves to you as a living sacrifice
    through Jesus Christ our Lord.
    Send us out in the power of your Spirit
    to live and work to your praise and glory.

3   Lord and heavenly Father,
    we your servants, desiring your fatherly goodness,
    ask you mercifully to accept
    our sacrifice of praise and thanksgiving;
    and to grant that,
    by the merits and death of your Son Jesus Christ,
    and through faith in his blood,
    we and your whole church
    may receive forgiveness of our sins
    and all other benefits of his passion.

And here we offer and present to you, O Lord,
ourselves, our souls and bodies,
to be a reasonable, holy and living sacrifice;
humbly beseeching you
that all we who are partakers of this holy communion
may be filled with your grace and heavenly benediction.

And although we are unworthy, through our many sins,
to offer you any sacrifice,
yet we pray that you will accept this,
the duty and service that we owe,
not weighing our merits but pardoning our offences,
through Jesus Christ our Lord;
by whom and with whom, in the unity of the Holy Spirit,
all honour and glory are yours, Father almighty,
now and for ever.

4   Eternal God, heavenly Father,
you have graciously accepted us as living members
of your Son our Saviour Jesus Christ,
and you have fed us with spiritual food
in the sacrament of his body and blood.
Send us now into the world in peace,
and grant us strength and courage
to love and serve you
with gladness and singleness of heart;
through Christ our Lord.

5   Most gracious God,
     you have made us one with all your people
     in heaven and on earth.
     You have fed us with the bread of life,
     and renewed us for your service.
     Now we give ourselves to you,
     and ask that our daily living
     may be part of the life of your kingdom.
     May our love be your love,
     reaching out into the life of the world;
     through Jesus Christ our Lord.

6   Almighty and everliving God,
     we heartily thank you that you graciously feed us,
     who have received these holy mysteries,
     with the spiritual food of the precious body and blood
     of your Son our Saviour Jesus Christ;
     and assure us thereby
     of your favour and goodness towards us,
     and that we are true members
     of the mystical body of your Son,
     the blessed company of all faithful people;
     and are also heirs, through hope, of your eternal kingdom,
     by the merits of the precious death of your dear Son.
     And we humbly beseech you, heavenly Father,
     so to assist us with your grace,
     that we may continue in that holy fellowship,
     and do all such good works
     as you have prepared for us to walk in;
     through Jesus Christ our Lord,
     to whom, with you and the Holy Spirit,
     be all honour and glory, now and for ever.

7　Father,
you graciously feed us
who have received these holy mysteries
with the bread of life and the cup of eternal salvation.
May we who have reached out our hands
to receive this sacrament
be strengthened in your service;
we who have sung your praises
tell of your glory and truth in our lives;
we who have seen the greatness of your love
see you face to face in your kingdom.
For you have made us your own people
by the death and resurrection of your Son our Lord
and by the life-giving power of the Spirit.

See also:

Grant, O Lord Jesus . . . No 6 in 'A Treasury of Prayers',
People's Book, page 214.

Words of Mission

The sentence of the day, or words from the psalm or other reading
for the day, or one of the following:

1   Be strong and of good courage, do not be afraid;
    for it is the Lord who goes with you.
    Your God will not fail you or forsake you.

    Deuteronomy 31:6

2   God has shown you what is good.
    What does the Lord require of you
    but to do justice,
    and to love kindness,
    and to walk humbly with your God?   *Micah 6:8*

3   You are the light of the world.
    Let your light so shine before others
    that they may see your good works
    and give glory to your Father who is in heaven.

    Matthew 5:14, 16

4   Go and make disciples of all nations,
    baptising them in the name of the Father
    and of the Son and of the Holy Spirit,
    teaching them to observe all that I have commanded you;
    and lo, I am with you always,
    to the close of the age.   *Matthew 28:19, 20*

5   You shall receive power
    when the Holy Spirit has come upon you;
    and you shall be my witnesses in Jerusalem
    and in all Judea and Samaria
    and to the end of the earth.   *Acts 1:8*

6   I appeal to you, by the mercies of God,
to present your bodies as a living sacrifice,
holy and acceptable to God,
which is your spiritual worship.   *Romans 12:1*

7   Be watchful, stand firm in your faith,
be courageous and strong.
Let all that you do be done in love. *1 Corinthians 16:13, 14*

8   God has given us the ministry of reconciliation.
So we are ambassadors for Christ,
God making his appeal through us. *2 Corinthians 5:18, 20*

9   Whatever you do, in word or deed,
do everything in the name of the Lord Jesus,
giving thanks to God through him.   *Colossians 3:17*

10   Christ suffered for you, leaving you an example,
that you should follow in his steps.
Rejoice in so far as you share Christ's sufferings,
that you may also rejoice when his glory is revealed.
         1 Peter 2:21; 4:13

11   Go forth in the name of the Lord.
This is God's commandment:
that we should believe in the name of Jesus Christ
and love one another,
just as he has commanded us.   *1 John 3:23*

Blessings

1   The Lord bless you and keep you;
the Lord make his face to shine upon you,
and be gracious unto you;
the Lord lift up his countenance upon you,
and give you peace.   *Numbers 6:24-26*

2   May the God of steadfastness and encouragement
grant you to live in such harmony with one another,
in accord with Christ Jesus,
that together you may with one voice
glorify the God and Father of our Lord Jesus Christ;   *Romans 15:5, 6*

and may almighty God bless you,
the Father, the Son and the Holy Spirit.

3   May the God of hope
fill you with all joy and peace in believing,
so that by the power of the Holy Spirit
you may abound in hope;   *Romans 15:13*

and may almighty God bless you,
the Father, the Son and the Holy Spirit.

4   The grace of the Lord Jesus Christ
and the love of God
and the fellowship of the Holy Spirit
be with you all evermore.   *2 Corinthians 13:14*

When said together by all:

5   **The grace of the Lord Jesus Christ
and the love of God
and the fellowship of the Holy Spirit
be with us all evermore. Amen.**

6   Grace and peace be with you all,
and love with faith,
from God the Father and the Lord Jesus Christ;

Ephesians 6:23, 24

and the blessing of God almighty,
the Father, the Son and the Holy Spirit,
be upon you and remain with you always.

7   The peace of God, which passes all understanding,
keep your hearts and minds
in the knowledge and love of God,
and of his Son, Jesus Christ our Lord;

Based on Philippians 4:7

and the blessing of God almighty,
the Father, the Son and the Holy Spirit,
be upon you and remain with you always.

8   May the God of peace sanctify you wholly;
and may your spirit and soul and body
be kept sound and blameless
at the coming of our Lord Jesus Christ;

1 Thessalonians 5:23

and may almighty God bless you,
the Father, the Son and the Holy Spirit.

9   May our Lord Jesus Christ himself,
and God our Father,
comfort your hearts and establish them
in every good work and word;   *2 Thessalonians 2:16, 17*

and may almighty God bless you,
the Father, the Son and the Holy Spirit.

10   May the Lord of peace
     give you peace at all times and in all ways.
     The grace of our Lord Jesus Christ
     be with you all evermore.   *2 Thessalonians 3:16, 18*

11   May the God of peace
     who brought again from the dead our Lord Jesus,
     by the blood of the eternal covenant,
     equip you with everything good;
     that you may do his will,
     working in you that which is pleasing in his sight,
     through Jesus Christ, to whom be glory for ever;
                                        Hebrews 13: 20, 21

     and may almighty God bless you,
     the Father, the Son and the Holy Spirit.

12   The blessing of God almighty,
     the Father, the Son and the Holy Spirit,
     be upon you and remain with you always.

13   May almighty God bless you,
     the Father, the Son and the Holy Spirit.

14   The almighty and merciful Lord,
     Father, Son, and Holy Spirit,
     bless you and keep you.

15   The love of the Lord Jesus draw you to himself;
     the power of the Lord Jesus strengthen you in his service;
     the joy of the Lord Jesus fill your hearts;
     and the blessing of God almighty,
     the Father, the Son and the Holy Spirit,
     be upon you and remain with you always.

16   The grace of Christ attend you;
the love of God surround you;
the Holy Spirit keep you;
this day and for ever.

17   God the Father make you holy in his love;
God the Son enrich you with his grace;
God the Holy Spirit strengthen you with joy;
the Lord bless you and keep you in eternal life.

SEASONAL BLESSINGS

Advent

18   Christ the Sun of righteousness shine upon you
and make you ready to meet him when he comes in glory;
and the blessing of God almighty . . .

Christmas

19   Christ the Son of God gladden your hearts
by his coming to dwell among us,
and bring you his peace;
and the blessing of God almighty . . .

Epiphany and Transfiguration

20   Christ the Son of God be manifest to you,
that your lives may be a light to the world;
and the blessing of God almighty . . .

Lent

21   Christ give you grace to grow in holiness,
to deny yourselves,
and to take up the cross and follow him;
and the blessing of God almighty . . .

Passiontide

22   Christ our crucified Saviour draw you to himself,
that you may find in him a sure ground for faith,
a firm support for hope,
and the assurance of sins forgiven;
and the blessing of God almighty . . .

Easter

23   The God of peace,
who brought again from the dead our Lord Jesus,
that great shepherd of the sheep,
make you perfect in every good work to do his will;
and the blessing of God almighty . . .

Ascension and Christ the King

24   Christ our King pour upon you his abundant gifts,
make you faithful and strong to do his will,
and bring you to reign with him in glory;
and the blessing of God almighty . . .

Pentecost

25   The Spirit of truth lead you into all truth,
give you grace to confess that Jesus Christ is Lord,
and to proclaim the word and works of God;
and the blessing of God almighty . . .

Trinity Sunday

26   God the Holy Trinity make you strong
in faith, hope and love,
defend you on every side,
and guide you in truth and peace;
and the blessing of God almighty . . .

All Saints' Day

27 God give you grace to follow the saints
in faith, hope and love,
and to know the fruit of the Holy Spirit
in your lives;
and the blessing of God almighty . . .

Christian Unity

28 Christ the Good Shepherd,
who laid down his life for the sheep,
draw you and all who hear his voice to be one
within the one fold of his love;
and the blessing of God almighty . . .

Dismissals

1   Go forth into the world in peace;
    be of good courage;
    hold fast that which is good;
    render to no one evil for evil;
    strengthen the faint-hearted; *Matthew 28:19*
    support the weak; *Mark 5:34*
    help the afflicted; *Psalm 27:14*
    honour all people; *Romans 12:9-11, 17*
    love and serve the Lord, *1 Thessalonians 5:14, 15*
    rejoicing in the power of the Holy Spirit. *1 Peter 2:17*
    Amen.

2   Go out into the world in peace.
    Love the Lord your God
    with all your heart,
    and with all your soul,
    and with all your mind.
    This is the first and greatest commandment.
    1 John 3:22, 23

    And the second is like it:
    Love your neighbour as yourself. *Matthew 22:37-39*
    Amen.

3   Go forth and live a life that is pleasing to God.
    And this is God's commandment:
    that we should believe in the name of Jesus Christ
    and love one another,
    just as he has commanded us. *1 John 3:23*
    Amen.

4   Go into the world in the power of the Holy Spirit
     to fulfil your high calling as servants of Christ.
     Amen.

5   Go in peace to serve the Lord,
     in the name of Christ.
     Amen.

6   Go in peace to love and serve the Lord.
     Amen.

7   Go out into the world in the power of the Spirit;
     in all things, at all times,
     remember that Christ is with you;
     make your life your worship
     to the praise and glory of God.
     Amen.

Acknowledgments

Acknowledgments

Over the last few years, ecumenically and internationally, English-speaking churches have witnessed a convergence in both the liturgical shape of orders of service and in translations of texts which churches have in common.

During the years of preparation of *Uniting in Worship*, The Assembly Commission on Liturgy has enjoyed a growing relationship with many other worship commissions and committees in the English-speaking world. These groups include the following:

The Australian Consultation on Liturgy (ACOL)
The Liturgical Commission of The Anglican Church of Australia
The worship committees of other member churches of The Australian Consultation on Liturgy
The English Language Liturgical Consultation (ELLC)
The Faith and Order Committee of The Methodist Church, U.K.
The General Synod Liturgical Commission of The Church of England, U.K.
The Church of Scotland Panel on Worship, U.K.
The Committee for Doctrine and Worship of The United Reformed Church, U.K.
The Doctrine and Worship Committee of The Anglican Church of Canada
The Worship Office, Division of Mission in Canada, The United Church of Canada
The Board of Congregational Life, The Presbyterian Church in Canada
The Standing Liturgical Commission of The Episcopal Church, U.S.A.
The Office of Worship, The Presbyterian Church (U.S.A.)
The International Commission on English in the Liturgy – A Joint Commission of Catholic Bishops' Conferences
The Section on Worship, The General Board of Discipleship, The United Methodist Church, U.S.A.
The Office for Church Life and Leadership, The United Church of Christ, U.S.A.
The Faith and Order Committee of The Methodist Church of New Zealand
The Worship Committee of The Presbyterian Church of New Zealand

These groups have generously shared published resources, journals and newsletters, and exchanged correspondence with us. Our indebtedness to some of these groups for the amount of material taken from their publications is very great. But all the groups listed above have in some way assisted our work. While much of the content of *Uniting in Worship*, particularly the orders of service, is the original work of the Commission, members of the above groups will recognise a phrase here or a sentence there which has been inspired by their own work.

Scripture quotations are from the *Revised Standard Version of the Bible*, copyrighted 1946, 1952, © 1971, 1973 by the Division of Christian Education of the National Council of the Churches of Christ in the U.S.A., and used by permission. A number of very small changes to the R.S.V. text have been made for the sake of inclusive language.

The English translations of *The Lord's Prayer, Apostles' Creed, Nicene Creed* (adapted), 'Lord, have mercy', 'Glory to God in the highest', 'Lift up your hearts', 'Holy, holy, holy Lord', 'Lamb of God', 'Glory to the Father', 'We praise you, O God', *Song of Zechariah, Song of Mary* and *Song of Simeon* were originally prepared by the International Consultation on English Texts (ICET) and revised in 1987 by the English Language Liturgical Consultation (ELLC).

The Selections from The Psalter and other excerpts from the psalms used elsewhere are taken from *The Psalter* of *The Book of Common Prayer*, 1979, of The Episcopal Church, U.S.A. Other resources from *The Book of Common Prayer* include some of the canticles and litanies, some prayers in Resources for the Liturgical Year and Resources for Leading Worship, and prayers in several orders of service. Used with approval.

Four of the litanies are from *The Worshipbook Services*. Copyright © 1970, The Westminster Press, Philadelphia, PA, U.S.A. Adapted and used by permission.

Two great prayers of thanksgiving and one other prayer in The Service of the Lord's Day and some prayers in Resources for Leading Worship are from *The Service for the Lord's Day - (Supplemental Liturgical Resource 1)*. Prepared by The Office of Worship, The Presbyterian Church (U.S.A.) Copyright © 1984, The Westminster Press, Philadelphia, PA, U.S.A. Used by permission.

The two prayers of thanksgiving in both services of baptism have been inspired by work published in *Holy Baptism and Services for The Renewal of Baptism - (Supplemental Liturgical Resource 2)*. Copyright © 1985, The Westminster Press, Philadelphia, PA, U.S.A.

Two prayers in The Marriage Service are from *Christian Marriage - (Supplemental Liturgical Resource 3)*. Copyright © 1986, The Westminster Press, Philadelphia, PA, U.S.A. Used by permission.

ACKNOWLEDGMENTS   671

Some of the canticles and litanies, some of the collects in Resources for the Liturgical Year and other prayers used in orders of service are from *The Book of Alternative Services* of The Anglican Church of Canada, copyright © 1985, The General Synod of The Anglican Church of Canada. Used with permission.

The Commission expresses grateful thanks to the Anglican Book Centre, Toronto, the publisher of *The Book of Alternative Services*, for the model this book has provided in size, lay-out and type-style for *Uniting in Worship*.

There are excerpts from the English translation of the *Rite of Marriage* © 1969, International Committee on English in the Liturgy, Inc. (ICEL); the English translation of the Good Friday Reproaches and the Exsultet (Easter Proclamation) from the *Rite of Holy Week* © 1970, ICEL; the text of 'Christ Has Died' and the English translation of 'Dying, you destroyed our death' from *The Roman Missal* © 1973, ICEL. All rights reserved. Altered with permission.

Some of the collects in Resources for the Liturgical Year are the English translation of the collects from *The Roman Missal* © 1973, International Committee on English in the Liturgy, Inc. All rights reserved.

Two Great Prayers of Thanksgiving from *A Sunday Liturgy* and one Great Prayer of Thanksgiving from *The Celebration of Marriage* are used by permission of The Worship Office, Division of Mission in Canada, The United Church of Canada. The statement of faith beginning *'We are not alone . . .'* is used by permission of the same church.

Some of the prayers in Resources for Leading Worship have been adapted from prayers in *Service Book*, 1969, of the United Church of Canada. The Commission gratefully acknowledges the model that the two complementary books, *Service Book*, 1969, provided for *People's Book* and *Leader's Book* of *Uniting in Worship*.

Some prayers in The Service of the Lord's Day, including the prayer beginning *'Father of all, we give you thanks and praise . . .'*, some prayers in The Marriage Service and The Funeral Service and some prayers in other orders of service are from *The Alternative Service Book*, 1980, copyright ©, The Central Board of Finance of the Church of England. The Litany and other prayers in the Resources sections of *Uniting in Worship* are also from *The Alternative Service Book*. Material from that book is reproduced with permission.

Some of the prayers in A Treasury of Prayers are from *The Book of Common Prayer*, 1662. The Commission gratefully acknowledges that this book is the heritage of The Church of England and affirms that, other than the Bible itself, no other book has provided so great an enrichment both of English literature and also of christian devotion in the Reformed tradition.

The form of The Covenant Service is based on that in *The Methodist Service Book*, 1975. One Great Prayer of Thanksgiving in The Service of the Lord's Day, one prayer in The Marriage Service, some prayers in The Funeral Service and three thanksgivings and other prayers in Resources for Leading Worship are also from *The Methodist Service Book*. Used by permission of The Methodist Faith and Order Committee and The Methodist Publishing House, London.

One great Prayer of Thanksgiving and other prayers in The Service of the Lord's Day are from the text of Second Order of The Holy Communion of *An Australian Prayer Book*, 1978, copyright, The Anglican Church of Australia Trust Corporation. Some prayers in The Marriage Service, The Funeral Service, Resources for Leading Worship and A Treasury of Prayers are also from this book. Some of the collects in Resources for the Liturgical Year are from *An Australian Prayer Book* or *Alternative Collects*, both published by the Anglican Information Office. Reproduced with permission.

The Ordination Prayer in Ordination of a Minister of the Word is based on *An Ordinal – The United Methodist Church*. Copyright © 1979 by The Board of Discipleship of The United Methodist Church. Used by permission.

Some of the collects in Resources for the Liturgical Year and some of the prayers in Resources for Leading Worship have been written by The Revd Dr Peter Gardner, a minister of The Presbyterian Church of New Zealand and a valued consultant to the Commission. Used with permission.

The Commission gratefully acknowledges the work of Liturgy Training Publications, Chicago, Illinois, in publishing a 3-year cycle of opening prayers, based on the *Roman Lectionary*. This initiative in the U.S.A. has encouraged the Commission to prepare a similar 3-year cycle of collects, based on the readings in *Common Lectionary*. Some of the collects included in Resources for the Liturgical Year are the opening prayers prepared by The Revd Peter Scagnelli and published by Liturgy Training Publications; other collects prepared by the Commission have been inspired by his work.